Official Publisher Partnership

# OCR LAW for GCSE

Chris Turner
Andrew Shepherd
Sue Teal
Craig Beauman

HODDER
EDUCATION
AN HACHETTE UK COMPANY

Orders: please contact Bookpoint Ltd, 130 Milton Park, Abingdon, Oxon OX14 4SB.
Telephone: (44) 01235 827720. Fax: (44) 01235 400454. Lines are open from 9.00 – 5.00,
Monday to Saturday, with a 24 hour message answering service. You can also order through our
website www.hoddereducation.co.uk

If you have any comments to make about this, or any of our other titles, please send them to
educationenquiries@hodder.co.uk

*British Library Cataloguing in Publication Data*
A catalogue record for this title is available from the British Library

ISBN: 978 0 340 98430 7

First Edition Published 2009
Impression number    10 9 8 7 6 5 4 3 2 1
Year                          2012 2011 2010 2009

Hachette UK's policy is to use papers that are natural, renewable and recyclable products and made from
wood grown in sustainable forests. The logging and manufacturing processes are expected to conform to
the environmental regulations of the country of origin.

Artwork by Ian Foulis and Oxford Designers and Illustrators
Cover photo © Stockdisc
Typeset by Dorchester Typesetting Group Ltd
Printed in Malta for Hodder Education, an Hachette UK Company, 338 Euston Road,
London NW1 3BH

# CONTENTS

# PREFACE

This book is the recommended text for the new OCR GCSE Law. The authors are all Principal Examiners who have had experience of writing GCSE Law papers and so you will be able to gain a good idea of the type and level of information that you are required to know for the course and the types of activities that you are likely to see and have to complete in the exams.

The simple aim of the OCR GCSE Law is to be an accessible, relevant and, above all, enjoyable course of study for both students and their teachers. The types of assessment activity hopefully mirror these aims. The book also provides a potential progression route to A Level Law.

The book contains many practical examples of the law in action. Most often these are from decided cases. For readers that might wish to read about those cases at greater length the name is given at the bottom. These can then be found in more advanced text books.

Each section of the book also contains an 'aims and objectives' at the start of a chapter so that you have a brief idea of the understanding that you are trying to build and what you are expected to do with it. Each section also contains a Key Fact chart at the end summarising the most important points contained in the section, and these can also act as a revision aid.

As authors and examiners we all hope that you will gain much enjoyment in reading about the law, and also from your study of the law, and find that it that has been worthwhile.

# ACKNOWLEDGEMENTS

The authors and publishers would like to thank the following for permission to reproduce copyright material:

The Independent for the article on p119; Human Resources Guide for the article on p120; Arthritis Care for the article on 123; Russell Jones and Walker Solicitors for the articles on p123 and p150; Daily Mail for the article on p125; Thompsons Solicitors for the article on p126; article on p127 © Telegraph Media Group 2009. © Crown Copyright material is reproduced with the permission of the controlled of HMSO.

Every effort has been made to track and acknowledge ownership of copyright. The publishers will be glad to make suitable arrangements with copyright holder whom it has not been able to contact.

# THE NATURE OF LAW; CRIMINAL COURTS AND CRIMINAL PROCESSES

# CHAPTER 1

# THE NATURE OF LAW

## Aims

The aim of this chapter is to:

- provide basic definitions of law
- look at the basic classifications of English law
- define the differences between criminal and civil law
- examine why we need law
- examine how laws are made: the role of Parliament, delegated bodies, the courts and membership of the European Union.

## 1.1 Definitions of law

The word 'law' could be described as being:

> **❝** a set of rules that allows us to do certain things and prevents us from doing others. **❞**

If you were asked to give an example of law you might probably use examples of criminal law such as murder or robbery. However, the English and Welsh legal system is much more than that. It not only provides citizens with individual rules and regulations; it also provides us with the framework within which the rules operate and with a means of enforcing those rules through the courts. Without the basis of a sensible system of rules, we would be confused over our rights and responsibilities.

A strong legal system will *create law* and *enforce law* to try to provide an answer to any problem. The law guides us from the moment (and before!) we are born through to death. Think about every time you buy an item from a shop, for example a sandwich. From the point when the materials used to make the sandwich are created, to the way it is delivered to the shop that sells them, to the way it is stored in the shop, to the way it is displayed in the shop, to the way it is packaged and labelled, to the method and time it is sold to you, the law covers how this is to be done. Even the person who has sold you the sandwich is governed by the law, a kind of law called employment law.

Many of the links in this chain are covered by what is called civil law – especially contract law, but it may be that the criminal law is broken if, for example the sandwich, is spoiled or out of date.

If a person were to deliberately take such an item without paying for it, then the criminal law could provide a solution. In criminal law this is known as theft.

The law is enforced by the courts and its aim is either:

- to punish and to prevent certain actions (criminal law), or
- to compensate a person (contract law) by placing them in the position they were in before the problem arose.

## 1.2 The basic classifications of English law

The English legal system provides different types of law to govern different situations. Our system of law is divided into public and private law. Public law is that which affects the *whole of society at any one time*, for example criminal law, while private law (or civil law) is that which affects *individuals and businesses*, for example in contract law as and when the need to use it arises.

## 1.2.1 Criminal law

The main type of public law is criminal law. The purpose of the criminal law is to stop certain types of act (or failures to act) that would cause physical danger to others, or cause distress. For example, murder can be defined as:

> ❝ the intentional and unlawful killing of a human being. ❞

If a person breaks the criminal law, then the legal system allows that he will be punished in some way. Depending on how serious the crime is, the defendant, once convicted, will usually face a fine, imprisonment or both.

## 1.2.2 Civil law

The purpose of the civil law is to settle disputes between individuals and/or businesses. There are many different types of civil law. The most common types of civil law are:

• contract
• consumer
• tort
• family
• employment.

The purpose of the civil law is to settle these disputes by trying to place the individuals in the position they would have been in before the dispute arose. This is known as restitution.

Contract law: when individuals or business enter into an agreement both parties generally want the other to carry out what they have agreed in the way they have agreed it. If the parties intended to be legally bound by the agreement, then usually this is called a contract. If either party fails to carry out their obligations, then the other party can seek help through the courts under contract law.

Consumer law: this allows customers to purchase goods and services in a safe and secure manner with the knowledge that if anything goes wrong with the goods or services, they have rights that

will be protected under the law. Much of this law is driven by EU legislation.

Tort law: a tort is a civil 'wrong' and in many cases complements criminal law. The criminal law will punish the defendant, but tort law can financially compensate the injured party. A claim under tort law usually arises where someone is injured as the result of another person's carelessness, or 'negligent act'. There are many types of tort, but negligence (failure to do something) is the most common.

Family law: this covers areas like marriage and divorce, death and inheritance.

Employment law: whenever we are employed to do a job or a person wants to employ another person to work for them, the Law provides rules and boundaries that both employers and employees must adhere to.

## 1.2.3 The differences between criminal and civil law

It is really important as a student of Law to have an understanding of the differences between criminal and civil law. There are many. The main ones are summarised below:

The different types of law: the reason we have criminal law is to maintain order in a civilised society, while the reason why we have civil law is to ensure that individuals can resolve disputes in an orderly manner – to be placed in the position they would have been in, had the dispute not arisen. This usually involves asking for compensation in the form of money.

Who starts the case? In the criminal law, following the police investigation the Crown Prosecution Service (CPS) is the main organisation responsible, if necessary, for taking the case to court on behalf of the state. In criminal law the CPS is known as the prosecution or prosecutor and the person accused of committing the crime is the defendant.

In civil cases it would be the responsibility of the individual, known as the claimant, alleging a failure to carry out obligations under an agreement, to start proceedings in court, while the person against whom the allegations are made is again the defendant.

Where is the case heard? In criminal law, the cases would be heard in either the Magistrates' Court or the Crown Court, depending on the seriousness of the crime. In the civil law the most likely court for the claim to start in would be the County Court or the High Court. This would depend this time not on seriousness, but on how much compensation the injured party is claiming.

Proving the defendant's legal responsibility: in order to prove whether the defendant in criminal law carried out the crime, the magistrate or Crown Court Judge must be satisfied that the evidence proves beyond reasonable doubt that the defendant committed the crime. In civil law this level of proof is much lower. Here the claimant has only to prove on a balance of probabilities that the defendant has broken or breached his agreement and therefore owes him some form of compensation, or, simply to carry out the agreement as planned. This requirement in a court case is known as the burden or standard of proof.

The conclusion of the case: if the defendant in a criminal case is proved to have committed the crime, then he will be found guilty. In consequence, depending on the seriousness of the crime, he will usually be either fined or sent to prison. In civil cases if the defendant is deemed to be responsible for the broken agreement, then he will be found liable and asked to pay the claimant damages: usually money. It may be that the claimant wants the defendant simply to stop doing something, such as to stop a neighbour making too much noise. In this case the court can grant an injunction stopping the defendant from carrying out the act – in this case the noise.

## 1.3 Why do we need law?

To maintain law and order: the law prevents people from doing what they want whenever they want as this could conflict with what other citizens want. Citizens need to feel safe and protected in their communities and conflict between citizens could lead to violence.

Protecting individual freedoms: if citizens did not have freedoms such as the right to free speech or freedom of movement then they would have their lives unnecessarily restricted. It is important for us to be able to say what is on our minds or to visit places where we want or need to go. Also, we should be responsible and live our lives in harmony. In order to live our lives in such a way, we must have the ability to control our lives as well as possible.

Regulating relationships: if two or more citizens enter into an agreement and at some point disagree over what the agreement was, then the law must be able to step in to regulate a successful outcome. In family law the creation of a marriage through to its termination in divorce or judicial separation or even after the death of a spouse is guided by the law.

Setting standards: in all areas of life it is important to set a level or standard that someone must achieve and if he was to fall below that standard, then the law may have to intervene. For example, when driving a car the driver must pay attention to the road around him and drive according to what he sees: specific attention must be paid to the speed of the vehicle and to not using a mobile phone when driving.

## 1.4 How are laws made?

In England and Wales the law comes from a variety of different sources. The four main sources are:

- Acts of Parliament
- delegated legislation
- European law
- judge-made law, called Judicial Precedent.

## 1.4.1 What is the role of Parliament?

The United Kingdom (UK) is a democracy. This means that the supreme lawmakers, the people who run the country, are elected officials, representing the majority view of the public. Acts of Parliament are passed by our elected Parliament. Statute law and legislation are different ways of describing Acts of Parliament.

When making laws (this is called 'passing legislation') the UK's Parliament is made up of three separate parts. These are the House of Commons, the House of Lords and the Monarch. Each of the three parts plays an important role in the creation and passing of new laws in this way.

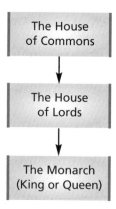

**Figure 1.1** Passing legislation

## Legislative process

This means the process in Parliament and, in particular, the different stages through which new laws have to go before they can be passed and introduced into English Law. The process by which Parliament changes or introduces a new law can take a very long time.

## The pre-legislative process

Before a new law is debated in Parliament, the Government will usually put its ideas together and produce a document called a Green Paper asking for the public's opinion. This is known as the consultation period and it is the Government's attempt to include the public in the process of changing law and to encourage democracy. Green Papers are published on the Internet for interested parties to share their thoughts with the Government. Once the consultation process is over, the Government may include some changes suggested from the consultation process before publishing a White Paper. This is the Government's firm proposals on what it wants to do in order to change the law.

The next stage is the actual writing or drafting of the proposed Act. This is done by lawyers working on behalf of the Government. Once this is done the resulting document is called a bill. The bill is debated through the variety of stages in Parliament. If it passes all the stages, then the bill becomes an Act and the new laws are therefore passed into English law.

## Types of bill

### Public bill

The vast majority of bills that are introduced into Parliament are these types of bill and are developed by the Government in order to change the law as they see fit. The Hunting Act 2004 is a recent example. This Act prohibits, with certain exceptions, all hunting of wild mammals with dogs.

### Private Members' bill

It is not only the Government who are allowed to introduce a bill. Any MP can, in theory, introduce a bill into Parliament. Twenty MPs are selected from a ballot at the beginning of the parliamentary year to try to introduce a bill that is important to them. There is a similar process for members of the House of Lords to introduce such bills. However, because parliamentary time is limited for such bills, the chance of a Private Members' bill becoming an Act is very slim. A noticeable Private Members' bill that succeeded in becoming law is the Forced Marriage (Civil Protection) Act 2007 introduced by Lord Lester of Herne Hill, a member of the House of Lords, to protect the victims in forced marriages and help to remove them from the situation.

### Private bills

Where public bills affect the general public, this type of bill affects only an individual or company or perhaps a local authority – not the whole country. This is where individuals, companies or local authorities ask for permission to carry out their role in conflict with existing law or in excess of it. In the north-east of England, The Tyne Tunnel Act 1998 was passed to allow the Tyne and Wear Passenger Transport Authority to build a new and much needed second tunnel for traffic to move north and south across the River Tyne; this following the massive increase in volume of traffic since the first tunnel was opened in 1967.

 **ACTIVITY**

### Activity 2

Identify the most appropriate bill for each of the following three scenarios. Fill in the table with the most appropriate sentence from the list below.
- Public bill
- Private Members' bill
- Private bill.

| Scenario | | Most appropriate bill |
|---|---|---|
| A | An MP wishes to introduce a controversial bill which is not a priority for the Government. | |
| B | A local authority wishes to build a new road bridge across a river to reduce congestion on another road bridge. | |
| C | The Government introduce a bill into Parliament to ban motor cars from all city centres. | |

Table 1.1

# The legislative process in Parliament

A bill is normally started in the House of Commons, but can be started in the House of Lords going through the same stages:

## First reading

Here, the bill is introduced into the House of Commons. The name and purpose of the bill is read out. There is no debate at this point, but a verbal vote is taken whether the bill should pass this stage. If enough MPs vote yes, then the bill moves to the next stage.

## Second reading

This is the main chance for MPs to debate the bill. MPs are able to raise points in favour of or against the bill's proposals. Here the main proposals are debated and the minister responsible for the bill will have a chance to answer any points raised during the debate. At the end of the second reading, another vote is taken and if there is a majority in favour of the bill, it will pass on to the next stage.

## Committee stage

This is an opportunity to look at each part of the bill in close detail. The Committee is made up of up to 50 MPs from all political parties in proportion to the number of MPs in the Commons. Clearly, the existing Government will have the most members sitting on the Committee. Usually, the MPs are chosen if they have a specific skill or interest in the bill. The Committee can suggest and vote on amendments to the bill. If this is the case, any amendments have to be debated in the next stage.

## Report stage

Here, the Committee reports back to the Commons on any suggested amendments to the bill. This stage acts as a 'safety net' to the Committee stage. The amendments are debated in the Commons and again voted on. New amendments can be suggested by MPs at this stage. If there were no suggested amendments from the Committee stage, then there is no report stage.

## Third reading

This provides the final vote on the bill in the Commons and the final draft of the Bill before being sent to the House of Lords.

## The House of Lords

The bill passes through the same stages as it does in the Commons. The only exception is the Committee stage where the whole House sits rather than a small number, as in the Commons. There is the same chance to debate amendments as there was in the Commons. If it does recommend amendments, then the bill will have to go back to the Commons to debate and vote on them.

## The Royal Assent

Once the bill has passed the Lords, then, as a matter of formality, the monarch gives consent

## ACTIVITY

### Activity 3

Using the grid below, complete the table by inserting a number from 1 to 7 next to each stage that indicates where the stage comes in the legislative process.

| Stage of legislative process | Order number |
|---|---|
| Committee stage | |
| Royal Assent | |
| First reading | |
| Third reading | |
| Report stage | |
| House of Lords | |
| Second reading | |

Table 1.2

to the passing of the bill so that it becomes an Act of Parliament and therefore a new law of the land.

## Is legislation the best way to pass laws?

It may be that legislation is the most democratic way of passing new laws or amending existing laws. Parliament can legislate on any issue it wants, and if the law needs changing, then Parliament can amend the law as it sees fit. There are clearly problems, particularly the time it takes to pass laws.

## The problems with using legislation to pass laws

### Time taken to pass legislation

Looking at all the stages that need to be passed, it would not surprise you to learn that the legislative process is a slow process which can take months and even years to complete. For example, the Human Rights Act 1998 was introduced as a Green Paper in 1996, and did not receive Royal Assent until late in 1998. However, if there is a national emergency and a new law or laws need to be passed quickly, then Parliament can debate a bill in a matter of hours, providing that there are no major objections. One of the quickest passings of an Act was the Northern Ireland Act 1972. This was passed in a little over seven hours, following a court decision made earlier that day. The Government felt that the decision threatened the stability of law and order in Northern Ireland and moved quickly.

### Difficult language

Legislation has to be written in such a way that makes it straightforward to read and understand. The reality is sometimes different and a common criticism is the complex language used in drafting legislation, and what exactly each word or phrase means.

### European influence on legislation

Having joined the European Economic Union, now called the European Union (EU), in 1973, another criticism is that the UK Government has removed its total ability to pass laws on any subject it wants. The UK Parliament is no longer able to pass laws on what it thinks is best for the UK if it conflicts with existing European law. This has led to calls for the UK to leave the EU. In the case of *Factortame v Secretary of State* (1991) the European Court of Justice stated that the Merchant Shipping Act 1988 conflicted with existing EU law and was invalid.

### More than one Act dealing with the same issue

Sometimes an Act can be amended by later legislation and therefore more than one Act of Parliament needs to be read together.

### Finding the correct law

As there are many thousands of Acts of Parliament it may be difficult for the public to find what they are looking for. The Internet has speeded this up, with Government websites providing such information.

---

**ACTIVITY**

**Activity 4**

One of the main criticisms of the legislative process is the length of time it takes to pass a bill through Parliament.

Identify three other criticisms of the legislative process.

Criticism 1

.........................................................

Criticism 2

.........................................................

Criticism 3

.........................................................

## 1.4.2 The role of delegated bodies

In this section we will explore the different types of and reasons for delegated legislation, and any potential disadvantages of it.

## What is delegated legislation?

Where someone delegates a task, he is asking someone else to carry it out on his behalf. This could be for a variety of reasons. It might be quicker for the other person to carry out the task; perhaps it will be cheaper; or perhaps the person to whom the task is being delegated is simply more qualified or experienced to carry out the task.

Delegated legislation is where the Government allows the final law to be made by an individual or organisations, rather than the Government itself. This does not mean that those passing delegated legislation can pass what they want; there are controls placed on the process. In the majority of cases Parliament will pass an Act called a Parent Act. This provides a framework within which the finer detail is drawn up by the other bodies and then passed in different ways depending on the type of delegated legislation.

## What are the types of delegated legislation?

There are four main types of delegated legislation and each has its own function:

1.  Orders in Council
    These are rarely used and only passed when Parliament is not sitting, and usually passed in emergency situations. The Parent Acts that give the power to pass this type of delegated legislation are the Emergency Powers Act 1920 and Civil Contingencies Act 2004.

The Orders are drawn up and passed by the Queen sitting with the Privy Council. The Privy Council is made up of the Prime Minister, senior politicians and Law Lords.

2.  Statutory instruments
    Here the power to make laws is granted by Parliament to individual Government departments. This means that the minister responsible for the department and their civil servants will pass delegated legislation that relates to the work of that department. The Parent Act will give guidance, but not the specific detail. For example, the Education (Student Loans) Act 1990 allowed students studying for degrees to apply for loans to help them meet the costs of studying. How much money is available is decided by the minister responsible for education and they will set the amount available.

3.  Bylaws
    This type of delegated legislation is usually passed by local authorities. These bodies can only pass legislation in the area they control. For example, in the north-east area of North Tyneside the local authority issued a bylaw banning the consumption of alcohol in certain streets and other areas on the coast in order to reduce and prevent the amount of disorderly behaviour caused by alcohol. Also, other public bodies such as Network Rail or the London Underground can pass bylaws that affect the running of their services.

4.  European Regulations
    The Regulations are made by the European Commission and enforced into English law by delegated legislation in the form of a statutory instrument under the European Communities Act 1972.

**ACTIVITY**

## Activity 5

Identify the most appropriate type of delegated legislation for each of the following three scenarios. Fill in the table with the most appropriate type from the list below.
- Order in Council
- Statutory instrument
- Bylaw

| Scenario | Situation | Most appropriate type of delegated legislation |
|---|---|---|
| A | A local train operator wants to prevent commuters bringing prams onto its trains | |
| B | The Government wants to pass legislation quickly, following a major terrorist attack | |
| C | A government minister wants to increase the amount of child benefit for parents under an existing Act. | |

Table 1.3

# The advantages of delegated legislation

### The future needs of the country

When Parliament passes legislation, it cannot see any changes in society in the future, such as changes in attitudes or opinions. Delegated legislation can be used to amend legislation more quickly and effectively. If there were to be another terrorist attack such as that which happened in the USA in 2001 (9/11) or the one which happened in 2005 in London (7/7) when Parliament is not sitting, then Orders in Council could be passed quickly to begin a state of emergency.

### Quick response

Since the passing of delegated legislation is much quicker than using the parliamentary process, those responsible can react quicker in times of necessity.

### Expertise

Ministers from specific departments can pass legislation using the expert opinions of the civil servants who work for them. Members of Parliament come from different backgrounds so, during the parliamentary process, MPs without the knowledge of the area concerned would have to have the law explained to them.

### More parliamentary time

As the passing of delegated legislation takes the process of lawmaking away from the complete control of the parliamentary process, Parliament can spend its time dealing with the passing of day-to-day or controversial legislation.

### Local geographical knowledge

For a Parliament based in London to legislate on local issues would be time consuming. Instead, it makes far more sense to allow locally elected councillors to pass laws that affect their area.

The local councillors who live in the area have the necessary understanding of local issues and are best placed to pass the bylaws.

## The disadvantages of delegated legislation

### Lack of control

As the power to pass the law is delegated there must be some degree of control to ensure that those people passing the law are not acting illegally or unfairly. There is some available control from Parliament and the courts, but it is argued that because of the sheer volume of delegated legislation, it is difficult to keep track of it all.

### Overused

Each year more than 3,000 statutory instruments are used to pass laws via delegated legislation. It has been argued that in the past, certain governments would use this method of lawmaking in order to avoid the lengthy Parliamentary process to pass contentious legislation 'by the back door'.

 **ACTIVITY**

### Activity 6

Read the following passage and fill in the missing words from the list below:

There are a variety of types of delegated legislation including Orders in .............................. An Act of Parliament, known as a ...................... Act provides the framework for the types of delegated legislation to be passed. Local authorities can pass laws that affect them on a local level, these are called ..............................

bypasses

public

council

bylaws

parent

concert

### Undemocratic

A common criticism of delegated legislation is that many people or bodies who pass laws here are not democratically elected. Clearly, local councillors are elected, but civil servants working for a government minister and who advise him/her on the detail of a statutory instrument are not. This therefore allows anyone who works for that body or organisation to have an input into how we lead our lives.

## 1.4.3 The role of the courts – judicial precedent

Historically the decisions of judges are an important source of law and this remains so today. If the Act fails to define the words or it is unclear what Parliament meant when it passed the Act, judges while sitting in court have been asked to rule on what the Act means or to clarify whether something in particular satisfies as being part of a definition. In the higher courts such as the House of Lords, the judge makes a judgment at the end of the case that sets out his reasoning for coming to his conclusion. This decision will bind future courts where the facts are the same or similar. This is called judicial precedent and is also known as case law. This, depending on the court and judge, is usually made available to the public in the form of a law report.

If a defendant has disagreed with the judge's interpretation of the law, they may ask permission for another, more senior judge, to re-look at it.

### The judge's decision – the judgment

If a senior judge makes a decision, his judgment will usually create a law that other judges have to follow in the future. In the judgment, the part of the judge's decision that is his legal reasoning that lays down his decision, forms the judicial (judge-made) precedent. It is this part of the judgment that will normally be followed, or will bind, later (similar) cases. This is known as the *ratio decidendi*, which means 'the reason behind the decision'. If the judge takes the opportunity to talk about other areas of law that are linked but are not directly relevant to the facts of the present case, then this is known as *obiter dicta* – which means other things said 'by the way'.

Lawyers will use the *ratio decidendi* from previous cases to support their cases and argue in court that the decision in an earlier case must be followed.

## The three types of precedent

There are three different types of precedent. Original precedent is where a court makes a decision as to what the law is for the very first time. This could be because a new law has been passed and this is the first ever opportunity for a court to give its opinion. It may also be that the court makes a ruling in the absence of an Act of Parliament to guide the courts. This is done rarely by the courts as, because they are not elected, they could be criticised for acting 'above their powers'. However, there are some notable examples of where the courts have felt obliged to create new original precedent. In *Donoghue v Stephenson* (1932) the House of Lords held that a manufacturer owed a duty of care to consumers who use their products and are injured even if they did not buy them themselves.

Binding precedent is the part of the decision which will bind future courts. Judges in the courts will generally follow previous decisions, in other words, precedent, on the grounds of certainty. Whether they can ignore or have to follow previous decisions depends on where that judge sits in which court in the hierarchy of the courts. Persuasive precedent is a decision that has been made by a previous court but, for a variety of reasons, a later court does not have to follow. This would be most common where a court lower in the hierarchy of the courts has decided a point of law, then a case with similar or the same facts comes before a court higher in the hierarchy. Here, judges can follow the precedent and create a binding precedent if they wish, but they do not have to if they do not want to.

In looking at judicial precedent there are three important parts to consider: the principle of *stare decisis*, the court's hierarchy and law reporting.

## Stare decisis

One of the main advantages of judicial precedent is that if a senior judge has made an earlier decision as to the law on a particular matter, then you can be fairly certain that this is the definition that the courts will use in future. If, however, that judge got it wrong, then it can be changed by another judge. However, in order to change precedent there must be a series of rules, otherwise any judge could change any earlier decision and there would be no certainty in the law. The main rule of precedent is *stare decisis*, which means 'stand by the decision'. Therefore, for the reason of certainty, rather than have any judges making any decision they want, they are told to follow the previous decision of judges. This makes the law certain so that clients can be advised by lawyers.

## The hierarchy of the courts

The courts' hierarchy is divided up into the civil courts and criminal courts. The lower courts, termed 'inferior courts', differ largely between the civil and criminal courts. Where there is similarity in the structure of courts is at the top of the hierarchy where the courts are the same. The higher up the hierarchy, the more important the judge's decision is and therefore the more likely that the judge's decision is binding on the lower courts. Therefore, precedent binds the lower courts, and sometimes the higher courts themselves. Since joining the European Union in 1973, the highest court in our hierarchy of courts is the European Court of Justice (ECJ), which hears appeals from English courts on matters of European law that affect us. When the ECJ makes a decision, as it is top of the hierarchy, it binds all of the courts below it.

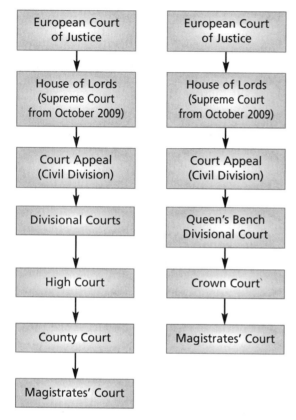

**Figure 1.2** Diagram of hierarchy of civil and criminal courts

The House of Lords (Appellate Committee) sits at the top of the domestic courts in the English legal system and is the most senior superior court along with the Court of Appeal and the High Court. Below these courts sit the inferior courts which consist mainly of the Crown Court, County Court and the Magistrates' Court.

## The House of Lords (Appellate Committee)

The House of Lords (not to be confused with the second chamber of Parliament) is the most senior domestic court in England and Wales. The Lords are bound by decisions that are made in the ECJ. This has caused a lot of controversy in this country. One of the most important functions of the House of Lords is where its judges – the Law

Lords – sit and hear appeals from lower courts asking for clarification or interpretation of the law. Because it sits at the top of the English hierarchy of courts, its decisions are very important and the courts below must follow its decisions or rulings. Importantly, if the House of Lords makes a decision, it is able to change its mind at a later date and overrule the previous decision. This has not always been the case.

Up to the end of the nineteenth century the House of Lords had allowed themselves the power to overrule its own decisions and not be bound by previous decisions, to allow flexibility. In 1898 in *London Street Tramways Co Ltd v London County Council* the Lords decided that certainty in the law was more important than flexibility and decreed in that case that they would be bound by their previous decisions. The *only* exception to this rule would be if the Lords made a decision by mistake and clearly got the law wrong. In that case the decision could be overruled and thus put right.

The responsibility of law reform was put on Parliament – if the Lords made a decision that they wanted to change (and now could not), it was up to Parliament as supreme lawmaker to pass an Act of Parliament to change the law. This caused problems, most notably in *DPP v Smith* (1960), where the Lords decided that the definition of the word 'intent' was to be decided objectively, which contradicted the existing common law which had looked at it from a subjective perspective.

Unable to amend their own decision and in reaction to criticism of the decision in *Smith*, Parliament passed the Criminal Justice Act 1967 which changed the ruling in *Smith*.

Following criticism the Lord Chancellor, Lord Gardiner, issued in 1966 a Practice Statement which allowed the Lords to change their minds in certain limited circumstances and change previous decisions they had made – when 'it is right to do so'. This allowed the Lords to go back to the more flexible position that they had been in before 1898 – they could amend the law in appropriate circumstances. Initially, the Lords were reluctant to use the Practice Statement. In 1972 in a civil case *Herrington v British Railways Board*, the Lords were asked to reconsider the earlier case of *Addie v Dumbreck* (1929).

Both cases concerned the liability of owners of land to child trespassers who are injured on their land. In *Addie* the Lords had decided that an owner of land would only be liable for injury to such children if they deliberately injured the child or were reckless in allowing the child to get injured. Therefore, the owner of land would not be liable to a young child who strayed onto the defendant's land and was injured by the child's own actions. In *Herrington*, a child had trespassed onto the defendant's land through a hole in a fence of which the defendant was aware, and was seriously injured on railway lines. The Lords used the 1966 Practice Statement to modify the decision in *Addie*. They said the test as to whether the defendant owed a duty to the child trespasser was extended to *whether they had done all they could* to protect a trespasser. As the defendant had not (as they knew there was a hole in the fence), then they were liable to the child.

The Lords were somewhat reluctant to use the Practice Statement in criminal cases. This was to ensure that the law was more certain, since the liberty of individuals is at stake. The first criminal case that used the Practice Statement was in *Shivpuri* (1986), which overruled a case decided by the Lords only a year earlier in *Anderton v Ryan* (1985). A more recent example is in *R v G and R* (2003), which overruled the previous decision in *R v Caldwell* (1982) over the true test of the meaning of recklessness.

## Supreme Court

Following the passing of the Constitutional Reform Act 2005, a new Supreme Court will be created in October 2009. This will replace the House of Lords and become the highest appeal court in the United Kingdom, hearing appeals from England, Wales, Scotland and Northern Ireland. The creation of the Supreme Court is in direct response to criticism that because the Law Lords sit as judges in the House of Lords (Appellate Committee) and also sit in the upper House of Parliament where they can take part in the debate and enactment of Government legislation, this is seen as a conflict of interest.

## The Court of Appeal (Civil Division)

Below the House of Lords in the hierarchy is the Court of Appeal, which must follow decisions made by the ECJ and the House of Lords/Supreme Court. The Court of Appeal is split into a Civil Division and a Criminal Division dealing with the respective areas of law. The Court of Appeal (Civil Division) is bound also by its own rulings unless one of the three exceptions in *Young v Bristol Aeroplane Co Ltd* (1944) applies. The exceptions are:

- where two previous decisions of the Court of Appeal contradict each other. Here the Court of Appeal can choose which of the two decisions to follow and which one to ignore
- where a previous Court of Appeal decision conflicts with a decision made (usually later) by the House of Lords. Here, because of the hierarchy of the courts, the Court of Appeal must follow the House of Lords decision and ignore its own earlier decision
- where a decision has been made *per incuriam*. This means without care or by mistake. Here, the Court of Appeal may simply have made a mistake and this is amended by a later Court of Appeal case.

## The Court of Appeal (Criminal Division)

The Criminal Division is bound by the same three exceptions in *Young* as the Civil Division. Since the ultimate punishment for a crime is prison, the Court of Appeal Criminal Division has been more flexible in allowing itself to overrule its own previous decision if it feels that the law has been 'misapplied or misunderstood'.

## The Divisional Courts

Next in the hierarchy is the three Divisional Courts. They deal with specific areas of law and are again bound by those courts above them in the hierarchy and by their own decisions, unless one of the exceptions in *Young* applies.

## The High Court and the inferior courts

The High Court is again bound by the decisions of all the courts above it in the hierarchy. It normally binds itself, but judges can, if they wish, depart from previous High Court decisions, provided that there is no precedent set by those courts above it. The inferior courts – the Crown Court, County Court and Magistrates' Court – do not technically create precedent. It could be possible for the Crown or County Court to create an 'original' precedent that a Magistrates' Court would have to follow.

 **ACTIVITY**

### Activity 7

Consider the following situations in the superior courts. Assuming the facts of each case to be similar, decide whether the later case is bound by the previous decision.

1. Case X was decided by the House of Lords in 1945. Case Y comes before the House of Lords in 1963.

2. Case X was decided by the House of Lords in 1945. Case Y comes before the House of Lords in 1970.

3. Case X was decided by the Court of Appeal (Criminal Division) in 1985. Case Y comes before the Court of Appeal (Criminal Division) in 2000.

4. Case X was decided by the European Court of Justice in 1975. Case Y comes before the Supreme Court in 2009.

## Law Reports

All superior courts' decisions are published both on paper and electronically on the Internet. The only way a court (especially a lower court), a lawyer or an individual researching law can understand precedents is if they are correctly and accurately recorded.

## How does precedent work?

### Following a precedent

As we know from what we've read so far, the main rule of precedent is that courts must follow the previous decisions of courts higher in the hierarchy of the courts where the facts of both cases are the same or similar.

### Distinguishing

One way a lower court can avoid following a precedent is by drawing a distinction between the current case and the earlier case. It would do this by saying that the facts of the current case are different from the facts of the earlier case the other party is trying to use and therefore is not bound by it. In *Merritt v Merritt* (1970) the court was asked to follow the previous precedent in *Balfour v Balfour* (1919), a case with similar facts, which had said that an agreement made between a husband and wife had no enforceability in law because there was no intent to create legal relations. Such an agreement was deemed to be merely a domestic arrangement with no legal enforceability. However, in *Merritt* the court distinguished *Balfour* by saying that the difference between the two cases was that in *Merritt*, while still married they had separated (in *Balfour* they had not) and therefore the agreement must have legal enforceability. The court therefore distinguished the two cases based on their specific facts.

### Overruling

Sometimes a judge will decide that the precedent in a previous case was wrongly decided. When he makes this decision he is said to overrule the

## ACTIVITY

### Activity 8

There are three main ways in which a court can avoid a previous decision. Identify the most appropriate type of avoidance for each of the following three scenarios. Fill in the table with the most appropriate type from the list below.
- distinguishing
- overruling
- reversing.

| Scenario | Situation | Most appropriate type of avoiding a previous precedent |
| --- | --- | --- |
| A | The Supreme Court in 2009 disagrees with the decision of the High Court in 1990. | |
| B | The High Court in 2007 decides not to follow a Court of Appeal decision made in 1975 because of differences in the facts. | |
| C | The Supreme Court hears an appeal from the Queen's Bench Division and disagrees with their decision. | |

Table 1.4

previous decision and make a new binding precedent in its place. This was the case in *Shivpuri* (1986). A previous case's decision can only be overruled by a court more senior in the hierarchy.

### Reversing

Both distinguishing and overruling cases involves considering different cases at different times. The process of reversing involves the same case. If a lower court decides a precedent, say in one of the Divisional Courts, and the case is asked to be heard in a higher court, called an appeal, then if the judge in the higher court feels the lower court made the wrong decision, he can change or 'reverse' the decision of the lower court to that he thinks is correct.

### Adapting

It may be that a higher court thinks that a previous decision is largely correct but wants to amend or adapt the earlier decision rather than overrule it. The House of Lords in *Woollin* (1998) agreed largely with what the Court of Appeal had said earlier in *Nedrick* (1986) when again trying to define what is meant by the word intent. In *Woollin* the House of Lords slightly amended the definition from *Nedrick* to make the law, in their opinion, more certain.

## What are the benefits of a system of precedent?

### Certainty in the law

As previous decisions are reported accurately, those interested in understanding the law can say with some degree of accuracy and certainty what the law is on a given point. Similar cases are treated in the same way. Thus, judges have clear preset rules to follow allowing clarity and consistency of their decisions in similar fact cases.

## Real situations

As precedent is made in response to real life situations it makes it easier to understand, knowing how it relates to the real facts of the case. There is therefore no need to imagine how a precedent would operate when a judge has to decide on actual real facts.

## The law is allowed to develop

As courts are able to avoid previous decisions or overrule incorrect ones, the law can grow and change with the times.

## It allows the correcting of mistakes

If a previous court has clearly made a mistake when making a precedent, there is the opportunity to rethink the law in a later case.

# What are the problems caused by a system of precedent?

## Sheer volume of case law

With the many hundreds of cases reported each year, keeping up-to-date knowledge of the existence of precedent can be difficult. The use of the Internet and Web resources has made it easier to check, but it is still difficult to keep track of all decisions made.

## Rigidity

Despite the ability to change the law, many judges are reluctant to do so. If a lower court has rigidly to apply the law set in higher courts, then the system in fact becomes inflexible. This in turn leads to a slowness of growth in the law.

## The law can only develop if a new case comes before the courts

As precedent is 'judge made' law, the judge can only rule on questions and facts that lie before him. Judges cannot create binding precedent that

is unconnected with the case – this would be for Parliament to do through an Act of Parliament.

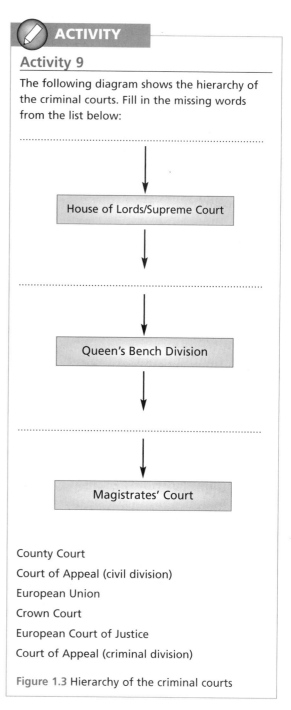

### ACTIVITY

### Activity 9

The following diagram shows the hierarchy of the criminal courts. Fill in the missing words from the list below:

..........................................................................

↓

House of Lords/Supreme Court

↓

..........................................................................

↓

Queen's Bench Division

↓

..........................................................................

↓

Magistrates' Court

County Court

Court of Appeal (civil division)

European Union

Crown Court

European Court of Justice

Court of Appeal (criminal division)

**Figure 1.3** Hierarchy of the criminal courts

## Continued application of bad law

If a higher court has made a mistake, then the lower courts have to follow that decision (see *DPP v Smith* above) until a higher court later overrules the earlier precedent.

# 1.4.4 Membership of the European Union

The important areas to understand here are: what are the lawmaking institutions and what types of law are passed by them?

## Why European law?

The UK joined in 1973 what is now known as the European Union (EU). Originally set up following the Second World War, the EU was an attempt by many western European countries to rebuild their economies by working closely together. The idea was that these countries would be more prosperous when working together than working apart. These countries decided that they would share a common framework of laws, originally in areas of employment law and in trading goods and services between the countries. As time progressed, European laws were introduced to cover other areas such as health and food safety and sex discrimination laws. It is therefore European law that holds together this framework of cooperation. The EU is currently made up of 27 Member States which include the United Kingdom, France and Germany.

There have been moves to adopt a common criminal law among EU member countries, but this has been strongly resisted by the UK and other EU states, as they feel that the criminal law should be unique to that country and reflect its own opinions and attitude to crime, not those of another country with different traditions or tolerances.

## The institutions of European lawmaking

Different to the UK's Parliament, the running of the EU is carried out by four bodies or institutions:

- the Council of Ministers
- the European Commission
- the European Parliament
- the European Court of Justice.

### The Council of Ministers

This is the main lawmaking body of the EU. Its main responsibility is in the coordination of the EU's economic policy. Each member state has one representative on the Council, normally the Foreign Secretary. It can be the case that a specific issue is being discussed, for example agriculture, so each member state would send a government minister responsible for agriculture to the Council. When it comes to voting on new EU laws, each country is given a number of votes that are weighted against its population. The UK currently has 29 votes, whereas a smaller state such as Malta, for example, has only three votes.

### The European Commission

This body's main function is to propose new laws for the Council to discuss. There are currently 27 Commissioners who are appointed from member states with the agreement of all the member states for five-year terms. They each agree to put aside any personal interests relating to their own countries and work for the benefit of all member states. Other key responsibilities for the Commissioners are to investigate large companies trading within the EU to make sure they are operating fairly and to make sure agreements made by the EU are adopted and carried out by the member states. If not, the Commissioners have the power to refer those states to the ECJ.

## The European Parliament

The main function of the Parliament is to discuss and comment on the proposals made by the Commission or any other European legislation. Each Member of the European Parliament (MEP) is elected by the citizens of the member states, similarly to general elections. This is done once every five years.

## The European Court of Justice

Since the EU has its own law, it also has its own court. While the House of Lords remains the highest appeal court in the UK, parties can further appeal to the ECJ on matters that are covered by European law. It consists of 27 judges who are not bound by the system of precedent in the way English domestic courts are. Therefore, the ECJ can create new precedent by interpreting European law and change their minds when they wish. Following a decision, this will bind all domestic courts in the EU member states and therefore creates binding precedent.

## The sources of EU law

It is important that we first understand that there are three main sources of EU law. Second, we need to know how they are used within the English legal system. Problems arise where there is conflict between our own domestic law and EU law and, in such circumstances, EU law takes priority over domestic law.

## The primary source – treaties

### Treaties

Treaties are a primary source of law and as such are the most important source of EU law. They are signed by the Heads of Governments providing the framework to create and manage the relationships between members of the EU. In essence it is the treaties which empower the institutions and dictate the direction the EU wishes to follow on specific policies. Treaties are directly applicable to domestic law and, once signed, automatically become part of the English law. The Treaty of Rome (1957) created the EU. When Parliament passed the European Communities Act 1972, section 2(1) allowed British citizens to rely on any rights granted under the Treaty. For example:

 **EXAMPLE**

Here the defendant had complained that her employer was paying her less money to do her job than the man who had previously carried out the same job. She successfully argued that this practice was in breach of Art 141 of the Treaty of Rome, which guaranteed equal pay for equal work.

*From the case of Macarthys Ltd v Smith (1979)*

 **EXAMPLE**

However, in this case the ECJ said that it was acceptable for a man to be paid more than a woman if she were to take time off from work for maternity leave and therefore was not in breach of Art 141.

*From the case of Cadman v Health and Safety Executive (2006)*

A treaty is therefore similar to a Parent Act and provides the framework, while regulations and directives provide the detail.

# The secondary sources – regulations and directives

## Regulations

These types of law are similar to an Act of Parliament and relate to a specific issue. They are issued by the Commission. Like treaties, regulations under Art 249 of the Treaty of Rome are automatically incorporated into the domestic law of the member states when passed.

## Directives

Directives are set by the Commission to direct member states as to what the law should achieve on a particular issue. It is then up to the member states to pass their own legislation to incorporate the purpose of the directive. Each directive is given a time limit within which the member state must implement the law.

 **EXAMPLE**

Here, the Government banned the claimant from entering the country. She argued under Art 39 that the ban breached her right to freedom of movement between member states. However, the British Government was able to rely on a directive that stated that they could ban such a person if they felt her conduct was against the public good.

*From the case of Van Duyn v Home Office (1975)*

European Court of Justice Precedent – When the ECJ makes a ruling, this becomes an important source of law in that such a decision binds all EU domestic courts.

 **EXAMPLE**

Here, Spanish fishermen challenged the Merchant Shipping Act 1988, which had restricted their trawlers from using British water to fish in. The ECJ ruled that EU law allowed EU citizens to work anywhere in the EU and therefore the 1988 Act conflicted with EU law and could not be enforced.

*From the case of R v Secretary of State for Transport ex parte Factortame (1990)*

 **ACTIVITY**

### Activity 10

Identify the most appropriate type of source of EU law for each of the following four scenarios. Fill in the table with the most appropriate type from the list below.

- treaty
- regulation
- directive
- ECJ.

| Scenario | Situation | Most appropriate source of EU law |
|---|---|---|
| A | The European Commission pass a law restricting teenage working hours. | |
| B | The heads of EU countries wish to increase the number of countries into the EU. | |
| C | The most senior court in the hierarchy of the English courts makes a ruling. | |
| D | The European Commission decide to pass a new law but leave the detail to the individual EU state. | |

Table 1.5

# CHAPTER 2

# THE ROLE OF THE POLICE

## Aims

The aims of this chapter are to:

- examine the balance between citizens' rights and the detection of crime
- examine the police's powers of stop and search, arrest and detention at a police station.

In this chapter we will look at how the law tries to balance the police's need to investigate crime against our right to freedom and liberty. The main three areas to understand are the police right to:

- stop and search
- arrest
- and detain suspects.

However, this must then be balanced with how an individual's rights are protected against any potential abuse of power.

## 2.1 The balance between citizens' rights and the detection of crime

The Human Rights Act 1998 covers our individual freedoms. This means (with certain limitations) that we can go where we want, when we want, without fear of being stopped from doing so. The right to liberty cannot be taken away from a citizen unless, for example, he has broken the criminal law, and his right to liberty can be suspended (while under arrest) then potentially denied (while in prison). The police have a right to investigate crime and to arrest citizens whom they feel have contravened

the criminal law. The public have the right not to be harassed or bothered by the police if they have not committed any crimes. Clearly, mistakes can and have been made when citizens have been arrested and it is the law relating to police powers that has tried to balance out the rights of both sides.

The police operate under a legal framework which is part common law but mainly statutory under the Police and Criminal Evidence Act 1984 (PACE84). There are further statutes that give the police the power to stop and search suspects for more specific items, for example controlled drugs under the Misuse of Drugs Act 1971.

There are eight Codes of Practice under PACE84 that deal with specific areas: Code A covers stop and search powers; Code C deals with the detention and questioning of suspects; while Code G covers the powers of arrest.

## 2.2 Stop and search

### 2.2.1 The police's powers

The police clearly must have a right to question anyone they think is acting suspiciously, without having to arrest him.

Section 1 PACE84 gives the police power to stop and search *persons or vehicles in a public place*. The police may search any person or vehicle or anything inside the vehicle for stolen or prohibited articles. Prohibited articles are described as any offensive weapon, for example a knife or any item made or adapted for use in a burglary, theft or criminal damage.

## 2.2.2 The public's safeguards

To provide safeguards for the public, the police, in carrying out the stop and search, must have reasonable suspicion that the suspect is carrying a stolen or prohibited article or that the vehicle contains such.

Section 2 PACE84 provides further safeguards for the public. The police, if not in uniform, must provide documentary evidence (such as a warrant card) proving that they are a police constable. The police must inform the suspect of their name and the name of the police station to which they are attached and, importantly, the reason for the search.

 **EXAMPLE**

In this case the police did not state their names, station or reason for the search when they stopped and searched the claimant. Consequently, when they searched him they had acted unlawfully.

*From the case of Osman v DPP (1999)*

Further safeguards are also made. During a search in a public place, the police can only request that the suspect removes his *outer coat, jacket or gloves*. Also, the police must make a record of the stop and search. A common criticism of the stop and search is that the police tend to stop and search certain groups of people, for example ethnic minorities, far more than others.

## 2.2.3 Code of Practice A – stop and search

This part of PACE provides guidance as to the manner in which the police carry out stop and search and is another safeguard. The important part of Code A is paragraph 2.2, which states:

66 Reasonable suspicion cannot be based on personal factors alone without reliable information on, or the suspicious behaviour of the suspect;

Therefore the police cannot stop and search a suspect simply on the basis of their race, age, appearance, or because they have a previous conviction. 99

 **ACTIVITY**

### Activity 1

During a stop and search, carried out under the Police and Criminal Evidence Act 1984, the police can only ask a person to remove certain articles of clothing in a public place. Identify these three items from the list below.

- hat
- gloves
- outer coat
- trousers or skirt
- jacket
- sunglasses.

Item 1

.................................................................

Item 2

.................................................................

Item 3

.................................................................

I thought the police could only ask for the removal of coat and gloves.

## 2.3 Arrest

If the suspect is stopped and searched and found to be carrying such items, the police may wish to question him further. One way of doing this is by arresting him and taking him to the police station. It may be that the police see the suspect carrying out an offence, for example robbery, and therefore naturally arrest him as a result.

## 2.3.1 The police's powers

The powers are contained in s 24 PACE84, which was amended by s 110 of the Serious Organised Crime and Police Act 2005. Section 24 now states that the police can arrest anyone in:

- The Future:
  1. Who is about to commit an offence, or that they have reasonable grounds for suspecting they are about to commit an offence, or
- The Present:
  2. Who is in the act of committing an offence, or that they have reasonable grounds for suspecting they are committing an offence.
- The Past
  3. Who has actually committed an offence, or that they have reasonable grounds for suspecting they have actually committed an offence, or
  4. Where the police have reasonable grounds for suspecting an offence may have been committed.

## 2.3.2 The public's safeguards

The necessity test

In order to carry out the arrest, the police must clearly have reasonable grounds for believing it necessary to make the arrest in one of the following situations:

- to find out the suspect's name or address
- to prevent the person causing physical injury to themselves, causing injury to another or to prevent the suspect receiving injury from another
- to protect a child or vulnerable person
- to allow a prompt and effective investigation of the offence
- to prevent the suspect from disappearing while the offence is investigated.

## 2.3.3 Code of Practice G – arrest

This stresses that a lawful arrest must clearly satisfy *two* elements:

a) a person's involvement or suspected involvement or attempted involvement

b) reasonable grounds for believing that the person's arrest is necessary.

The police must also inform the suspect as soon as possible that they are arresting them and why, even if this is obvious. There is a stock phrase that is used by the police in television programmes such as *The Bill* but it is also acceptable for the police to say, which is 'you're nicked!' However, such slang phrases must be clearly understood by the suspect.

 **ACTIVITY**

### Activity 2

Read the following scenario and give two reasons why PC Malik's actions were not lawful.

Billy is in the park playing football when PC Malik, who is in uniform and on duty at the time, decides to stop and search him because he knows Billy has a criminal conviction for burglary. PC Malik tells Billy to remove his T-shirt straight away. When Billy refuses, PC Malik arrests him. Billy asks why he is being arrested, and PC Malik responds: 'You'll find out in court!'

## 2.4 Detention

In many cases it is important to take the suspect to the police station to interview him in order to gather information before the police decide to take the case further. Like stop and search and arrest, there is further assistance for the police and protection for the public under PACE84. The main rules govern the time limits for which the police can detain a suspect, and how the police treat the suspect while detained.

### 2.4.1 The police's powers: the detention clock

The police are obviously allowed to detain suspects, but PACE84 provides the following time limits on detention:

- start of detention – upon arrival at the station the custody police officer decides whether the suspect should be detained.
- six hours – the first review of the suspect must be made no later than six hours after arrival.
- 15 hours, then every nine hours. A second interview must be conducted at 15 hours, then regular reviews must be made no later than every nine hours after this.
- 24 hours – generally, the police can detain a suspect initially for 24 hours. The suspect must be charged or released at this point.
- 36 hours – the police can detain the suspect for a further 12 hours after the initial 24, if charged with a serious offence. This can only be authorised by a senior officer, for example a superintendent. At 36 hours the suspect must either be released or charged with a serious offence.
- 96 hours – If the police allege that the suspect has committed a serious offence and they need more time to gather information, then they can ask for permission to interview the suspect for a longer period. This can be up to 96 hours (four days).

- 28 days – terrorist suspects are allowed to be detained for up to 28 days. In October 2008 there was an unsuccessful attempt by the Government to introduce legislation to allow terrorist suspects to be detained for up to 42 days without charge.

### 2.4.2 The public's safeguards

There are two key safeguards under ss 56 and 58 of PACE84 and under Code of Practice C when a suspect is detained. Code C provides further safeguards:

#### The right to have someone informed of the detention (s 56)

This is to enable a person who has an interest in the welfare of the suspect to be duly notified. This person, for example a spouse or parent, is notified as soon as possible of the fact and reason for the arrest. This can be delayed for up to 36 hours if the police believe such notification could hamper their investigation.

#### The right to legal advice (s 58)

The suspect must be informed of this right by the custody officer and can choose their own solicitor, or one will be appointed free of charge while they are detained. The suspect will sign the custody record to acknowledge that they understand this right. Again, the right to legal advice can be delayed for up to 36 hours for similar reasons as in s 56 above.

#### The right to consult the Codes of Practice

Under Code C the suspect is allowed to have a copy and to read the Codes while detained.

#### Adequate facilities to interview the suspect

Under Code C the suspect must have adequately lit, heated and ventilated accommodation while in the police cell and in an interview room. They are also entitled to breaks from interviews with meals and at least eight hours of rest in each 24 hours.

## Tape or video recording of the interview

All police interviews must be tape recorded. Some are video recorded, but this is rare. Two copies of the recording are kept. One is a working copy for police or court use, while the other is sealed and stored for safety. This is an attempt to prevent either the police or the suspect denying anything that was said or discussed during the interview.

## An appropriate adult present

If the suspect is under 17 or has a learning difficulty or disability, then 'an appropriate adult' must be present during the interview as well as the suspect's solicitor. This would normally be a parent or guardian, or could be a social worker. In *R v Aspinall* (1999) it was decided that a person suffering from schizophrenia should have an appropriate adult present. That would be the case, even if the suspect appeared to understand what was going on.

## The right to silence

The suspect can choose to remain silent during the interview and refuse to answer questions. Sections 34–39 of the Criminal Justice and Public Order Act 1994 allows the refusal to answer questions during interview to be raised in any subsequent trial. A jury could therefore think that the suspect remained silent to hide information to avoid a conviction. This has been strongly criticised by human rights groups

## Freedom from oppression

Section 76 of PACE84 states that evidence gained under torture, inhuman or degrading treatment or the use of threats or violence is inadmissible as evidence in court.

---

✏️ **ACTIVITY**

**Activity 3**

State three rights that a person is entitled to when they have been detained at a police station:

Right 1

......................................................................

Right 2

......................................................................

Right 3

......................................................................

---

## 2.5 Search powers at the police station

## 2.5.1 Further gathering of evidence

Searches – When the suspect is brought to the police station, the police need to know what items they are carrying with them. Many items will be confiscated from them if the police believe they could injure themselves, others or use them to help them escape. The custody officer can authorise a general or non-intimate search which looks into pockets or under hats, for example. Two further types of search can be carried out:

## Strip searches

This involves the '*removal of more than the outer clothing*'. This search is to find and remove items from the suspect that they must not be allowed to keep or if there is reasonable suspicion that they are carrying such an article. The search must be carried out away from the gaze of the public and only carried out by police of the same gender. The suspect is not expected to remove all of their clothes at the same time.

## Intimate searches

This is 'a search which consists of the physical examination of a person's body orifices other than the mouth'. It can only be authorised by a high-ranking police officer if the police believe that the suspect has hidden on him an item he could use to cause physical harm to himself or others or is suspected of being in possession of a Class A drug such as heroin. Searches for drugs can only be carried out by a suitably qualified person such as a doctor or a nurse, while a search for any other article can also be carried out by another 'person' as authorised by a high-ranking police officer.

---

### ✎ ACTIVITY

### Activity 4

1. It is important that the police have powers to investigate crime. Some people however think that the police have too many powers.

   Identify three ways in which the law tries to balance individual rights with police powers.

   Way 1.................................................................................................................................

   Way 2.................................................................................................................................

   Way 3.................................................................................................................................

2. Consider the following statements and state in the box next to each whether you think the statement is true or false.

| Statement | Response |
|---|---|
| The Police and Critical Evidence Act 1984 is the main piece of legislation covering the police's powers. | |
| The police are able to stop and search a youth on the basis that they are wearing a hooded top. | |
| The police can arrest someone who is about to commit a crime or provided that they have reasonable suspicion that they are about to commit a crime. | |
| The police are able to detain a suspect for up to 24 hours without interviewing him. | |

Table 2.1

# CHAPTER 3

# THE CRIMINAL COURTS

## Aims

The aims of this chapter are to:

- discuss pre-trial matters
- look at the different classification of offences
- define the basic criminal trial process
- understand the criminal appeals process
- look at paying for criminal legal services.

If something is taken to court the first important consideration is what exactly the suspect is accused of doing. Once this is decided, then this dictates in which criminal court the case will start. Second, when the correct court is decided, then there is a procedure to follow which directs the case through that court. There may also be a disagreement at the end of the trial which requires the defendant to appeal against the decision to a higher court in the hierarchy for a more senior judge to consider the case.

## 3.1 Pre-trial matters

In criminal trials it is not the victim who pursues the suspect through the courts; it is the Crown Prosecution Service (CPS) on advice from the police. Once the police have interviewed the suspect and believe there is sufficient evidence to convict the suspect, the file is then handed to the CPS. The CPS decides whether it is in the public's interest to prosecute the suspect and whether there is indeed sufficient evidence for a likely conviction. The CPS must find the defendant guilty 'beyond all reasonable doubt' in criminal trials. This is termed the burden of proof in a criminal case.

## 3.2 Classification of offences

Criminal offences can be classified in many different ways. This could be by type, such as offences against the person, for example murder; or offences against property, for example theft. The most common way to classify offences is to divide the crimes into levels of seriousness. There are three broad categories of offence.

1.  Summary offence
    These are relatively minor offences, and are tried only in a Magistrates' Court. They are dealt with usually by three magistrates who act as judge and jury. Examples include assault and battery and exceeding the speed limit. More serious offences are normally tried in the Crown Court but before such a trial, the magistrates may be called upon to decide the issue of a defendant's liberty and their request for bail, rather than staying on remand in custody awaiting trial. These offences will carry a fine or a limited time in prison, usually up to a maximum of six months.

2.  Indictable offences
    These are the more serious, complicated offences tried only in the Crown Court. Examples of such offences are: murder, manslaughter and robbery. These offences carry heavy sentencing possibilities including life imprisonment and unlimited fines.

3. Triable either way

These offences can either be tried in the Magistrates' Court or in the Crown Court. Normally the defendant is asked how he pleads to this offence. If guilty, then the magistrate may be able to deal with the whole case. If the defendant pleads not guilty, then the magistrates may, using a process known as committal proceedings, send the defendant to Crown Court for a full trial under the Magistrates' Courts Act 1980. It may be that the magistrates decide they can hear the trial but send the defendant to the Crown Court for sentencing as they feel their powers are insufficient. Examples of triable either way offences are theft and actual bodily harm (ABH).

## 3.3 Basic criminal trial process

## 3.3.1 In the Magistrates' Court

All criminal cases will begin in the Magistrates' Court regardless of how serious the crime is. The vast majority, around 95 per cent, will be fully dealt with in that court. Only around 5 per cent of cases are so serious that they must be sent to the Crown Court for the full trial. If it is a summary case, then it can be dealt with usually in one sitting or hearing. However, for many summary cases there can be a delay where the defendant pleads not guilty and the case has to be put back or adjourned until a later date. This is normally to allow the prosecution to gather further evidence or to call witnesses.

 **ACTIVITY**

### Activity 1

Match the type of criminal offence to the most appropriate criminal court that would hear the case. Place the appropriate number next to each letter in the grid below.

| A | |
|---|---|
| B | |
| C | |

| 1 | John is charged with common assault after he threatens his wife with a hammer |
|---|---|
| 2 | Shulpa is charged with ABH when she deliberately breaks Omar's leg with a cricket bat |
| 3 | Claire is charged with murder after she violently stabs Steve to death |

| A | Either the Magistrates' Court or the Crown Court |
|---|---|
| B | Crown Court |
| C | Magistrates' Court |

Table 4.1

The procedure for a summary case depends on whether the defendant pleads guilty or not guilty.

## Not guilty

Here the prosecution begins the case by outlining the crime that the defendant is alleged to have carried out. This is followed by the prosecution, if necessary, calling their witnesses to ask them questions in court about the crime. At this point if prosecution witnesses are used, the defence is entitled to ask them questions. This is known as cross-examining. After the prosecution witnesses are called, the defence can call their own witnesses to give evidence and these witnesses again can be cross-examined by the prosecution. After hearing all the evidence, the magistrates will make a decision whether or not the defendant is guilty of the crime. If they feel he is not guilty, the defendant is free to leave court. If the magistrates believe the defendant is guilty, he will be sentenced by the magistrates. It is possible that the magistrates will ask for reports about the defendant and look at previous convictions before deciding.

## Guilty

If the defendant pleads guilty the prosecution will read out the facts of the case in court. If the defence agrees to the facts, then the background and reasons behind him committing the crime can be looked at. Importantly, previous convictions or the defendant's mental health can be looked at. This may make the sentence worse or better. Once the facts and background are established, the magistrate will sentence the defendant.

## 3.3.2 In the Crown Court

The Crown Court deals with cases that involve very serious offences and those triable-either-way offences that the magistrates do not think they have sufficient power to try. If the defendant has

pleaded guilty, then a single judge known as a circuit judge or a part-time judge known as a recorder will hear the facts and evidence and decide the appropriate sentence. If the defendant pleads not guilty, then the case will be heard by a judge and jury. The jury will decide whether the defendant is guilty or not guilty based on the evidence. If they find him guilty, then the judge's ultimate role is to pass sentence. In high-profile criminal cases, a High Court Judge will normally preside over the case. For example, during the Soham murder trial of Ian Huntley in 2003, Mr Justice Moses, a High Court Judge, sat in the Old Bailey.

## Not guilty

If the defendant pleads not guilty then the process is similar to that in the Magistrates' Court where the prosecution states the charge against the defendant and calls witnesses. The defence then cross-examines these witnesses. When this is finished, it is possible for the defence to argue that there is insufficient evidence to convict and they can ask the judge to halt the trial. If the judge disagrees, then the defence must make their opening speech outlining the defendant's counter argument. The defence then calls witnesses who, in turn, can be cross-examined by the prosecution. Finally the prosecution make their closing speech arguing the defendant's guilt followed by the defence's closing speech pointing out problems with the prosecution argument.

After this the trial judge summarises the case to the jury and will talk through any criminal law that needs explaining, such as definitions of offences. The jury then retire to a private room to discuss the evidence and decide on the defendant's guilt. The jury then returns their verdict. If their verdict is guilty, the judge will sentence the defendant accordingly. If the verdict is not guilty, the judge will release the defendant.

## 3.4 Appeals

In both the Magistrates' Court and the Crown Court, the defendant can appeal against the magistrates' or judge's decision in certain circumstances:

### From the Magistrates' Court

The usual appeal route from the summary trial held in the Magistrates' Court is direct to the Crown Court where the defendant appeals against either the *verdict* of being found guilty or against the *sentence* that the magistrate has decided. Only the defendant is able to appeal on these two grounds and this means that there will be a full retrial in front of a circuit judge and two magistrates in the Crown Court, but without a jury. At the end of the appeal hearing, the verdict can be reversed or the sentence reduced or even increased. It may be that the Crown Court send the case back to the magistrates for further consideration and a retrial. If it becomes apparent in the appeal at the Crown Court that there is a point of law in dispute, then the case can be referred to the Queen's Bench Division (QBD) Divisional Court for clarification. This is known as a case stated appeal.

### Case stated appeal

The other route of appeal available to the prosecution or the defence from the Magistrates' Court is by way of case stated. Here, either the prosecution or defence teams appeal over a point of law crucial to the case, or argue that the magistrates have acted outside their powers. This is known as acting *ultra vires*. In either case, either side must make a written request for clarification to the Queen's Bench Division Divisional Court for their opinion on the point of law. The final route of appeal is from the QBD to the House of Lords for ultimate clarification of the law.

### From the Crown Court

Under the Criminal Appeals Act 1995 these appeals are made to the Court of Appeal (Criminal Division). Appeals come in two types: against *verdict* or against *sentence*. With certain exceptions, only the defendant can appeal against the verdict. The main reason for appeal here is where the defendant appeals on a point of law – similar to that from the Magistrates' Court. The other more recent available appeal route against verdict is where the conviction is found to be unsafe, usually when new evidence becomes available after the trial. Following the 1995 Act the Criminal Cases Review Commission (CCRC) was set up to investigate miscarriages of justice and refer any unsafe guilty verdicts to the Court of Appeal to hear the case again. The permission from the Court of Appeal is needed first. Again this court may allow the appeal, dismiss the appeal or order a retrial. In November 2007, Barry George was granted the right to appeal against his sentence for murder of the popular TV presenter, Jill Dando. New evidence had been obtained by the defence team to suggest that his conviction was unsafe. The CCRC referred the matter to the Court of Appeal who quashed his conviction and ordered a retrial. Mr George was subsequently cleared of the murder in August 2008 following the retrial.

It is also possible to appeal from the Crown Court against the sentence passed. Again, permission is required from the Court of Appeal or the trial judge. It is usually the defence who appeal on the basis of an unduly lengthy sentence, but it is possible for the Attorney General (the Government's chief legal adviser), on behalf of the prosecution, to appeal against a sentence that is seen to be too lenient. There is a further possible appeal route to the House of Lords if the Court of Appeal think there is a point of law certified as being one of general public importance that requires clarification.

## Activity 2

Look at the statements below. Using the list of criminal courts decide which is the most appropriate court to which the parties to a criminal trial would appeal.

House of Lords/Supreme Court

Court of Appeal (Criminal Division)

Crown Court

Queen's Bench Divisional Court

European Court of Justice

High Court.

1. The defendant appeals against the verdict of guilty in the Magistrates' Court.

   Court appealed to:

   .................................................................

2. The prosecution appeal on a point of law raised at the Magistrates' Court:

   Court appealed to:

   .................................................................

3. The defendant appeals against the sentence passed on him in the Crown Court:

   Court appealed to:

   .................................................................

# 3.5 Paying for criminal legal services

The right to legal advice is absolutely key to a fair legal system. Paying for legal advice has always been expensive. People on a low income or who are unemployed may not be able to pay high legal costs. This can be a problem and can historically cause prejudice to them. Since 1949 the administration and allocation of 'free' legal advice (in other words, paid for by the Government and not the defendant) was the responsibility of the Legal Aid Board. However, because of criticisms of the Board, mainly due to the fact that the people at whom it was aimed were not receiving it, the Access to Justice Act 1999 replaced the Board with the Legal Services Commission. This set up the Criminal Defence Service (CDS). The CDS guarantees that defendants get the

66 advice, assistance and representation as the interests of justice require. 99

This help includes:

- free legal advice from a solicitor for the defendant at the police station while being questioned
- free legal advice and representation from a solicitor at the Magistrates' Court
- payment for the cost of a solicitor preparing a case and initial representation for certain proceedings at a Magistrates' or Crown Court
- provision of the full legal representation for the defendant in criminal cases at all court levels.

## The duty solicitor

The provision of the duty solicitor at a police station following an arrest has nothing to do with the financial circumstances of the defendant. PACE84 *guarantees* the right to legal advice to a defendant here. Once granted by the police, the request is passed to the Defence Solicitor Call Centre. If the offence with which the defendant is charged is less serious, such as drink driving, then the advice given by the duty solicitor will be via the telephone. However, if the defendant is charged with a more serious offence or deemed vulnerable, then he is entitled to be advised by a solicitor in person.

# CHAPTER 4

# SENTENCING

## Aims

The aims of this chapter are to:

- identify the aims and objectives of sentencing
- define the types of sentencing available for adults
- define the types of sentencing available for young people
- look at factors influencing sentencing.

The term sentencing is defined under s 142 of the Criminal Justice Act 2003 as:

> 66 . . . any order made by a court when dealing with an offender in respect of his offence . . . 99

In order to understand how the entire criminal process comes to a conclusion, we must look at how, once the defendant is found guilty of the offence, they are to be punished and what is the purpose of the punishment. In the English legal system we refer to the punishment as 'sentencing'. This does not simply refer to sending someone to prison as it also includes fines and types of punishment that deliberately keep offenders out of prison to serve their punishment in the community in which they live. Historically, the main type of punishment was either to execute the criminal or to send him to prison, sometimes for even minor offences such as shoplifting. As society has progressed and attitudes have changed, the ways in which defendants are punished have changed.

## 4.1 Aims and objectives of sentencing

If the defendant is convicted following a trial or pleads guilty to the charge, the magistrate or judge has a range of sentencing options available. Which option the judge chooses depends on a variety of factors. These factors include:

- which type of crime was committed
- the seriousness of it
- the circumstances in which the crime was carried out.

The court is also restricted by the maximum (or minimum) sentence available by law.

The court passing the sentence must therefore decide what purpose the sentence should achieve. Should it punish the offender, reform or rehabilitate them, make the offender financially compensate his victim, try to deter crime in the future, or simply protect the public from the defendant? The sentence will be a combination of these aims. Each purpose can work in conjunction with the other, or be used on its own. Section 142 of the Criminal Justice Act 2003 sets out the five main purposes and states:

> 66 Any court dealing with an offender in respect of his offence must have regard to the following purposes of sentencing. 99

1. Punishment of offenders
   Traditional right-wing governments have always called for a lack of tolerance of offenders and have made sure that the emphasis in sentencing was on a firm hand

in punishing the offender. This purpose of sentencing is to ensure that retribution is taken out on offenders in order to seek clear revenge for what they have committed.

2.  Reform and rehabilitation of offenders
    This view perhaps contradicts punishing offenders, but provides a useful alternative. Rather than sending the offender to prison, this sentence's aim is to change the patterns of behaviour and break the cycle of offending. This provides a strategy for the future, particularly with young offenders, but it still has its part to play for the older, more 'professional' criminals.

3.  Reparation by offenders to their victims
    Here, the offender is required to make some kind of compensation available to the victim. The usual means is by paying the victim a sum of money or perhaps to return stolen goods. Reparation can either be to the victim themselves, or, in the case of carrying out community service (such as graffiti removal), to society as a whole. Celebrities such as singer Cheryl Cole and model Naomi Campbell have carried out community service as punishment for crimes.

4.  Crime reduction through deterrence
    Here, the purpose is either aimed at the individual to prevent further crime, called individual deterrence, or for general deterrence to send a clear message to society of making an example of the offender's crime. A common criticism of general deterrence is that criminals are not put off by lengthy sentences if caught and convicted. If they were, then there would be no more crime as people would be scared of the punishment! It seems more as though the criminal weighs up the likelihood of being caught against the consequences of the punishment if caught.

5.  Protection of the public
    If the public are clearly at risk from the offender, perhaps because they have a violent nature or they have committed sexual offences, the court must pass a custodial sentence. It may be that the offenders are given sentences that prevent them from going to certain places where they have committed crimes in the past, such as town centres or football matches.

## ACTIVITY

### Activity 1

When a judge or magistrate passes a sentence he will look not only at the types of sentence available but also he will decide how the punishment will fit the crime.

1.  Identify three of the aims of sentencing which are set out in the Criminal Justice Act 2003.
    Aim 1

    Aim 2

    Aim 3

2.  Discuss what the three aims of sentencing identified in 1 above are seeking to achieve.

## 4.2 Sentencing for adults

An adult offender is described as anyone over the age of 21 years old. The three main types of sentence available to adult offenders are:

* custodial
* community
* fines.

There are also other miscellaneous types of sentence such as disqualification from driving, where the offender commits an offence while driving a motor vehicle and is consequently banned from driving. As an example they may be travelling in excess of 100 mph on the motorway or may be caught drink driving.

## 4.2.1 Custodial sentences

This type of sentence is normally reserved for the most serious of offences and its purpose is to punish the offender by removing his right to liberty. Section 152 of the Criminal Justice Act 2003 imposes some restrictions on the court when deciding whether to pass a custodial sentence:

> 66 The court must not pass a custodial sentence unless it is of the opinion that the offence . . . was so serious that neither a fine alone or a community sentence can be justified. 99

The judge's ultimate responsibility while in court is to pass the sentence appropriate for the defendant. The sentence the judge passes depends on the crime committed. Most crimes punished by prison carry a discretionary sentence. This means that the sentence set is decided by the judge, based around the maximum sentence allowed by an Act of Parliament for that crime.

It is also possible for the judge to issue a suspended sentence. Rather than be sent to prison, the offender is allowed to remain free, but on condition that he does not commit another crime during the period of suspension. If he is convicted of a further crime during this period then the first crime will be taken into account when the defendant is sentenced for the second crime.

A judge can also issue an intermittent sentence. Here offenders can serve custodial sentences on weekends in order to fit around their jobs or families. This is an alternative to full-time custodial sentences.

## 4.2.2 Community orders

This type of sentence's aim is to reform the offender's behaviour, away from prison, while enforcing reparation to the community or, in some cases, to the victim themselves. The idea is to create an individual punishment that relates to the offender themselves. These requirements can include a combination of the following:

- unpaid work for between 40 and 300 hours on a specified project
- participation in any specified activities
- programmes aimed at changing offending behaviour
- prohibition from certain activities
- curfew order
- exclusion from certain areas
- residence requirement
- mental health treatment
- drug treatment and testing
- alcohol treatment
- supervision order
- attendance centre order (if under 25 years).

## 4.2.3 Fines

One of the most common ways of punishing offenders is in the form of fining the offender. Here, the offender must pay the court an amount of money as compensation for what he has done. This punishment is most commonly used in the Magistrates' Court owing to the less serious nature of crimes. The fines can be up to a maximum of £5,000 for those aged 18 or over. This can rise up to £20,000 for breaches of health and safety regulations. There is the option to fine offenders in the Crown Court where there is the possibility of unlimited fines, depending on the offence committed.

## 4.2.4 Discharges

These sentences are either a conditional discharge, where the defendant is released on condition that they do not commit further offences during a set period of up to three years; or an absolute discharge, where the suspect is free to go without condition. Here the suspect would or may have committed a crime but was unaware of it and no sentence is appropriate.

## 4.3 Sentencing for young people

Statute law states that any child under the age of 10 years old cannot be guilty of a criminal offence because he cannot understand the true nature of his actions. Therefore, he cannot face a criminal charge or conviction. A young offender is therefore defined as being between the ages of 10 and 20 years old. The main aim of sentencing young offenders is reformation in order to stop any continuation of the cycle of criminal activities.

## 4.3.1 Custodial sentences for young offenders

The use of custodial sentences for young offenders is used only as a last resort. If they are to be given a custodial sentence, they are not detained in a prison. Instead, they would be detained in secure accommodation in either a young offenders' institution, under the care of the local authority, or in a secure training centre.

### Young offenders' institution

These places accommodate 18 to 20-year-olds. The offender can serve the maximum allowable for that offence, but if they reach the age of 21 during that time, they will be sent to an adult prison.

### Local authority secure children's homes

These homes are run by local authority social services departments. The homes are normally used to house young offenders aged 12–14, girls up to the age of 16, and 15–16-year-old boys who are assessed as being vulnerable to crime.

### Secure training centres

These centres provide secure accommodation for youths up to the age of 17. The aim is to provide an environment where the young offenders can be rehabilitated through education for 25 hours a week, 50 weeks of the year.

## 4.3.2 Community sentences for young offenders

The main community sentences for young offenders are:

### Action plan order

This is imposed on offenders under the age of 18 and addresses the individual needs or reasons why the offender has committed crimes. It lasts for up to three months and aims to rehabilitate the offender through education.

### Attendance centre order

This requires the young offender to attend, usually on Saturdays, an attendance centre which is organised by the police or probation service and focuses on an organised programme of physical activities or education and training.

### Supervision order

This applies to offenders aged 18 and under who are placed under the supervision of either the probation service or the local authority and can be placed on such an order for up to a maximum of three years. Conditions such as curfews can therefore be placed on this order.

### Reparation order

This is where the young offender must repay the victim in some way following his conviction or repay the community in some way. This could be a financial payment directly to the victim, or to the community as a whole by, for example, carrying out graffiti removal or clearing wasteland. It applies to any offender aged 18 or under.

 **ACTIVITY**

## Activity 2

Identify the most appropriate sentences for each of the following three scenarios. Fill in the table with the most appropriate sentence from the list below.
- Intermittent custody
- Discretionary life sentence
- Fine up to £1,000
- Disqualification from driving
- Mandatory life sentence
- Conditional discharge.

| Scenario | | Most appropriate sentence |
|---|---|---|
| A | Jill, aged 17, steals milk from a shop for her baby son because she has no money. | |
| B | Akbar, aged 26, robs a bank using a shotgun. | |
| C | Norman, aged 78, is convicted of speeding while driving at 70 mph in a 30 mph zone. | |

Table 3.1

## 4.3.3 Fines

It is also possible for the young offender to be issued with a fine. Those aged between 10 and 13 years old can face a fine up to a maximum of £250; while those aged 14–17 can face a maximum of £1,000. If the defendant is aged 18 or over, they can face the maximum fine available for the crime they have committed.

## 4.4 Factors influencing sentencing

In addition to the aims of sentencing, the Criminal Justice Act 2003 and the Sentencing Guidelines Council provide further guidance as to what factors also need to be taken into account when passing a sentence.

## Determining the seriousness of an offence

The court must look at how much the offender was to blame for the offence, and how much harm was caused intentionally or was foreseeable. If the offender has any previous convictions then this must be looked at as being an aggravating factor (in other words making it worse) if the court considers it to be relevant to the current conviction, taking note of the time lapse between the convictions.

## Reduction in sentences for guilty pleas

When passing the sentence a judge must take into consideration if the defendant pleaded guilty. This could be before or during the trial. The court will look at at which stage the defendant pleaded guilty and can reduce the sentence accordingly. It can be possible for the offender to have their sentence reduced by a third if they plead guilty at the earliest opportunity.

## Offences that are racially or religiously motivated, or related to disability or sexual orientation

If the offence was racially or religiously motivated or the offender demonstrated that the hostility was due to the victim's sexual orientation or disability, then this will be seen as an aggravating factor and allow the sentence to be increased.

## Further aggravating and mitigating factors

The court will also look at certain factors that will increase the sentence called aggravating factors, or look at circumstances that can reduce the sentence called mitigating factors. For example, if someone has committed common assault, when considering an appropriate sentence the court might be thinking about some of the following factors:

| Aggravating factors | Mitigating factors |
|---|---|
| If there was use of a weapon to frighten or harm the victim | Was the person committing the assault provoked (this is called provocation)? |
| If the offence was planned or sustained | Was there only a single push, shove or blow? |
| If there was head-butting, kicking, biting or attempted strangulation | |

Table 3.2

 **ACTIVITY**

### Activity 3

Consider the following situations and in the box next to it decide whether there have been any mitigating or aggravating factors:

| Situation | Mitigating | Aggravating |
|---|---|---|
| Andrew kills his wife after she attacked him for being late. He says that she regularly beat him up | | |
| Candice, 16, robs an elderly lady as she leaves the post office with her pension money | | |
| Clare carries a knife when she burgles a house, knowing that a young mother and her two children will be upstairs | | |
| Raj deliberately drives above the speed limit and through a red stop light to get to a hospital. He argues that this was because his passenger suffered a heart attack | | |

Table 3.3

# CHAPTER 5

# LAY PEOPLE IN CRIMINAL JUSTICE

## Aims

The aims of this chapter are to:

- look at magistrates' qualifications and their role in the criminal courts
- discuss the appointment and the training of magistrates
- look at jury qualification and the jury's role in the Crown Court
- discuss the selection of juries
- decide upon the advantages and disadvantages of using juries in the criminal courts.

The English legal system has long supported the belief that ordinary members of the public (sometimes called lay people) should be involved in the legal process. This keeps the system of justice fair and open and prevents any criticisms of any court's decisions being made 'behind closed doors'. Involving unqualified or lay persons in the courts allows trial by people such as you and me – that is to say, the law being enforced on behalf of the people, by the people.

## 5.1 The role of the magistrate

Each magistrate or Justice of the Peace is expected to sit for at least 26 half-days each year. Magistrates normally sit and carry out their role as part of a bench of three magistrates. While all three are involved in deciding the verdict, only the chairperson will deliver the verdict. The other two magistrates are known as 'wingers'. The magistrates' main role is to decide upon the guilt of the defendant. As they are legally unqualified they have access to the advice of a legally qualified clerk, usually a solicitor, who sits in court with the magistrates. The role of the magistrate is split mainly between criminal work and a small amount of civil matters:

## Criminal matters

Over 95 per cent of all criminal cases are dealt with by magistrates, either in the Adult Court or in the Youth Court. Their work here involves:

- deciding on whether or not a defendant is guilty
- deciding on applications for bail
- passing sentences relevant to the offence with which the defendant is charged
- authorising arrest and search warrants for the police
- hearing cases in the Youth Court where young offenders aged 10–17 are tried. Here, there must be at least one male and one female on the panel of three unless it is impractical.

## Civil matters

Around 4–5 per cent of cases deal with civil matters. The magistrates' main civil work is in relation to family matters, but not exclusively:

- making orders for the residence of and contact with children
- proceedings relating to the care and control of children
- the enforcement of financial penalties such as non-payment of court fines and orders such as those in respect of non-payment of council tax

- hearing appeals against local authority licensing decisions such as for the refusal to grant licences for off-licences and betting shops.

---

**ACTIVITY**

### Activity 1

Magistrates hear the vast majority of criminal cases in the English legal system. In the space below explain THREE of the roles that magistrates have in the criminal matters:

Role 1

..................................................................

Role 2

..................................................................

Role 3

..................................................................

---

## 5.1.1 The reasons for using magistrates

There are many benefits of using magistrates in the English legal system:

**They are representative of society as a whole**

The Lord Chancellor and Secretary of State for Justice, who ultimately appoints magistrates, requires that each bench should broadly reflect the community it serves. Magistrates have, therefore, to be appointed so that there is a balance of gender, ethnic origin, geographical spread, occupation, political party membership and life skills experience.

**They have sound local knowledge**

Since magistrates will generally live in or around the area where they hear cases, then it is assumed that they have good knowledge of local issues and can respond in court in dealing with such matters. If, for example, an area has a high number of thefts from cars, then the magistrates can sentence any defendants in accordance with the law and how the local area feels about such crimes.

**The cost**

A professional judge in the Crown Court will earn a salary of around £120,000 per year (at December 2008); therefore, the fact that a magistrate receives no salary would suggest that this is a massive saving to the taxpayer and allows the volume of cases to be dealt with relatively cheaply.

**The speed of hearings**

Since the cases involve minor crimes, the magistrates can deal with a huge volume of cases in a short period of time. On a typical day, a bench of three magistrates could hear and resolve four or five cases an hour.

## 5.1.2 The magistrates' qualifications

While there is no requirement of legal experience or any specific academic qualification for magistrates, in 1998 the Lord Chancellor issued guidance on six key qualities that prospective magistrates should have:

- good character
- understanding and communication
- social awareness
- maturity and sound temperament
- sound judgement
- commitment and reliability.

There are some other more formal qualifications to become a magistrate:

- The candidate must be aged between 18 and 65 years. Someone who becomes a magistrate before the age of 65 can serve until they are 70, but they must then retire.
- The candidate must be able to sit in court for at least 26 half-days per year.
- The candidate must have no serious criminal record. Criminal convictions such as minor motoring offences may not automatically disqualify the candidate.
- The candidate must not be an undischarged bankrupt (they have been declared bankrupt and have not yet paid off the debt).

 **ACTIVITY**

### Activity 2

Using the grid below, complete the table by inserting either qualified or unqualified next to the person's profile to show whether they can or cannot be appointed as a magistrate and the reason why:

| Person | Response | Reason |
|---|---|---|
| Kelly, 26, has several convictions for burglary going back five years. | | |
| Lorraine, 61, is a retired doctor. | | |
| Michael,15, is a schoolboy. | | |
| Norma, 42, has just been released from hospital, having been treated for a serious mental illness. | | |

Table 5.1

- The candidate must not be a member of the Armed Forces or hold any job (for example, a police officer) that might conflict with their work.
- The candidate must not be any person whose physical or mental infirmity means that they cannot carry out the duties of a magistrate.

## 5.1.3 The appointment of magistrates

Magistrates are ultimately appointed by the Lord Chancellor on the advice of local advisory committees. The candidates start by completing an application form that is available on the Internet. If the applicant is suitable, references will be followed up and at least one or usually two interviews will be conducted before a decision is made whether or not to appoint.

Following criticism of this appointment procedure, the Constitutional Reform Act 2005 has put into place temporary arrangements for the appointment of magistrates. In the short term any recommendations on the appointment of magistrates continue to be made by local advisory committees. These are then passed to the Lord Chief Justice for approval, before being submitted to the Lord Chancellor to make the appointment.

## 5.1.4 The training of magistrates

All magistrates undergo basic training before they can be expected to sit in court for the first time. They have mentors appointed for their first two years and are given regular appraisals on how they are doing. Training and appraisal are continuous throughout every magistrate's time on the bench. Much of the training is to allow the magistrates to keep up to date with any new and relevant legislation or sentencing policy, particularly following the passing of the Human Rights Act 1998.

## 5.1.5 The disadvantages of using magistrates

Despite clear advantages of using lay persons as magistrates, this must be balanced with possible criticisms:

## They may have no sound local knowledge

Until the Courts Act 2003 magistrates had to live within 15 miles of the court in which they sit. The Act removed this requirement to increase the availability of magistrates to sit where they are needed, so now magistrates from different areas can sit in any Magistrates' Court.

## There may not be a broad cross-section of citizens involved in dispensing local justice

It is often argued that magistrates do not reflect the broad cross-section required by the Lord Chancellor. They are frequently from the middle classes, professional backgrounds or are retired. Very few young magistrates sit on the bench.

### ✎ ACTIVITY

**Activity 3**

1. Discuss three advantages of using magistrates in criminal cases:

   Advantage 1

   .................................................................

   Advantage 2

   .................................................................

   Advantage 3

   .................................................................

2. Discuss three disadvantages of using magistrates in criminal cases:

   Disadvantage 1

   .................................................................

   Disadvantage 2

   .................................................................

   Disadvantage 3

   .................................................................

## There can be inconsistencies in sentencing

Geographical differences are said to be reflected in sentencing. Historic government data from 2001 suggested that some Magistrates' Courts were more lenient in sentencing than in other areas for the same types of crime. The Government's White Paper *Justice for All* gave various examples from these statistics: some 39 per cent of domestic burglars sentenced in Leeds were sent to prison, compared with only 21 per cent in nearby Teesside.

## 5.2 Juries

If a criminal case goes to the Crown Court and the defendant pleads not guilty, then a jury is used.

A jury consists of 12 ordinary members of the public who are selected at random from the electoral register. This lists all adults over 18 years old eligible to vote in local and national elections. Jurors are notified by a letter called a summons, which notifies them that they have been selected for jury service and means they are legally required to attend court. Jurors will hear the more serious indictable criminal cases such as murder, manslaughter or robbery. On rare occasions a jury could be called to sit in on civil cases, usually concerning the tort of defamation in the County Court or the High Court.

## 5.2.1 Jury qualification

Not everyone can sit on a jury. The Juries Act 1974 (amended by the Criminal Justice Act 2003) lists the basic qualifications:

1. A juror must be registered as a parliamentary or local government elector and not younger than 18 years old or older than 70 years.
2. A juror must have been ordinarily resident in the UK, the Channel Islands or the Isle of

Man for a period of at least five years since reaching the age of 13.

3. A juror must not be a mentally disordered person.

4. A juror must not be disqualified from jury service.

A fine can be payable if a juror who does not meet any of these qualifications sits on a jury.

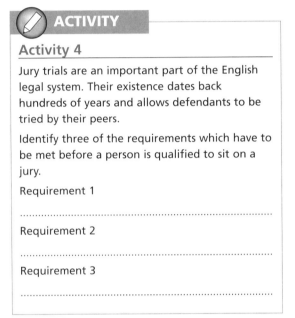

**Activity 4**

Jury trials are an important part of the English legal system. Their existence dates back hundreds of years and allows defendants to be tried by their peers.

Identify three of the requirements which have to be met before a person is qualified to sit on a jury.

Requirement 1

.....................................................................

Requirement 2

.....................................................................

Requirement 3

.....................................................................

## Mentally disordered persons

The Criminal Justice Act 2003 describes 'mentally disordered' as:

66   1. A person who suffers or has suffered from mental illness, psychopathic disorder, mental handicap or severe mental handicap and on account of that condition either:

    a) is resident in a hospital or similar institution; or

    b) regularly attends for treatment by a medical practitioner.

2. A person who is for the time being looked after under s 7 of the Mental Health Act 1983.

3. A person who, under the Mental Health Act, has been determined by a judge to be incapable, by reason of mental disorder, of managing and administering their property and affairs. 99

## Persons disqualified

In some cases a previous criminal conviction can prevent a person sitting on a jury. The Criminal Justice Act 2003 disqualifies some people permanently from jury service and some for 10 years:

Disqualified permanently:

1. A person who is on bail in criminal proceedings, or

2. A person who has at any time been sentenced in the UK to:

    a) imprisonment for life, detention for life or custody for life, or

    b) detention during her Majesty's pleasure or during the pleasure of the Secretary of State, or

    c) imprisonment for public protection or detention for public protection, or

    d) a term of imprisonment of five years or more or a term of detention of five years or more.

Disqualified for 10 years:

1. Anyone who has served any part of a sentence of imprisonment or a sentence of detention in the last 10 years, or

2. Had passed on them a suspended sentence of imprisonment in the last 10 years, or

3. Had a community order or other community type sentence against them in the last 10 years.

 **ACTIVITY**

**Activity 5**

Members of the public can either be qualified or disqualified from jury service. Identify whether the following statements about juries are true or false by putting a tick in the appropriate box.

|  | TRUE | FALSE |
|---|---|---|
| Police officers are not allowed to sit on a jury. |  |  |
| A person who has previously been to prison for more than five years cannot sit on a jury. |  |  |
| A student can be excused from jury service if she is sitting an important exam at the same time. |  |  |

Table 5.2

## Deferral and excusal

There may be occasions where the juror may have a valid reason why they may not wish to sit on the jury. Potential reasons for an excusal could be:

- someone who has served on a jury within the last two years
- someone who has insufficient understanding of English
- someone who is part of a religious order and whose views are too different to be compatible with jury service
- a teacher or a student, particularly during exam time
- full-time serving members of the Armed Forces will be deferred or excused in cases where their commanding officer certifies that their absence would be prejudicial to the efficiency of the Service in question. In other words, if them attending jury service would mean they weren't carrying out their duties to the best of their ability
- anyone who is hearing-impaired and would require an interpreter.

## 5.2.2 The role of juries

Juries play a vital role in the English legal system. Jury service is one of the most important civic duties that anyone can be asked to perform. Each of the 12 members of the jury will be asked to consider the evidence presented and then apply their common sense in order to determine whether or not the defendant is guilty based on the facts of the case presented in court. The decision and all the reasoning behind their verdict must be done in private. The jurors are allocated a room in which they can discuss the case. Even when they have finished carrying out the jury service, they must not discuss their reasons with anyone outside or after the trial.

## 5.2.3 The selection of juries

### Before trial date

The Jury Central Summoning Bureau is responsible for organising the summonsing letters that are sent out requesting citizens to attend as jurors. They use information from local electoral registers and a central computer generates the lists of citizens to summon. The summons informs the potential juror of the date they are to attend and provides a comprehensive list of qualification and disqualification information.

## Jury vetting

This is a process whereby the prosecution and the defence can see the list of potential jurors. From this list, and in order to keep a fair trial, both sides may ask for further checks or vetting to be carried out. Either police checks into the jurors' background can be routinely made to ensure that there are no disqualified jurors who may sympathise with the defendant, or checks can be made into the jurors' background if the case involves issues of national security or terrorism.

## Selection in court

At the beginning of the trial the jury of 12 people must be selected. The court clerk divides the jurors into groups of 15 and each juror is given a number. The court clerk will then draw out cards, randomly from a box, which contain a number. The first 12 numbers called form the jury. The first person called will act as the foreperson of the jury. It is possible for the prosecution or the defence to challenge the suitability of an individual juror (challenge to the cause) or the entire jury (challenge to the array).

## 5.2.4 The advantages and disadvantages of using juries in the criminal courts

### Advantages

**The jury are independent**
The jury's decision is their own and they cannot be influenced or forced into a decision. In *Bushell's Case* (1670) a jury was imprisoned by a judge as he had directed the jury to convict the defendants. The jury refused to convict them and they were imprisoned. They were subsequently released on appeal.

Do you think I ought to challenge that juror on the end?

**It gives the public confidence in criminal trials**
The public must feel confident in the democracy of the jury process in that any decisions on serious criminal cases, whether or not the defendant is guilty, rests in the hands of ordinary members of the public selected at random, rather than tried purely by a judge.

**The jury room is private**
Since the jury must decide the guilt of the defendant in private, no one other than the jury can become involved with the decision-making process. This leaves no doubt that the decision is based purely on the facts.

**The jury are neutral towards the defendant**
As jurors are picked at random from the electoral roll there is little chance that all jurors would be especially biased against the defendant. If it was obviously the case, then the defence could challenge the jury.

**Costs are low**
Juries are not paid for their service other than their expenses. This keeps down the overall cost to the taxpayer while maintaining an open and efficient system of justice.

## Disadvantages

### There can be a lot of secrecy
The jury decide the verdict in the jury room and in secret. Therefore, the jury does not have to give a reason for their decision.

### Doesn't everyone have some bias?
To assume that each juror is not biased, or has no prejudices in some way would be too simplistic a view of human nature, and dangerous to assume in all cases.

### There can be too much media influence
If the case has received a lot of TV and newspaper coverage, it would be very difficult to find a jury that had not heard about the case and could be influenced in some way.

### There can be a lack of understanding
As juries normally have no legal training, everything in court has to be explained in very simple terms and this may prolong a trial. This can then lead to delays and increased court costs.

 **ACTIVITY**

### Activity 6

1. Read the following passage and fill in the missing words from the list below.
   - High Court
   - Crown Court
   - twelve
   - nine
   - points of law
   - facts.

   Juries are mainly used in the ......................... ........................... and sit in groups of ........................... In criminal trials the jury's role is to decide the case's ................. where the defendant has pleaded not guilty.

2. Following the Criminal Justice Act 2003 certain types of people who were previously excused from jury service have become eligible to sit on juries, for example doctors, solicitors and judges.

   Identify three reasons why allowing a judge to sit on a jury has been criticised.

   Reason 1

   ....................................................................

   Reason 2

   ....................................................................

   Reason 3

   ....................................................................

# CIVIL COURTS AND CIVIL PROCESSES. CIVIL LIBERTIES AND HUMAN RIGHTS

# CHAPTER 6

# CIVIL COURTS AND PROCESSES

## Aims

The aims of this chapter are to:

- explain the civil court structure and the functions of the various courts
- explain the track system and how to bring a claim
- assess some of the recent reforms of the civil justice system
- explain the routes of appeal available in civil cases
- describe the various sources of advice for civil problems and the funding for civil legal advice.

## 6.1 The different courts

Civil courts are arranged in a 'pecking order' (or 'hierarchy') with a distinction between 'courts of first instance' (a court where a case is first heard) and appellate courts (a court which only hears appeals). The diagram on page 50 represents this hierarchy and the tables below describe the roles and work of these courts. The tricky one to understand is the High Court because it is *both* a court of first instance and an appellate court all rolled into one. The diagram should help.

 **ACTIVITY**

### Activity 1

Research task

Civil law has lots of strange words that you need to get used to. Make a glossary (your own mini law dictionary) to help you gain a better understanding. You can use a traditional law dictionary such as the *A–Z Law Handbook*, 3rd edn, by Martin and Gibbins, Hodder, and/or online law dictionaries such as Law Guru (http://www.lawguru.com/). Start with the following terms and add more as you come across them in your studies:

| | | | | |
|---|---|---|---|---|
| defendant | claimant | litigation | jurisdiction | appellate |
| probate | contentious | libel | remedy | slander |
| equity | dissolution | negligence | hierarchy | appellant |
| damages | injunction | sue | allegation | disclosure |
| adversarial | inquisitorial | trusts | ATE | ADR |
| injunctions | *pro bono* | *inter alia* | tribunal | statutory |
| clause | contract | tort | matrimonial | probate |

Table 6.1

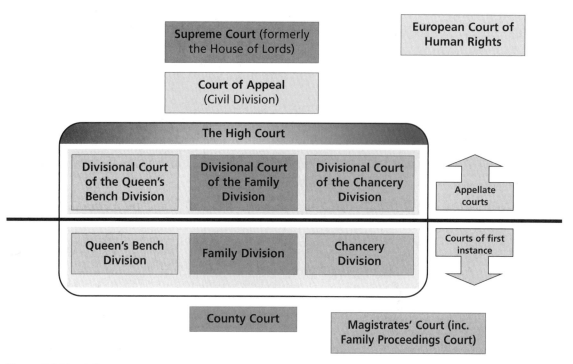

Figure 6.1 The civil courts

| The Supreme Court |
| --- |
| • replaced the House of Lords in October 2009<br>• the highest court in England and Wales for all UK cases<br>• only matters arising under the Treaty of Rome can be referred past the Supreme Court to the European Court of Justice<br>• hears appeals from the Court of Appeal<br>• hears 'leapfrog' appeals from the High Court. |
| **The Court of Appeal (Civil Division)** |
| • hears appeals from the High Court and the County Court and certain tribunals. |
| **The High Court**<br>**Divisional Court of the Chancery Division** |
| • hears appeals from the County Court in bankruptcy and land registration. |
| **Divisional Court of the Family Division** |
| • hears appeals from the Family Proceedings Court in the Magistrates' Court<br>• hears appeals from the County Court on family matters. |
| **Divisional Court of the Queen's Bench Division** |
| • hears appeals from the County Court, Crown Court and Magistrates' Court by way of case stated and an Administrative Court hears applications for judicial review. |

Table 6.2 Appellate courts

| The Chancery Division of the High Court |
|---|
| Hears cases concerning: land; mortgages; equity and trusts; contentious probate (eg disputed wills); tax and revenue; companies; partnerships; breach of trust; deeds and intellectual property (eg copyright, patents and trade marks) |

| The Family Division of the High Court |
|---|
| Hears cases concerning: matrimonial (all matters relating to marriage like separation and divorce); final dissolution (ending) of civil partnerships; children (all matters relating to children such as adoption and fostering); cases about domestic violence and family homes; and cases relating to medical treatment cases – for example, fertility, abortion and surrogacy issues |

| Queen's Bench Division of the High Court |
|---|
| Hears high-value or complex cases concerning: tort (especially specialist areas like defamation); contract; and cases involving non-payment of a civil debt and actions for possession of land or property. (Also houses an Admiralty Court, Technology and Construction Court and a Commercial Court) |

| The County Court |
|---|
| Hear cases concerning: torts such as negligence (especially personal injury cases) and nuisance; contract and consumer disputes; landlord and tenant disputes; land law; equity and probate; insolvency (bankruptcy); taxation; matrimonial – divorce, dissolution of civil partnerships and separation; domestic violence; children – adoption, fostering and care proceedings; and non-employment-related sex and race discrimination. |

| Magistrates' Court (Family Proceedings Court) |
|---|
| Hears cases concerning: minor family matters concerning: child welfare, child custody and contact with children. Matrimonial issues such as the payment and non-payment of maintenance and matrimonial violence. The Magistrates' Court also deals with some minor civil issues such as non-payment of civil debts like council tax and utility bills and hearing licensing appeals against local authority decisions. |

Table 6.3 Courts of first instance

## 6.2 Bringing a claim

### 6.2.1 Background

The civil justice system has traditionally been too slow, too expensive, and too complicated. These problems led different governments to look into the problems in various reviews but the most comprehensive review was undertaken in 1994 by Lord Woolf. He published an important report called 'Access to Justice' which contained many recommendations that were brought into law through the Civil Procedure Act 1997. This act established the Civil Procedure Rules that now govern how a civil claim must be made.

The essence of the new rules is set out in part 1(1), known as the 'overriding objective', which aims to deal with all cases 'justly' by:

• ensuring parties are on an equal footing
• saving expense
• delivering proportionality
• ensuring speed and fairness
• allocating appropriate resources
• ensuring that parties give greater cooperation to the court.

 **ACTIVITY**

## Activity 2

Use Tables 6.2 and 6.3 to find out which would be the appropriate court for the following cases.

| Case | Court |
|---|---|
| Ahmed hasn't paid his council tax or his electricity bill. Now he is being taken to court. | |
| Bob's appeal against his sentence has just failed in the Court of Appeal but he's been given permission to appeal further. | |
| Christina is a top model who was seen coming out of a drug treatment centre by a press photographer. A story has been published saying she is a drug addict and many of her modelling contracts have been cancelled. In fact, she was only visiting a friend and the story is untrue. She wants to sue in defamation. | |
| Delyth is very concerned about a new bypass that the council wants to put through her local woods – an area of outstanding natural beauty which is home to lots of rare wildlife. She wants to challenge the way the council have failed to consult local people by having their decision judicially reviewed. | |

Table 6.4 **Name the court**

## 6.2.2 The three-track system

The overriding objective was to be achieved through a number of mechanisms but at the centre of them was a new three-track system. The key features of the three tracks are described in the chart below.

| Small claims track for claims under £5,000 (or £1,000 for housing and personal injury claims) | Fast track for claims between £5,000 and £15,000 | Multi-track for claims over £15,000 |
|---|---|---|
| Likely to be heard by a District Judge<br><br>This is supposed to be a quick, easy, informal, DIY court for minor civil issues<br><br>Cases are often heard informally in the judge's chambers around a table with the judge adopting an inquisitorial style where he | Likely to be heard by a Circuit Judge<br><br>This is, as the name suggests, supposed to be a 'fast' means of dealing with a slightly more formal civil issue<br><br>Cases are heard formally in open court with strict rules of evidence and oaths being taken | Likely to be heard by a senior Circuit Judge or a High Court Judge<br><br>This is the most formal track for complex and/or high-value claims (or lower value claims that involve complex points of law)<br><br>The essence of this track is the 'hands-on' judges using active |

| Small claims track for claims under £5,000 (or £1,000 for housing and personal injury claims) | Fast track for claims between £5,000 and £15,000 | Multi-track for claims over £15,000 |
|---|---|---|
| helps the parties to present their case and 'get to the truth' | Cases should take 30 weeks from allocation to trial. | case management rather than standard pre-trial procedures |
| There are no strict rules of evidence, oaths will not be sworn and cross-examination will be limited by the court | The trial itself is likely to be one day | Use of case management conferences and pre-trial reviews to set everything from timetables, disclosure of evidence, use and control of expert witnesses, legal directions and trial of specific pre-trial matters |
| Use of lawyers is discouraged and if you do use one, you will have to pay them out of your own money as costs are not normally awarded, nor is there any legal aid and expert witnesses are not generally allowed | Usually, lawyers would be used but with limits placed on costs or 'fixed costs'. The court also normally only allows one expert witness who is loyal to the court rather than to the claimant and/or defendant | The judge also aims to encourage an out-of-court settlement and can insist on the parties first trying ADR (see Chapter 7) |
| There may be a 'paper judgment' if both parties agree and this will mean that the parties need not attend | The speed is achieved through the use of strict timetables and standard pre-trial directions designed to stop time-wasting and running up costs | Trial dates are set early, strictly enforced and should take 72 weeks maximum from allocation to trial |

Table 6.5 Three-track system

### ACTIVITY

#### Activity 3

| Track feature | True | False |
|---|---|---|
| Hearings in the multi-track are informal. | | |
| The small claims track is the best place for a personal injury case of £50,000 in value. | | |
| Cases could take 72 weeks to be heard on the multi-track. | | |
| A disadvantage of using the fast-track is not knowing the maximum lawyer's costs. | | |
| In the multi-track the judge will encourage you not to come to court by urging you to try ADR. | | |
| A case in the small claims track can be heard without the parties being in court. | | |

Table 6.6 True or false three-track questions

## 6.2.3 Starting a claim

When an individual has a civil claim the starting point should be to try and resolve that claim through informal negotiation. If this fails there are a number of agencies who may be able to assist a claimant to resolve things without going to court (see section 6.4). If this fails, the claimant may have no choice other than to start a civil claim.

## 6.2.4 The N1 claim form and allocation to track

- First, obtain an N1 claim form (see Figure 6.5 on pages 56–57) available on the Internet or from your local County Court (http://www.hmcourts-service.gov.uk).
- Fill in the claim form, giving details of your claim and any useful information such as names and contact details of any witnesses, receipts, photographs and the general nature of your claim. Sign the form to swear that you are telling the truth, enclose the fee charged by the court and send it to the court.
- The court receives the claim form, checks that you have a valid legal claim and then sends a copy of the claim form to the defendant. When the defendant receives the claim form, they have three choices:

- ignore the claim and risk the judge deciding the case in the claimant's favour in their absence
- settle the claim in full – in which case the matter will come to an end
- decide to 'defend the claim' – this means there will be a court case and the defendant will either fight the whole claim or accept some liability and defend part of the claim.
- If the defendant defends the claim, then the court sends out an 'allocation questionnaire' to ask for more detailed information about the claim from both sides.
- A judge will then use the information in these questionnaires to allocate the case to one of the three tracks.
- At the end of the case there will be two possible outcomes:
  - claimant loses the case – claimant will have to pay his lawyer's costs as well as those of the winning side
  - claimant wins the case – claimant will be awarded a 'remedy' plus his lawyer's costs by the judge. Remedies in civil cases are usually money called 'damages' but can also include things like injunctions (a court order to do [or not do] something).
- Allocation to track is decided based on the financial value of the claim and the law involved – see Figure 6.2.

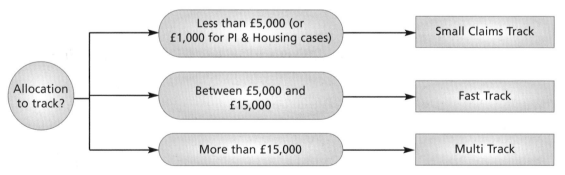

Figure 6.2 Allocation to track

Here is the process in a useful flowchart:

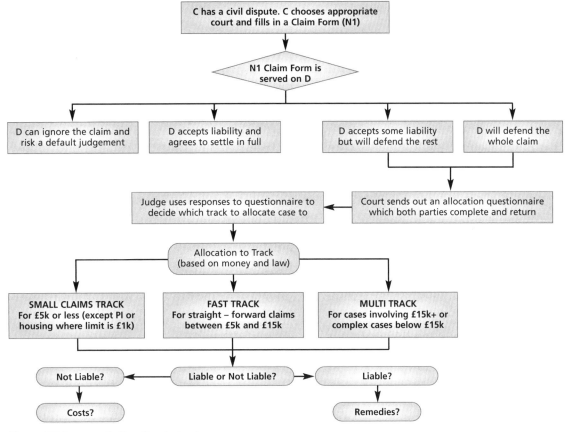

Figure 6.3 Process of allocation to track

## 6.2.5 Which court?

The court a case will be heard in is determined by the value of the claim and the seniority of the judges sitting in that court, but will usually be as follows:

Figure 6.4 Which court?

**Claim Form**

In the

|  | *for court use only* |
|---|---|
| Claim No. |  |
| Issue date |  |

Claimant

Defendant(s)

SEAL

Brief details of claim

Value

Defendant's name and address

| | £ |
|---|---|
| Amount claimed | |
| Court fee | |
| Solicitor's costs | |
| Total amount | |

The court office at

is open between 10am and 4pm Monday to Friday. When corresponding with the court, please address forms or letters to the Court Manager and quote the claim number.

NI Claim form (CPR Part 7) (01.02)                                                                                          *Printed on behalf of The Court Service*

**Figure 6.5** N1 claim form

| Claim No. |
|---|
|  |

Does, or will, your claim include any issues under the Human Rights Act 1998?    ☐ Yes    ☐ No

Particulars of Claim (attached)(to follow)

Statement of Truth
*(I believe)(The Claimant believes) that the facts stated in these particulars of claim are true.
*I am duly authorised by the claimant to sign this statement

Full name _____

Name of claimant's solicitor's firm _____

signed_____ position or office held _____
*(Claimant)(Litigation friend)(Claimant's solicitor)    (if signing on behalf of firm or company)

*delete as appropriate

Claimant's or claimant's solicitor's address to which documents or payments should be sent if different from overleaf including (if appropriate) details of DX, fax or e-mail.

### Activity 4

**Self-Examination Questions on civil process**

Which track *and* court are likely to be used with the following claims:

1. Alice has purchased a washing machine from Dodgy Dave's Electricals. It doesn't work. However, Dodgy Dave's refuses to give Alice a refund or replacement goods which she is entitled to under the Sale of Goods Act 1979.

2. Barinder has been the victim of a car accident because of the careless driving of reckless Eddie. Barinder wants to sue Eddie for personal injuries valued at £4,000 as well as repairs to his damaged car that cost a further £4,000.

3. Charlie, a famous actor and dedicated family man, has just read a story written and published by Freddie the Fly, a tabloid journalist, stating that he has been having a series of affairs with young actresses. The story is completely untrue.

## 6.2.6 Assessing the reforms

The Woolf Reforms are generally seen as a 'qualified success'. This means they have broadly done what they set out to achieve but not completely.

Some of the good things about the reforms are as follows.

- There is more cooperation between parties.
- Judges are now in charge of how cases are managed rather than being manipulated by lawyers in the sole interests of their clients.
- The system is slowly moving to a less adversarial style.
- Active judges now identify issues much earlier, rather than coming up during the case and causing more delay, which has increased early settlements.

- There has been a drop in the number of cases reaching the civil courts; costs are being kept down by case management; and the trial is shorter once they get there.

However, there are still some problems:

- Some lawyers argue that the new procedures are more complicated.
- The system has arguably shifted much of the emphasis to what happens before the trial and has become 'front-loaded'.
- The very strict approach to enforcing time limits has been claimed to be harsh in some cases and a possible abuse of Article 6 of the Human Rights Act 1998 (HRA) – the right to a fair trial.
- Although it has improved – delays, formality and lack of legal funding are still a problem.

## 6.3 Appeals

- An appeal happens when a claimant or defendant wants to challenge the decision made in their case.
- It is not possible to make an appeal simply because you do not like the outcome – it will be necessary for your lawyer to find some 'grounds' for appeal. This means that there will have to be an acceptable legal reason to ask another judge or a higher court to review the decision.
- In civil cases the starting point regarding appeals is the seniority of the judge who first heard the case.
- There will normally be only one level of appeal (the first appeal). It will only be possible to make a further appeal to the Court of Appeal (Civil Division) or the Supreme Court if 'leave to appeal' has been granted. This is special permission from a judge and will only be given if the case has a realistic chance of success and/or it involves a point which should be heard for some other good reason.

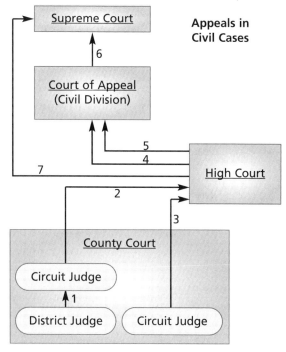

**Appeals in Civil Cases**

Figure 6.6 Various routes of appeal

| 5 | From a decision made by a High Court Judge the first appeal would be to the Court of Appeal (Civil Division). |
|---|---|
| 6 | Following (5) above there may be the possibility of a further appeal to the Supreme Court. |
| 7 | In exceptional circumstances there may be a possibility for an appeal directly from the High Court to the Supreme Court – this is known as a 'leapfrog appeal'. |

Table 6.7

 **ACTIVITY**

### Activity 5 Civil appeals

1. What is an appeal?
2. What is the difference between 'grounds of appeal' and 'leave to appeal'?
3. Which court would hear an appeal from the High Court?
4. Explain why a leapfrog appeal is sometimes necessary.
5. Which judge would hear an appeal from a decision by a District Judge made in a small claims track case?

• The so-called leapfrog appeal will be quite rare but, as seen in the diagram, involves an appeal going 'around' (avoiding) the Court of Appeal. This is done in cases where the rules of precedent mean that there would be no point appealing to the Court of Appeal as they would also be bound by the House of Lords.

The diagram above shows the appeal routes that you need to learn and the table below explains the various routes of appeal.

| 1 | From a decision of a District Judge the first appeal would be to a Circuit Judge. |
|---|---|
| 2 | Following (1) above, there may be a possibility of a further appeal to a High Court Judge. |
| 3 | From a decision of a Circuit Judge the first appeal would be to a High Court Judge. |
| 4 | Following (3) above there may be a possibility of a further appeal to the Court of Appeal (Civil Division). |

## 6.4 Funding and advice

Although there are some areas of civil law where we can represent ourselves quite well, most of us need some help and advice with our civil claim. Whether it is just some initial help to point us in the right direction or full representation in formal court proceedings – what are the options?

## 6.4.1 Sources of legal advice

1. Client-funded legal advice and assistance
   • If you can afford it, privately funded legal representation will give the best choice of lawyer.

- It can be very expensive so it excludes those who do not have the funds – even though they may have a good case. These people must rely on state-funded legal assistance.

2. State-funded legal advice and assistance
   - State-funded legal aid was first set up after the Second World War to redress some of the perceived inequalities between the rich and the poor and to address the argument that there was little point in having legal rights one could not afford to pursue.
   - The system was 'demand led', meaning that provided applicants passed certain tests about their financial eligibility and whether their case was worth funding, they would receive state assistance.
   - By the 1990s people had become more aware of their rights; the compensation culture had become established; and the legal aid budget was spiralling out of control – despite attempts to bring it under control it remained a huge financial burden.

Figure 6.7 Sources of legal advice

- In 1999 under the Access to Justice Act, the old system was scrapped in favour of a new Legal Services Commission.

**The Legal Services Commission**
The body now in charge of state-funded legal aid is the Legal Services Commission, which oversees both criminal and civil legal aid:

Figure 6.8 Legal Services Commission

**The Community Legal Service**
This is the new body now responsible for distributing civil legal aid. Unlike the old demand-led system, the CLS receives a fixed budget each year provided by the government (a supply-led system).

**Help provided by the Community Legal Service**
The Community Legal Service provides the following types of help:

- Legal help
  This can be used for obtaining preliminary help with things such as general advice, writing letters, negotiating with the other side, getting an opinion from a barrister and preparing written materials for court in case an appearance is necessary.

- Help at court
  This is used to fund someone like a solicitor or legal executive to represent clients in court

hearings short of a full trial – like a pre-trial hearing or a case conference.

- Legal representation
  This is the form of help most people would recognise as 'civil legal aid'. It provides representation that will allow you to take your case to court. It has two forms:
  - Investigative help
    where you are unsure about your chances of winning, you can use investigative help to 'test the strength' of a potential claim
  - Full representation
    which in principle can cover all the costs of taking a case to trial and appeal and may be available in family and civil cases as well as certain tribunals.
- Family mediation
  Mediation is a form of ADR (see section 7.3) which is particularly useful for family disputes over children, money and property. Family mediation provides funding for this type of dispute resolution even if it is only to find out whether mediation might be appropriate or not.
- Approved family help
  This provides help with a family dispute that may include using negotiation or other assistance – this comes under Family Help (Lower). More formally it might involve issuing legal proceedings or representing you in court in connection with proceedings, such as obtaining a consent order or disclosure of information from the other side – this is covered by Family Help (Higher).

**Means and merits testing**
Generally, all forms of civil legal aid will be means and merits tested under something called the Funding Code. These 'tests' are designed to make sure that (a) you are financially eligible for state-funded assistance; and (b) your case is worth spending state funding on.

- Means testing
  The LSC takes a look at your finances and decides:
  - how much disposable income you have (this is the money you have left each month after essential bills are paid)
  - how much disposable capital you have (this is how much the property and things like shares and savings you own are worth after a certain amount fixed by law is disregarded).
- The LSC decides, based on these figures, whether your case should be:
  - fully funded
  - partly funded (with you making a contribution)
  - not state-funded at all.

### ACTIVITY

**Activity 6 Internet activity**

In order to help people work out whether they would be entitled to any help the LSC has provided a really useful calculator on their website which you can try out with different figures to see how changes in circumstances might affect eligibility:
http://www.communitylegaladvice.org.uk/en/legalaid/calculator.jsp

- Merits testing

  This is also based on two simple principles which test the strengths and weaknesses of funding your case:
  - what are the chances of you winning your case?
  - would your case be likely to win more than it cost?

**No funding**
Testing is the main method of 'rationing' civil legal aid. However, the government decided in the Access to Justice Act 1999 that certain types

of case should not be funded at all; these include:

- personal injury cases arising from negligence (except medical negligence)
- cases arising in relation to running a business
- cases involving disputes about a company, partnership or trust
- boundary disputes
- defamation cases.

 **ACTIVITY**

### Activity 7 State-funded legal help

1. What is the name of the body in charge of civil legal aid?

2. What kind of assistance would you need in order to see a lawyer for some advice?

3. What kind of assistance would you need to fund a lawyer going to court for a pre-trial hearing?

4. What kind of assistance would you need to go to mediation for a family matter?

5. What is the difference between means and merits testing?

What are the options for those who cannot afford a private lawyer or who fail the eligibility criteria for state-funded assistance or who have a case which is excluded from funding arrangements?

3. Conditional fee arrangements (CFAs)

- Sometimes referred to as 'no win, no fee' arrangements – CFAs are one of the solutions to the lack of legal funding.
- They were made available in certain areas under the Courts and Legal Services Act 1990 but were promoted much more extensively by the government under the Access to Justice Act 1999.
- CFAs involve lawyers providing services to clients on the understanding that no fees will be paid unless they win the case.

- CFAs can be used in any area of civil law except family law and their use is specifically encouraged for personal injury (PI) cases where there is no longer any legal aid.

How do CFAs work?

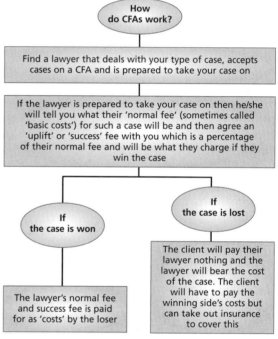

**Figure 6.9** How CFAs work

CFAs points to note

- Lawyers justify the success fee on the basis that they take the financial risk of losing the case.
- They are also working on the case without any income until (and if) they win.
- They will often operate on the basis that the more risky the case, the higher the uplift fee.
- The maximum uplift allowed by the CFAs Order 1998 is 100 per cent and most solicitors are now governed by rules of court which set maximum uplift percentages for certain types of case.

ATE insurance

- Special insurance is available called After the Event (ATE) insurance to cover the cost of losing and having to pay the winning side's costs.

## ACTIVITY

### Activity 8 CFAs

| | | | |
|---|---|---|---|
| ATE | | Success (or 'uplift') fee | |
| Lose the case? | | High risk | |
| Percentage of the 'normal fee' | | Type of insurance | |
| Loser pays the winners | | Advantage of CFAs | |
| Improves access to justice | | Lawyer gets nothing | |
| High uplift fee | | Costs | |

Table 6.8 CFAs matching exercise

- ATE insurance has become increasingly expensive for some cases and can put some people off.
- However, it is now possible to recover the cost of ATE insurance premiums as part of your costs as well as your lawyer's fees.

Advantages and disadvantages of CFAs

- Advantages
  - Some claimants are given access to justice where their case would not be funded by the state.
  - Time-wasters are 'filtered out' of the system as they will not find a lawyer prepared to take on the case.
  - Clients do not have the worry of facing a huge bill and they know their lawyer is focused on winning.
- Disadvantages
  - Cases that only have a slim chance of winning may still be worth pursuing, which denies some claimants access to justice.
  - A two-tier system is created where the best cases are taken by the best lawyers, leaving less valuable claims with less capable lawyers.
  - Those who cannot afford the ATE are left without access to justice.

4. Free and subsidised legal advice
   - Many law firms offer a free or subsidised initial interview.
   - The client is given some free advice about whether his claim is worth pursuing and the lawyers get potential clients, so both sides stand to gain.
   - Many solicitors' firms, barristers' chambers and individual lawyers will give up some of their time for free to help with things such as giving legal advice in Citizens' Advice centres – this is known as *pro bono* work.

5. Community Legal Service website – 'Community Legal Advice'
   - A really useful source of free legal advice has been brought about by the CLS website http://www.communitylegaladvice.org.uk/.
   - The site contains legal advice on a wide range of topics including benefits, consumer issues, family and personal, immigration, landlord and tenant, housing and homelessness, money and taxation, education, training and employment.

6.  Advice agencies – Citizens' Advice, CLACs and Law Centres

    Citizens' Advice

    - Citizens' Advice was started in 1939 and is now a familiar source of free and impartial legal advice. There are 426 bureaux with a workforce of 26,000 who deal with some 5.5 million queries each year.
    - Citizens' Advice also runs a successful online enquiry service called Advice Guide http://www.adviceguide.org.uk/ which has a mass of information available in several languages.
    - Citizens' Advice specialise in areas such as welfare rights, employment disputes, consumer law, landlord and tenant issues, family and rented housing problems.
    - They also work to support individuals and campaign in areas like immigration, human rights and discrimination.
    - In terms of legal advice, Citizens' Advice retain the services of both volunteer and paid professional lawyers as well as their trained volunteer staff.

    Community Legal Advice Centres (CLACs)

    - The Community Legal Service with assistance from various partners has set up a network of local Community Legal Advice Centres.
    - The aim is to achieve a national network (like a 'legal NHS') of centres which will coordinate and combine resources with other LSC service providers to provide access to legal advice, from basic advice to specialist representation.
    - The advice is in five social welfare law categories of community care, debt, employment, housing and welfare benefits.

    Law Centres

    - There are 54 Law Centres, mostly in big cities, which provide free legal advice and representation to both individuals and community organisations.
    - The main focus of Law Centres is in developing the rights of communities and trying to bring about changes in policy and legislation in areas such as housing, employment, immigration and nationality, discrimination, welfare rights, education, community care and health.
    - Law Centres target their work to help local communities in the greatest need, for example, the unemployed or low paid, disabled people and other minorities.
    - They use qualified and experienced staff, which means that they are able to pursue cases to the ultimate extent including, if necessary, the European courts.

7.  Trades Unions

    Most Trades Unions will retain the services of an employment law specialist but many unions also offer free or subsidised legal advice on other issues to their members.

8.  Charities

    Many charities will have a wealth of knowledge in specialised areas such as housing (SHELTER) or mental health (SCOPE). They also often retain the services of experts in these areas and can give quite specialised legal advice.

9.  Insurance companies

    It is possible to take out specific legal insurance but it is still uncommon in this country. However, legal insurance is often 'packaged' with other types of insurance like motor and household policies.

10. Claims Management Companies (CMCs)

    Claims Management Companies are companies who 'manage' civil claims. The vast majority deal only with personal injury cases. CMCs will field your initial enquiry, investigate your claim, take statements from you and witnesses, take photographs and assess your chances of winning before referring you to a lawyer (for which they receive a referral fee) and then arranging for ATE insurance (for which they are paid commission).

## ACTIVITY

## Activity 9 Legal funding crossword

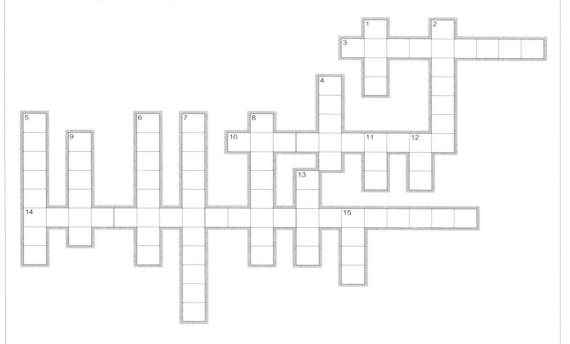

## Across

3. The body in charge of civil legal aid is the
_ _ _ _ _ _ _ _ Legal Service (9)

10. Income or capital could be this? (10)

14. All one word! The name of the website run by the Community Legal Service (20)

## Down

1. Free work done by lawyers is known as pro _ _ _ _ (4)

2. Access to this is what legal aid and advice is all about (7)

4. Different 'trades' have these and you might join one at work – they often give their members free legal advice (5)

5. The body in charge of legal aid is the Legal _ _ _ _ _ _ _ _ Commission (8)

6. You can't get legal aid for this type of injury any more (8)

7. This type of fee arrangement is sometimes also known as a 'no win – no fee' arrangement (11)

8. The most successful source of free legal advice and assistance is known as _ _ _ _ _ _ _ _ Advice (8)

9. CMCs manage these for you – for a price (6)

11. Three letters that stand for the type of insurance you take out in case you lose a CFA (3)

12. These 'Centres' are funded by the Lottery, big city councils and the Law Commission (3)

13. A financial test you will have to pass to get legal aid (5)

15. A scheme run by the Law Society to give free initial advice to accident victims (4)

**KEY FACTS**

- The civil courts are arranged in a hierarchy with a distinction drawn between courts where cases are heard (courts of first instance) and courts which only hear appeals (appellate courts) – knowing the hierarchy will be important!

- Civil process has been subject to a great deal of change, the key feature of which is the new three-track system, which allocates cases to different tracks based on their value – cases are then dealt with in a manner distinct to that track.

- The reforms are recognised as a qualified success with more cooperation and a less 'adversarial' style, but problems such as delay and funding still exist.

- The civil justice appeal system is based on the seniority of the judge who first hears the case.

- There is a system of state-funded legal aid but means and merits testing mean that it is inaccessible to many for whom a variety of alternative sources of advice exist.

# CHAPTER 7

# TRIBUNALS AND ADR

## Aims

This chapter aims to introduce you to:

- the reasons why ADR is needed
- the different types of ADR, examples of each and an evaluation of ADR
- the role and functions of tribunals and what their advantages and disadvantages are.

## 7.1 Reasons for not using courts

As discussed above in section 6.2 the Woolf Reforms were a response to a number of long-standing problems in the civil justice system. While the reforms have helped, many of these problems persist and are the reason that a number of alternatives to traditional 'court-based' dispute resolution have developed. Some of these problems are summarised in the mind map on page 68.

So, what are the alternatives? There are a number of options known collectively as Alternative Dispute Resolution (ADR) and they represent a range of increasingly formal methods of resolving a dispute without going to court.

## 7.2 Negotiation, mediation, conciliation and arbitration

Arbitration, conciliation, mediation and negotiation are the main types of ADR.

### 7.2.1 Negotiation

- Negotiation is the informal resolution of a dispute by the parties themselves.
- It might be something quite informal, such as taking goods back to a shop, or it can be very formal with the use of trained negotiators.
- Once instructed, most lawyers' initial approach to a dispute will be to continue any negotiations the client has started more formally.
- The fact that so many disputes are resolved without going to court shows the success of negotiation.

### 7.2.2 Mediation

- Mediation is negotiation with the help of a neutral third party (the 'mediator').
- The mediator 'facilitates' a solution between the parties.

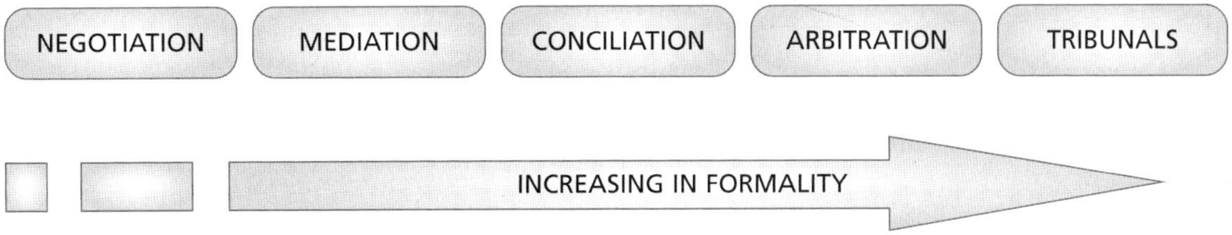

| NEGOTIATION | MEDIATION | CONCILIATION | ARBITRATION | TRIBUNALS |

INCREASING IN FORMALITY

Figure 7.1 Alternative dispute resolution

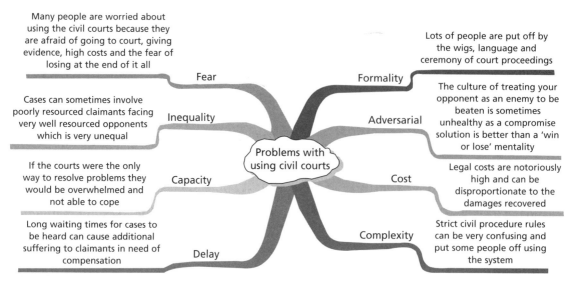

Many people are worried about using the civil courts because they are afraid of going to court, giving evidence, high costs and the fear of losing at the end of it all — **Fear**

Lots of people are put off by the wigs, language and ceremony of court proceedings — **Formality**

Cases can sometimes involve poorly resourced claimants facing very well resourced opponents which is very unequal — **Inequality**

The culture of treating your opponent as an enemy to be beaten is sometimes unhealthy as a compromise solution is better than a 'win or lose' mentality — **Adversarial**

**Problems with using civil courts**

If the courts were the only way to resolve problems they would be overwhelmed and not able to cope — **Capacity**

Legal costs are notoriously high and can be disproportionate to the damages recovered — **Cost**

Long waiting times for cases to be heard can cause additional suffering to claimants in need of compensation — **Delay**

Strict civil procedure rules can be very confusing and put some people off using the system — **Complexity**

**Figure 7.2** Problems with using the civil courts

- Some mediation takes place face-to-face with the mediator 'refereeing' the negotiations.
- In other situations the mediator will act as a 'go-between', trying to find some room for manoeuvre between the parties where a compromise can be agreed.
- The mediator will be trained but not necessarily in the subject-matter of the dispute. Rather, the mediator will have been trained in counselling so he can recognise opportunities for compromise.

## Examples of mediation

- Some schools use 'playground mediators' or 'peer mentors' where pupils have been trained

This is our latest form of mediation.

to intervene and resolve bullying.
- Many housing estates now use 'neighbourhood mediators'.
- One of the longest running and best recognised mediation providers is 'Relate' (http://www.relate.org.uk/) the relationship service that used to be called the Marriage Guidance Service.
- Formal commercial disputes now also commonly use mediation; for example, the Centre for Dispute Resolution (CEDR) deals with numerous commercial clients.

## 7.2.3 Conciliation

- Conciliation is similar to mediation but the mediator (or 'conciliator') is more actively involved in coming up with and proposing a solution.
- For this reason the conciliator will need training in mediation and some expertise in the subject-matter of the dispute.

## Examples of conciliation

- A well-known example of a conciliation service is ACAS (http://www.acas.org.uk) who provide dispute resolution services for disputes which arise between employers and employees.

**ACTIVITY**

### Activity 1 ADR

It will be useful to make a definition chart of each of the main types of ADR.

| Type of ADR | Definition |
|---|---|
| Negotiation | |
| Mediation | |
| Conciliation | |
| Arbitration | |

Table 7.1 ADR key definitions chart

## 7.2.4 Arbitration

- Arbitration is a formal, private and binding process.
- Parties voluntarily agree to have their dispute resolved by the decision of a pre-agreed third party known as the arbitrator (or an arbitration panel) who will be experts in the area concerned.
- Arbitration is more formal than negotiation, mediation and conciliation and most of the rules about arbitration are set out in the Arbitration Act 1996. In arbitration:
  - Both sides agree to be bound by the decision of the arbitrator.
  - The agreement to arbitrate should be in writing.

**ACTIVITY**

### Activity 2 ADR – AO3 Task

Some of the unit 2 ICT exam questions require short 'free text' answers. Try preparing for this by writing a short answer to the question below. Concentrate on developing your points by explaining them, giving examples or putting them into context as this is what the examiners will be looking for to award top marks.

Discuss the disadvantages (or advantages) of using ADR rather than using the courts.

- The agreement to arbitrate can take the form of a clause within the original contract, or can be made after a dispute has arisen.
- Advance agreements to arbitrate in commercial contracts are known as '*Scott v Avery* clauses' and a common example can be seen in Association of British Travel Agents (ABTA) forms.
- The arbitrator's decision is final and courts can enforce the 'awards' made.

### Examples of arbitration

- The Association of British Travel Agents (http://www.abta.com/home) who will organise arbitration between holidaymakers and travel agents in the event of a dispute.
- The Federation of Master Builders (http://www.fmb.org.uk/) who will organise arbitration between clients and builders and builders and other builders.

## 7.3 Tribunals

- Tribunals are the most formal way of resolving a dispute short of going to court. They are similar to courts and exist to resolve disputes in specific areas.
- Tribunals became a significant part of the dispute resolution system after the Second

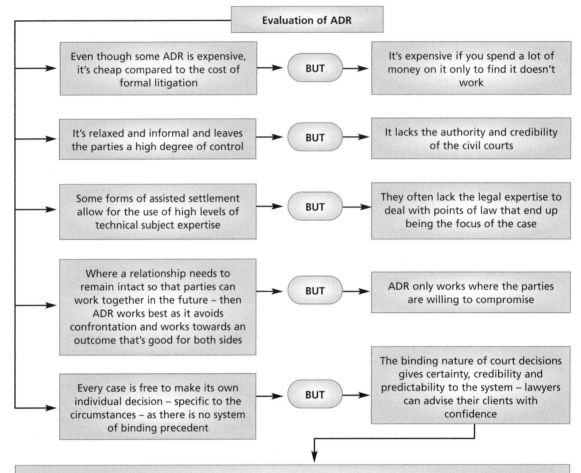

Figure 7.3 Advantages and disadvantages of ADR

World War. The post-war welfare state brought with it many new rights such as education, pensions, housing, sick pay, employment and other welfare rights.

- These new rights brought the potential for large numbers of disputes over entitlement. It was clear that the civil courts would not cope, so tribunals grew to provide a place to resolve disputes relating to such rights.
- There are now over 2,000 tribunals covering over 70 areas of dispute and over a million cases a year. They cover areas as diverse as immigration, social security, pensions, VAT

and duties, rent, mental health and employment.

- The main difference between tribunals and civil courts is that tribunals are often the only forum in which to resolve such disputes (ie they **must** be used).

## 7.3.1 Common features

- Most tribunals have a panel of three members: a legally qualified chairperson and two lay members who have expertise in the particular field of the tribunal.

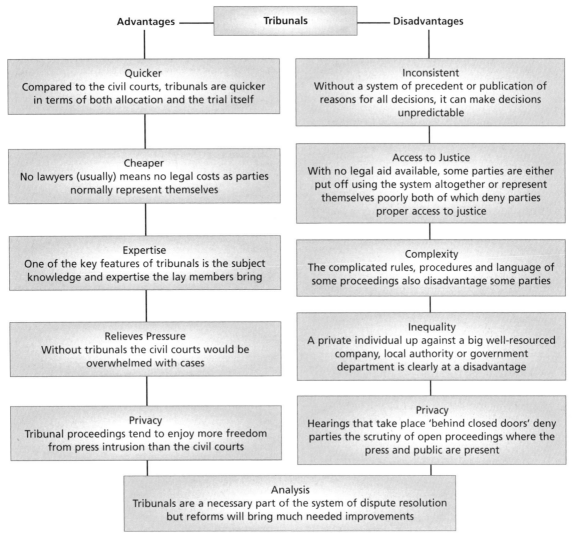

Figure 7.4 Advantages and disadvantages of tribunals

- The tribunal in which we are most interested (because it relates to Unit 3) is the Employment Tribunal. Here, the legally qualified chairperson would typically be assisted by a member of the Trades Union Congress (TUC) representing the interests of employees and another member who belongs to the Confederation of British Industry (CBI) representing the interests of employers.
- Procedures are quite formal (similar to court) and are governed by the Tribunals, Courts and Enforcement Act 2007.

- Legal aid is not available for most tribunals; they use an inquisitorial style like the small claims track and the use of lawyers is not encouraged.

## 7.3.2 The future shape of tribunals

- The rapid growth of tribunals which all operated separately and the standards required by the Human Rights Act 1998 led the government to ask Sir Andrew Leggatt to undertake a major review recently. He concluded that tribunals:

- lacked 'openness' and independence
- were no longer as user-friendly as they were intended to be
- were incoherent – with each having different rules and procedures.

The Leggatt Review contained proposals which are now part of the Tribunals, Courts and Enforcement Act 2007. Consequently, most tribunals will be transferred into a new single Tribunal Service with two new 'generic' tribunals: a 'First-tier' and an 'Upper' Tribunal.

## 7.3.3 Control of tribunals

- Tribunals will be administered by a centralised Tribunal Service established by the Ministry of Justice.
- Tribunals' decisions can be subject to Judicial Review.
- Under the Tribunals, Courts and Enforcement Act 2007 there is now a single appeal system which usually involves an appeal from First-tier to Upper Tribunal and then into the court system.

 **KEY FACTS**

- A number of problems which still persist in the reformed civil justice system make the use of ADR an attractive and necessary alternative to using courts.

- There are a range of different forms of ADR which increase in the degree of formality they employ: negotiation, mediation and conciliation are forms of assisted settlement as somebody helps you resolve your dispute but arbitration (and tribunals) are forms of 'alternative adjudication' as they involve submitting yourself to the judgement of a third party.

- Tribunals are nearly as formal as the civil courts and provide a forum in which to resolve a variety of disputes.

- Despite their disadvantages both ADR and tribunals are a very necessary part of our system of dispute resolution because they are quicker, cheaper and more accessible and 'user-friendly' than the courts.

 **ACTIVITY**

### Activity 3 Internet research activity

Of the many different types of tribunal, the one which would be especially useful for you to know about would be the Employment Tribunal as you will come across them again in Unit 3. On their website you will find a link to 'Publications' where you will find a further link to 'Guidance booklets'. You will find three of them particularly useful: 'Your claim, what happens next?', 'The hearing, guidance for claimants and respondents' and 'The judgment'.

Use the information in these booklets to make a summary flowchart describing the process of taking a case to an Employment Tribunal from making your claim right through to judgment and what you can do to appeal against a tribunal decision. Website address: http://www.employmenttribunals.gov.uk/

# CHAPTER 8

# THE LEGAL PROFESSIONS

## Aims

This chapter aims to introduce you to:

- the qualification and training routes of solicitors, barristers and legal executives
- the role, functions and organisation of solicitors, barristers and legal executives
- the system of regulation and complaints about the legal profession
- some of the problems associated with the legal profession.

## 8.1 Differences between barristers, solicitors and legal executives

- Unlike other countries we have two different kinds of lawyer, called solicitors and barristers, in the English legal system.
- Generally speaking, solicitors are 'general practitioner' lawyers who you might compare to a GP as they handle a broad variety of work; however, some solicitors do specialise quite narrowly.
- Similarly, barristers are generally 'specialist' courtroom lawyers who you might compare to a consultant – although some will cover a broad range of work and some never appear in court at all.
- In addition, both types of lawyer, but especially solicitors, rely on the support of legal executives who are qualified lawyers who work in a specialised area.
- The best way to understand the differences between these professions is to look at how they qualify and the roles they perform.

## 8.2 Training and qualification

See Figure 8.1 on the next page for an overview of the training routes for both solicitors and barristers.

### 8.2.1 Barristers' training – points to note

#### Academic stage

- Start with A Levels
- Do a Qualifying Law Degree (QLD), which is any degree that has covered the 'foundations of legal knowledge' (tort, contract, crime, land law, equity and trusts, EU law and public law) as authorised by a joint committee of the profession's governing bodies.
- Do a non-law degree and take a Graduate Diploma in Law (GDL) – in essence, the seven foundation subjects all taken in one year (full-time) or two years (part-time).

#### Vocational stage

- Take the Bar Vocational Course (BVC) – a skills-based course aimed at equipping student barristers with the knowledge and skills needed to be effective in court. The BVC will cover things such as: case-work skills, legal research, opinion-writing, advocacy, evidence and professional ethics.
- Join an Inn of Court. All barristers must join an 'Inn of Court' (there are four called: Inner Temple, Middle Temple, Gray's Inn and Lincoln's Inn) which is a sort of professional association that looks after the interests of its members as well as 'calling its members to the bar' and disciplining them where necessary.

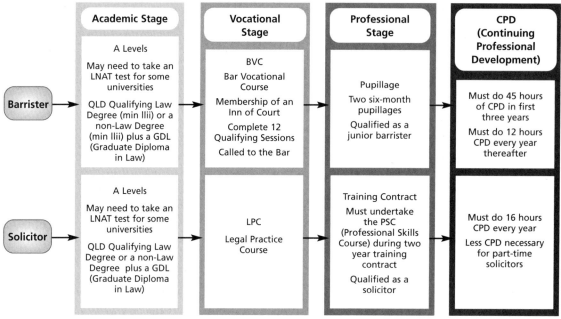

**Figure 8.1** Training and qualification

- All barristers must 'keep terms' or undertake a number of 'qualifying sessions'. This traditionally involves eating 12 dinners in your Inn of Court dining-hall in order to 'network', make contacts and to absorb the traditions of the profession. Because all the Inns are in London, it is possible to attend alternative 'qualifying sessions' (special residential weekends (both within and outside London)) which count as the equivalent to dinners.
- After the BVC the trainee barrister is called to the Bar and must then start the professional stage of training called pupillage.

## Professional training

- Pupillage involves doing two six-month training periods called 'sixes'.
- Both sixes are performed under the supervision of a 'pupil supervisor'.
- The first 'non-practising six' involves learning through observation and pupils will not generally take on any cases. The second 'practising six' might involve a little fee-earning work.

- Barristers are mostly self-employed so at the end of this training, and in order to practice, a barrister must get a tenancy (a vacant place) in a set of chambers (the shared offices from which barristers work).
- If a tenancy is not available, barristers will have to do a 'third six' or 'squat' in a set of chambers until they find a tenancy.

## Continuing Professional Development (CPD)

- All barristers must undertake continuing professional development. This involves 45 hours of CPD training in the first three years and 12 hours per year thereafter.

## 8.2.2 Solicitors' training – points to note

### Academic stage

- This will be the same as it is for barristers (above).
- In addition legal executives can become solicitors without taking the traditional academic route (see section 8.2.3).

## Vocational stage

- Trainee solicitors will have to take the Legal Practice Course (LPC).
- The one-year full-time course involves a combination of legal theory, practical skills and business skills including things such as business law and practice, litigation and advocacy, conveyancing of property, writing and drafting legal documents and interviewing and advising clients.
- From 2010 the LPC is changing to a qualification designed to offer more flexibility to providers and law firms who wish to 'tailor' LPC courses to produce the kind of trainee solicitors the profession needs.

## Professional training

- After the LPC, graduates will have to find a training contract.
- The training contract can be done in a variety of legal settings such as local government, the Crown Prosecution Service (CPS) and the Court Service – not just solicitors' firms.
- The training contract is a two-year period working under the supervision of a qualified solicitor and is regulated by the Solicitors' Regulation Authority.
- The training contract involves a sort of apprenticeship where trainees build on what they learnt in the LPC and put it into practice.
- Trainees will have to gain experience in at least three areas of legal work.
- The training contract includes a 20-day Professional Skills Course which is undertaken towards the end of the training contract to make sure you have attained the appropriate professional standards.
- Trainee solicitors have to be paid a minimum salary decided by the Solicicitors Regulation Authority (SRA) and from August 2009 it will be £16,790 outside London or £18,870 inside London.

## CPD

- All solicitors working more than 32 hours per week must do 16 hours of CPD a year and, when newly qualified, must attend a management course before the end of their first three years.

## 8.2.3 Legal executives' training – points to note

The training route for legal executives is set out in the diagram on page 77 below.

- Qualifying as a legal executive is a two-stage process involving study at levels 3 and 6 that can either be done at an Institute of Legal Executives (ILEX)-approved local college as an evening class or through distance learning.
- After stage 1 the student can apply for associate membership.
- After stage 2 associates can apply for graduate membership, which will improve their career prospects, earning potential and status within the profession.
- After five years of working under supervision, with at least two of those five years being after qualifying for membership, members can apply for fellowship. Fellows have many rights comparable to solicitors and barristers, such as earning fees, the right to appear in court, taking instructions and signing company cheques.

## 8.3 Roles

## 8.3.1 Barristers

- In 2008 there were 12,136 self-employed barristers with 7,681 of them working in London.
- The barristers' governing body is the General Council of the Bar (http://www.barcouncil.org.uk/) and for regulatory matters the Bar Standards Board (http://www.barstandardsboard.org.uk/).

- Barristers are specialist lawyers who give expert opinion on legal matters as well as being highly skilled courtroom lawyers.
- They have the right to appear (called 'rights of audience') in any court in England and Wales.
- They usually take their instructions from solicitors or other professionals but can take direct instructions from the public.
- Most barristers are self-employed and work from offices called chambers where they share the administration costs.
- After gaining sufficient experience a barrister can apply to become a Queen's Counsel which will improve their status and earning power within the profession.
- Barristers' work is wide-ranging and includes:
  - drafting legal documents and pleadings
  - managing cases during trial
  - researching relevant points of law to keep up-to-date in their specialist area
  - writing opinions and giving considered legal advice to solicitors and other professionals
  - preparing cases for court, holding client conferences, preparing legal argument, presenting opinions, pleadings and arguments to the judge and examining and cross-examining witnesses.

## 8.3.2 Solicitors

- In 2007-08 there were 108,407 solicitors in practice, of whom 82,557 were in private practice and 25,850 were employed outside private practice.
- The solicitors' governing body is the Law Society (http://www.lawsociety.org.uk/home.law) and for regulation matters the Solicitors Regulation Authority (http://www.sra.org.uk/consumers/consumers.page).
- The main role of a solicitor is to solve problems for their clients but this can be very diverse. Solicitors might work for:
  - the Crown Prosecution Service or Criminal Defence Service

- national or local government
- industry or private individuals
- small, medium and large firms of solicitors in private practice.
- the Court Service
- In private practice solicitors tend to work in firms from small sole-practitioner firms to huge multi-partner firms – both take instructions directly from members of the public and the private and public sectors.
- The work of solicitors varies enormously and might include:
  - conducting litigation including negotiation and advocacy in the lower courts (Magistrates' and County) and (for solicitor advocates) in the higher courts
  - providing general advice to the public and undertaking routine paperwork such as wills, probate, drafting contracts, letters, conveyancing, divorce petitions, etc
  - commercial work such as registering new companies, negotiating contracts, takeovers, mergers, acquisitions and giving tax advice.
- Although specialisation is associated with barristers, many solicitors increasingly specialise in areas like corporate and commercial law.
- Solicitors can also take a course to become solicitor-advocates which will entitle them to represent clients in the higher courts alongside barristers.

## 8.3.3 Legal executives

- There are 24,000 legal executives who are legally qualified professionals and work in a variety of legal settings like solicitors' offices, legal departments of local or national government, barristers' chambers, private companies, the CPS and the Court Service.
- The legal executives' governing body is the Institute of Legal Executives (http://www.ilex.org.uk/).
- Legal executives will usually specialise in a particular area.

## ACTIVITY

### Activity 1 Legal profession activity

Imagine you are a careers adviser. Abdur, Barrie and Chantelle come to see you. All three want to become lawyers but Abdur is very anxious about getting into debt and doesn't want to go away to university; Barrie loves the idea of the 'cut and thrust' of arguing cases in court but hates the idea of doing too much office work; and Chantelle wants to work in a job that gives her a variety of work to do.

Advise Abdur, Barrie and Chantelle which profession would be best for each of them, why, how long it will take and each of the various stages each of them will have to go through.

Write up your advice in the form of a careers guidance leaflet.

• They can have their own clients and, as fee-earners, their work is charged directly to the client.
• Common areas in which legal executives specialise include conveyancing (the legal side of buying and selling property ), probate (wills, trusts and inheritance tax), family law (divorce and children's matters) and civil litigation.
• Depending on their area of work their work

might include:
• advising clients and acting for them
• contacting other professionals or lawyers on behalf of clients
• researching and summarising legal information
• preparing legal documents such as wills and contracts.

## 8.4 Problems associated with the legal professions

### Training

Although the training itself represents a good mix of theoretical and practical skills, the cost has been heavily criticised. There is little or no funding available for the vocational stage of training which means that many able candidates are put off entering the profession.

### Supply and demand

Every year there are far more students graduating with LPCs and BVCs than there are training contracts and pupillage places available. Some people argue that this wastes valuable resources and talent.

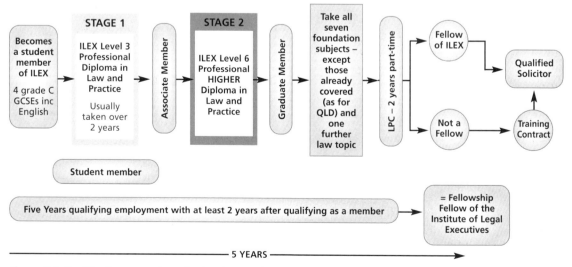

Figure 8.2 Qualification procedures for legal executives

## Ethnicity, gender and class

It is obviously important that the legal profession broadly reflects the community it serves so that it is properly and fairly representative. A less obvious but equally important reason is that the legal profession is where our judges come from and if the legal profession is not properly representative, then our judiciary will not be either.

### Ethnicity

Overall representation of ethnic minorities is a positive reflection of society itself at just over 10 per cent in both branches of the profession. However, at the senior levels of the profession the same is not true with considerably fewer ethnic minority QCs than white and fewer ethnic minority solicitors at senior partnership level than white.

### Gender

The picture here is similar. Women are represented very well at entry level in the profession but less well at senior levels. Interestingly 75 per cent of legal executive lawyers are women and more than 13 per cent represent black or minority ethnicities.

### Class

The legal profession has had a tradition of being seen as elitist. Recent research by the Centre for Market and Public Organisation (CMPO) confirms that lawyers tend to come from a more privileged background than other professions and that this gap is getting worse.

## A divided profession?

Solicitors and barristers used to be very separate professions with distinctly different roles. However, these distinctions have now largely disappeared through legislation like the Courts and Legal Services Act 1990, the Access to

Justice Act 1999 and the Legal Services Act 2007. Many argue that it is a waste of resources and confusing for the public to continue to train and retain two separate types of lawyer and that we should get rid of the distinction altogether.

## The future of the profession

The legal profession has been the subject of numerous government reports in recent years. Mostly, these revolve around how the profession regulates itself and with what are sometimes called 'monopolies'. A 'monopoly' is what happens when one body controls something to such a large extent that they can charge a very high price for their services because they have little or no competition.

In 2004 Sir David Clementi published a report into the legal profession which became the basis of the Legal Services Act 2007. The main areas that will be affected by the Act are (1) regulation where a new Office for Legal Complaints has been set up and a Legal Services Board is to be established to oversee regulation, and, (2) allowing for alternative business structures so that different legal services providers can form partnerships with each other and other professions, which was not allowed before.

## 8.5 Regulation

There are different ways of complaining about your lawyer depending on the type of complaint and how serious it is.

## Solicitors

- The first thing to do is to complain directly to the solicitor or their firm. It is best to do this in writing. SRA rules say they should have a written complaints procedure to follow. You can even get an online dispute form on the Law Society website.
- If this does not work you can go to the Legal

 **ACTIVITY**

## Activity 2

| Tick the appropriate column for the following | Barrister | Both | Solicitor |
|---|---|---|---|
| 1.  Have to get pupillage | | | |
| 2.  Have to get a training contract | | | |
| 3.  Have to do the LPC | | | |
| 4.  Need a QLD or other degree plus GDL | | | |
| 5.  Have to do the BVC | | | |
| 6.  Might be promoted to a partner | | | |
| 7.  Join an Inn of Court | | | |
| 8.  Governed by Law Society | | | |
| 9.  Regulated by the BSB | | | |
| 10. Need to 'eat dinners' to qualify | | | |
| 11. From degree to being qualified takes 6 years | | | |
| 12. From degree to being qualified takes 5 years | | | |
| 13. Need to do CPD when qualified | | | |
| 14. Become a solicitor without doing a degree | | | |
| 15. Have to do a Professional Skills Course | | | |
| 16. Might end up 'squatting' in some chambers | | | |
| 17. Regulated by the SRA | | | |
| 18. Could be disciplined by the 'Senate' | | | |
| 19. Could be investigated by the LCS | | | |
| 20. Can complain to Legal Services Ombudsman | | | |

Table 8.1 Legal profession end of topic quiz

Complaints Service (LCS) who are part of the Law Society but independent of it. They have numerous powers to reduce your bill, correct mistakes or order compensation. Serious complaints of misconduct can be referred to the Solicitors Regulation Authority who have the power to strike off a solicitor (stop them practising).

- If you wish to complain about the way the LCS handled your complaint, then you could go to the Legal Services Complaints Commissioner. The independent

Commissioner has powers to make sure the Law Society are handling complaints properly and can set standards and deadlines for the Law Society to follow and fine them if they fail.

- The final place to take your complaint is the Legal Services Ombudsman who is an independent government appointee who oversees the handling of complaints against all lawyers and has powers to order the Law Society to reconsider complaints as well as ordering compensation.

- Alternatively, you may take your lawyer to court and sue them. There are two main areas to consider. First, if your solicitor has failed to do something that was agreed then you can sue in breach of contract. Second, following a case called *Arthur J Hall v Simmons* (2000), you can sue your solicitor for negligence for work done in or out of court that falls below the standard of work of a reasonable solicitor.

## Barristers

- In the first place you should complain to the solicitor that instructed the barrister on your behalf. If you gave direct instructions, then you must complain directly to the barrister or his Head of Chambers. Again this should be done in writing.

- The next place to go is the Bar Standards Board who are an independent part of the Bar Council. They have a complaints team who investigate complaints and may refer a complaint to the investigations team who deal with disciplinary hearings. They have various powers including ordering apologies,

repayment of fees or compensation.

- Serious complaints can be referred to the Senate of the Inns of Court who have the power to administer disciplinary tribunals and ultimately 'disbar' (remove from the profession) a barrister.

- Finally, the Legal Services Ombudsman oversees complaints against barristers as well as solicitors and you can take your barrister to court and sue them in negligence or contract in the same way as you can a solicitor.

### KEY FACTS

- There are two distinct types of lawyer and, despite recent changes which blur the distinctions, they remain very separate in the way they qualify and train. They are supported by legal executives who act mainly in a supportive role but are gaining increasing independent recognition.

- Training involves a mix of academic theory and practical elements.

- Although roles vary, it is generally true that barristers tend to be courtroom-based specialists whereas solicitors' practice involves a broader range of activity and legal executives undertake specialist but supportive roles.

- Problems with the profession include not being accessible to able candidates because of the cost of training and the poor representation of women and ethnic minorities at senior levels with the associated impact on the judiciary.

# CHAPTER 9

# JUDGES

## Aims

This chapter aims to introduce you to:

- the qualifications and roles of the judiciary
- the appointment process and training of the judiciary
- some common criticisms of the judiciary, especially their composition.

## 9.1 Qualifications and appointment

Like the courts they work in, judges (or the judiciary as they are collectively known) are arranged in a hierarchy as detailed in the chart below:

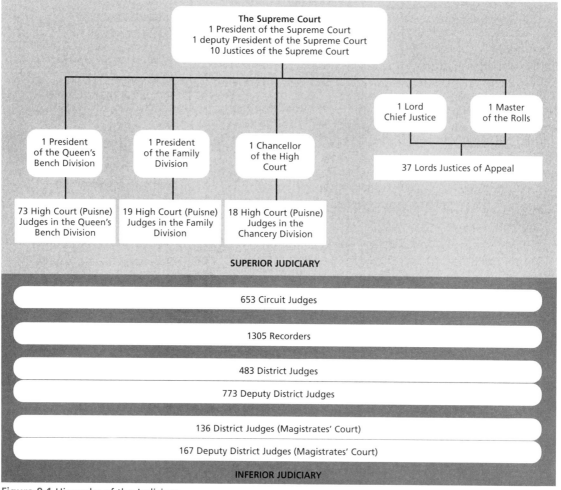

Figure 9.1 Hierarchy of the Judiciary

| Judge | Qualification | Court(s) in which they appear |
|---|---|---|
| Supreme Court Judges | 15 years Senior Court qualification (ie qualified to appear in the Supreme Court) or Held high judicial office for at least two years (eg a Court of Appeal Judge) | Supreme Court |
| Appeal Court Judges | 10 years High Court qualification (ie qualified to appear in the High Court) or Been a High Court Judge | Court of Appeal |
| High Court Judges | Seven years High Court qualification (ie qualified to appear in the High Court) or Been a Circuit Judge for at least two years | Three Divisions of the High Court Can sit with Appeal Court Judges to hear appeals Can sit in Crown/County Courts to hear important cases |
| Circuit Judges | Seven year Crown or County Court qualification (ie had the right to practise in the Crown/County Court) or Held judicial office for three years (eg been a Recorder, District Judge or Tribunal Chairman) | Crown Court to hear criminal cases County Court to hear civil cases |
| Recorders | Seven year Crown or County Court qualification (ie had the right to practise in the Crown/County Court) | Part-time judges who mainly sit in the Crown Court hearing criminal cases, although they are entitled to sit in the County Court on civil cases |
| District Judges | Five-year general qualification (ie been in practice as a solicitor or barrister for five years+) | Sit in the County Court and deal with civil cases |
| District Judges (Magistrates' Court) | | Sit in the Magistrates' Court dealing with all Magistrates' Court business – mainly criminal |

The Tribunals Courts and Enforcement Act 2007 has recently introduced the 'judicial-appointment eligibility condition'. This means eligibility for judicial office is no longer based solely on possession of rights of audience for a specified period. Judges have to show that: they have possessed a relevant legal qualification; for the requisite period; and that whilst holding that qualification they have been gaining legal experience.

Table 9.1 Appointment process and training of the judiciary

## 9.1.1 Bar monopoly

- Qualifying to become a judge is based on having served a certain amount of time in particular courts as a lawyer.
- At one time only barristers had the right to appear in all courts and because of this the Bar had a monopoly over judicial appointments so that judges were almost exclusively drawn from the barrister's profession.
- The Courts and Legal Services Act 1990 broke this monopoly by allowing solicitors rights of audience in all courts provided that they qualified as 'solicitor-advocates' so that they may now apply for all judicial positions if they meet the qualifications.
- The qualifications for becoming a judge depend on having served a 'proscribed period' of service as a lawyer with rights of audience in the relevant court. The details are set out in Table 9.1 on page 82.

## 9.1.2 Appointment

- Technically all judges are appointed by the Queen but in reality most appointments are made by the Queen on the direct recommendation of the Lord Chancellor who had, until recently, chosen and selected the candidates as well.
- The appointments used to be 'by invitation' from the Lord Chancellor's Department based on a secretive process which lacked transparency.
- In an important report called the Peach Report it was thought that the Lord Chancellor had too much influence over a rather secretive process and a recommendation was made that an appointments commission should be set up.
- Consequently, the Judicial Appointments Commission (JAC) was set up under the Constitutional Reform Act 2005.
- The JAC is an independent body that 'selects' people for appointment to judicial posts. It consists of 15 members including six laypeople and nine legal professionals.

---

**ACTIVITY**

**Activity 1**

| | | |
|---|---|---|
| Part-time Judge | | District Judge |
| High Court Judge | | Seven-year High Court qualification |
| Sits in the County Court only | | Supreme Court Judge |
| Circuit Judge | | Recorder |
| 15-year Supreme Court qualification | | Held judicial office for three years |

Table 9.2 Judiciary matching exercise

## 9.1.3 The appointment process

**Adverts and applications**

- Appointments are openly advertised so that anyone can apply.
- Applicants will need to possess certain 'generic' judicial qualities such as the ability to weigh evidence, sound powers of reasoning, impartiality and fairness and be able to show authority – these will need to be evident in the application.
- Applicants will also have to have the appropriate qualification (as in the chart above).

**Sifts**

- This process produces a short-list to be called for interview.

**Interviews**

- Interviews are intensive and applicants are questioned by a panel to assess whether they have the necessary skills, temperament and experience.
- The panel will include a judge and a layperson.
- Technical expertise may be assessed through a written exercise.
- Suitability for some roles will be assessed at a formal 'assessment centre' where applicants will undertake a range of exercises and role-plays as well.

**Consultation**

- There will be a thorough consultation where judges and other legal professionals who have worked with the applicant are asked for their opinions.
- These references will assist the JAC in assessing the applicant's suitability.
- For senior appointments, the Lord Chancellor will always consult senior judges.

**Appointments for successful applicants**

- The JAC does not appoint at the end of this process!
- Their job is to consult with the Lord Chief Justice and another very senior judge and then pass a list of suitable names to the Lord Chancellor, who will then make the final decision and select.
- However, the Lord Chancellor has limited powers to reject a candidate or ask the JAC to reconsider and must put his reasons in writing.

Figure 9.2 Appointment process

## 9.2 Role

The various roles of judges alter according to whether they are appeal court judges or trial judges and also, if trial judges, whether they are dealing with civil or criminal trials. The roles are summarised in the Tables 9.3 and 9.4.

| Supreme Court Judges . . . | Court of Appeal Judges . . . | Judges in the Divisional Courts of the High Court . . . |
|---|---|---|
| Sit in panels of 3, 5 or 7 and hear a small number (less than 100) of the most important civil and criminal appeals each year | Sit in panels in Civil and Criminal Divisions which act as final courts of appeal for most cases from lower courts. In doing so, they also develop the law through precedent and statutory interpretation | Listen to appeals from the Crown Court, County Court, Magistrates' Court and certain tribunals |
| Develop common law through the doctrine of precedent by considering important points of law | Have the power to uphold, reverse or overrule decisions of lower courts and, under certain circumstances, overrule their own earlier decisions | |
| Give final clarification regarding the meaning of statutes through statutory interpretation | In criminal cases they can overturn convictions, change the length of a sentence or order a retrial | |
| Have to refer some unclear points of EU law to the European Court of Justice | In civil cases they can make or alter awards | |

Table 9.3 Role of appellate court judges

| In courts of first instance judges generally . . . | In criminal trials, judges . . . | In civil trials, judges . . . |
|---|---|---|
| Supervise the trial<br><br>Rule on all points of law<br><br>Give legal direction on points of evidence<br><br>Manage pre-trial matters | Control pre-trial matters like Plea & Direction Hearings<br><br>Deal with applications for bail, bail renewals and changes to bail conditions as well as appeals against refusals of bail from the Magistrates' Court<br><br>Manage the trial and the jury, sums up the evidence and gives legal directions to the jury<br><br>If D is found guilty or pleads guilty then the judge sentences D<br><br>Can hear some appeals against sentence and/or conviction from the Magistrates' Court<br><br>Consider granting leave to appeal to higher courts | Use allocation questionnaires to allocate cases to appropriate tracks<br><br>Hear pre-trial matters and manage Case Management Conferences<br><br>Enforce timetables<br><br>Hear cases, weigh evidence and decide liability<br><br>Supervise the trial and direct juries in rare civil cases that use juries<br><br>Rule on all points of law<br><br>Give legal direction on points of evidence<br><br>Use an inquisitorial approach in small claims track cases to help litigants put their cases<br><br>Consider granting leave to appeal to higher courts |

Table 9.4 Role of trial judges

## 9.2.1 Training

Judges receive surprisingly little training. Newly appointed judges do receive initial training from the Judicial Studies Board. This consists of:

- a four-day residential course involving:
  - lectures
  - role play of managing a courtroom
  - mock sentencing exercises
  - meeting probation workers
  - racial awareness training.
- visiting at least two penal institutions like a prison or a young offender institute (YOI)
- shadowing an experienced circuit judge for two weeks.

Newly appointed recorders and circuit judges will then start their judicial careers in charge of a criminal court – even if they have never practised as criminal lawyers.

Occasional 'one-off' training may be necessary from time-to-time to update on new developments in the law (like new sentencing guidelines) or when significant new legislation is introduced such as the Human Rights Act 1998.

The superior judiciary receive no compulsory training, although they can attend voluntarily, and they have research days built into their terms of employment to allow them to keep up-to-date with the latest developments in their area.

## 9.3 Composition and background

Why is the composition of the judiciary important?

- It is generally accepted that the judiciary should broadly reflect the society that they serve.
- This is because judges make decisions which:
  - affect people's families
  - affect people's finances
  - affect people's human rights
  - affect people's liberty
  - hold the government to account
  - strike a fair balance between competing commercial interests.

- They can do these things better if they have some sympathy with the lives of the public whom they represent.

What is the composition of the judiciary?

- It is a fact that the judiciary *are* overwhelmingly:
  - white
  - male
  - middle-aged
  - middle-class
  - former barristers.

The evidence for this can be easily located in various sources including the judiciary's own website. Some key points are summarised in the table below:

| Judges are: | Evidence | Source |
|---|---|---|
| Overwhelmingly white (8.7% of judges should come from an ethnic minority background to accurately reflect society) | Only one superior judge out of 161 (less than 1 per cent) and only 122 (3.6 per cent) of the inferior judiciary | DCA Website Jan 2008 |
| Overwhelmingly male (should be 50 per cent to reflect society) | Only 14 superior judges are women (8.7 per cent) and only 650 (19.2 per cent) of the inferior judiciary | DCA Website Jan 2008 |
| Middle-aged | Average age of all judges = 60 Average age of Law Lords = 69 | Labour Research 2002 DCA Website Jan 2008 |
| Oxbridge educated | 60 per cent of judges in the Labour Research statistics were Oxbridge educated | Labour Research 2002 |
| Public school educated | 67 per cent of judges in the Labour Research statistics went to public schools | Labour Research 2002 |
| Former barristers | Only two superior judges (1.3 per cent) were former solicitors. All the rest were barristers and 90 per cent of circuit judges were also former barristers | DCA Website Jan 2008 |

Table 9.5

So, what is the problem?

There are two sides to this question:

- Some people believe that the judiciary should be made up of the best people for the job and if this happens to lead to a white, male, middle-aged and middle-class judiciary, then that is acceptable. This is sometimes called the 'meritocracy' argument.
- Other people believe that the judiciary is an exclusive group of self-perpetuating elites (sometimes called an 'oligarchy') who will hang on to power unless measures are taken to make sure that there are a representative number of women, ethnic and other minority groups represented.

What do you think?

**ACTIVITY**

### Activity 2 Judiciary research and ICT activity

The judiciary have an excellent website called 'Judiciary of England and Wales' which can be found here: http://www.judiciary.gov.uk. Click first on 'Key Facts', then on 'Statistics', where you will find the very latest data on numbers, gender, age and ethnicity. Next, click 'Key Facts' followed by 'Judicial Salaries Scales', where you will find the latest data on judges' salaries. Use the data from the two sources to make a data chart. Put the judges down the left column in order of seniority and then add the data on numbers, number of men/women, how many ethnic minorities there are, average age and salary.

Put the data into a spreadsheet and make some graphs and pie charts for your classroom.

## 9.4 Other criticisms

## Bias against women

- Some writers (see Helena Kennedy, *Eve was Framed* and Elliott and Quinn's *English Legal*

*System*) believe there is evidence of sexist attitudes among some of the judiciary. Also, research by Pat Carlen has suggested sexist attitudes in sentencing practice.
- The Judicial Studies Board does issue judges with the *Equal Treatment Bench Book* as part of their training and these may well be isolated incidents but, in what is quite a small profession with the power to remove people's liberty, they are still disturbing.

## Training

- The level of training is often criticised as insufficient – there can be few professions where so little training takes place before being entrusted with such important powers.
- Many lawyers will have had little experience of life outside legal practice.
- Being a good lawyer does not automatically mean you will be a good judge.
- Other countries, such as France, have a trained 'career judiciary' but there is no evidence that this produces 'better' judges.

## Establishment-minded and political bias

- It is often said that judges are 'establishment-minded' and that they side with the settled order of things such as supporting traditional property rights over individual rights and freedoms.
- Some case decisions would also suggest that judges have a political bias that favours right-wing politics (see the *Fares Fair* case, in which the judiciary were considered by many to have acted with political bias when they sided with the Conservative Party against a policy implemented by a democratically elected Labour Council based on a manifesto promise to reduce public transport fares).
- However, since the enactment of the Human Rights Act 1998 it would be true to say that the judges are now far more conscious of upholding individual rights and of acting without bias.

## Activity 3 Internet ICT activity

Use the same site http://www.judiciary.gov.uk. If you click on 'Learning Resources' you will find a selection of activities. Test yourself by taking the 'Myth Busting Quiz'? You could also listen to an interesting podcast interview with the Lord Chief Justice.

## KEY FACTS

- Judges are arranged in a 'hierarchy' divided into superior and inferior judges based on the courts in which they sit.

- Judges have different roles according to whether they sit in trial courts or appeal courts and, in trial courts, whether they deal with civil or criminal cases.

- Judges qualify based on serving a 'proscribed period' of practice as a lawyer and are appointed by an Appointments Commission who short-list for selection by the Lord Chancellor and appointment by the Queen.

- Judges have been criticised for not being representative of the community they serve, for secrecy, for lacking sufficient training and for being too conservative.

# CHAPTER 10

# BASIC FREEDOMS

## Aims

This chapter aims to introduce you to:

- the idea that certain fundamental freedoms exist
- the idea that they need protecting in law and that sometimes there are good reasons which justify restricting or limiting these freedoms
- how these freedoms are protected and the sources of these protections.

## 10.1 The idea of freedoms

Freedom is the absence of unwanted interference. Freedom has been an important concept since the earliest civilisations with wars, revolutions and civil wars being fought over the protection of freedom and against being enslaved or living under a totalitarian regime. Most philosophers and the great religions of the world also embrace the idea that man is born free and equal.

However, if man was to live without any rules there would be anarchy and so it is accepted that certain rules are a necessary part of any society. The way in which a state protects the freedoms of its citizens is known as the law of civil liberties. These rules are based on two concepts:

1. That certain basic freedoms should be provided and protected by the state; and
2. That certain restrictions have to be placed on these freedoms in some circumstances.

In a free society it is said that we should all be able to express ourselves freely but what if someone wanted to promote ideas that were distasteful or offensive to the majority? For this reason we have laws regarding obscene

publications that stop the publication of material such as child pornography.

 **ACTIVITY**

### Activity 1

Divide your class into two groups. Group A should decide what kind of classroom rules and behaviour should be protected as key class freedoms in a class charter which should be passed to group B. Group B should then decide what restrictions to these rules might be necessary. For example:

Group A say there should be no physical interference with other pupils (to avoid bullying) but Group B says there should be an exception when playing sports.

Group A say there should be a five-minute session after registration when anyone can say anything they like (to promote free speech and to circulate new ideas) but Group B says this should not include homophobic, racist or sexist comments, swearing or insulting other classmates' religion or beliefs.

Draw up your 'class charter' onto a poster and put it on the classroom wall.

## 10.2 The sources of freedoms

Many countries have written down all the rules they follow in a single document. This is known as having a written constitution. The constitution will contain all the fundamental freedoms and restrictions in that country. For example, the USA has a constitution which contains a Bill of Rights that guarantees, among other things, freedom of religion, speech, peaceful assembly and the freedom of the press. The UK does not have a written constitution. However, this does not mean that the UK does not protect or restrict fundamental freedoms; the rules can be found in a variety of sources:

## Statute law

These are laws passed by Parliament which were covered in Chapter 1. Examples of statutes that contain basic freedoms include:

- Magna Carta 1215 – which guaranteed the right to appeal against unlawful imprisonment (in something called the 'writ of habeas corpus') which is part of our freedom of the person
- The Bill of Rights 1689 – which guaranteed freedom of speech in Parliament without interference from the Crown
- The Human Rights Act 1998 – this very important Act did not 'invent' human rights but it did give legal effect to certain human rights contained in the European Convention on Human Rights – see section 11.1.

## Common law

This is the body of law developed by judges in the courts using the system of precedent described in Chapter 1. Examples of cases which establish important freedoms include:

- In *Entick v Carrington* (1765), Carrington broke into Entick's property by force claiming that he had a warrant to seize certain papers but the court held that the warrant had no lawful basis and Carrington was trespassing. The case is an important one in establishing freedom of the person as the police cannot enter premises without lawful authority.
- In *Bushell's Case* (1670), a jury was locked up without food or drink to try and force them to bring in a verdict against their will. The case underpins the right to a fair trial through ruling that a judge cannot interfere with the decision of a jury.

## European Law

In the last 50 years the influence of European law can be seen in two ways:

- Membership of the European Union – this has made a significant contribution to our laws on freedom from discrimination – especially in the workplace. A number of directives have been passed under Article 141 of the Treaty of Rome which ban discrimination on the basis of gender, sexual orientation, race and age.
- Membership of the European Convention on Human Rights – the provisions of this convention have now been brought into UK law through the Human Rights Act 1998 which is discussed below in Chapter 11.

The following list is not comprehensive but features the key freedoms recognised in English law.

## 10.3 Types of freedoms

## Freedom of expression

This freedom protects your right to express your opinions without interference through:

- speech
- books, articles, leaflets
- plays, films and dramatic productions
- broadcasts on television or radio
- the Internet
- artistic works.

It is important because it allows:

- the press to hold the government to account in a democracy
- companies and individuals to be held to account through public scrutiny
- education and information to be imparted, promoted and exchanged
- the right to seek and receive information and ideas.

## Freedom of the person

This freedom protects you from unlawful interference through:

- unlawful stop, search and arrest by the police or others
- unlawful detention, questioning and treatment by the police and others
- unlawful deportation
- forced labour or slavery.

It is important because it avoids:

- being arrested without reasonable grounds of suspicion
- being detained without authority
- being subjected to torture, inhuman or degrading treatment
- being deported to face death or personal danger
- misuse of mental health laws.

## Freedom of association and assembly

This freedom gives you the power to assemble and meet for a variety of reasons without interference from the state where you:

- meet to hold peaceful discussions or demonstrations
- form, join and participate in a trade union or other legal organisation
- use the highway to demonstrate, hand out leaflets or obtain signatures for a petition
- picket outside a place of work
- use a public footpath, road, bridleway or other right of way for a lawful purpose.

It is important because it allows:

- attention to be drawn to causes which concern us all like illegal or dangerous working conditions, mistreatment of animals or similar causes
- workers to demonstrate collective solidarity to employers
- like-minded groups to share and express their views and ideas

- lawful protest to demonstrate public feeling about issues such as wars or the use of nuclear weapons
- free access to the countryside where it does not interfere with private property rights.

## Freedom of thought, belief and religion

These freedoms allow you to have, express and change your religion, thoughts and beliefs without unnecessary restriction. They include:

- holding and expressing religious beliefs and other beliefs like veganism, agnosticism, humanism, pacifism and atheism
- taking public oaths in accordance with beliefs
- educational provision.

They are important because they allow:

- individual religious beliefs and practices to be respected
- education to take place in an appropriate setting
- non-discrimination regarding time off work, school or college for faith days
- recognition of cultural diversity
- freedom to wear religious clothing like turbans and hijabs without discrimination.

## Freedom of information

This is an increasingly important area in the ever-changing technological environment in which we now live. This freedom makes sure that:

- personal data held about you is lawful
- surveillance by police and others is subject to lawful controls
- listening devices and covert observation devices are used lawfully
- intercepting email communications and other personal information like fax messages is lawful
- police files and records held about you are lawful
- you have the right to access information held about you.

These freedoms are important because:

- increasing amounts of information about us is now held on computers and it may be inaccurate
- we are subject to more surveillance than many other citizens in other countries
- we are unlikely to challenge mistaken information of which we are unaware
- our privacy is a fundamental right.

These freedoms are important and are established in many different areas of UK law besides the Human Rights Act. The importance of this cannot be overstated. For example, Article 6 of the Human Rights Act 1998 guarantees the right to a fair trial but does not mention the 'right to silence' which is a freedom that has been protected in English law for hundreds of years and is still protected under the Criminal Justice and Public Order Act 1994.

 **ACTIVITY**

### Activity 2: Civil Liberties AO2 – Applying Your Knowledge

The following are all based on genuine cases. Which freedom is being interfered with in each one?

1. An antiques dealer was wrongly accused of handling stolen goods, based in part on evidence gathered by having his telephone tapped by the police.

2. In 1987 the *Guardian* newspaper published extracts from a book called 'Spycatcher' which contained allegations that MI5 had conducted unlawful activities. The government tried to silence the *Guardian* by issuing an injunction (a legal way of preventing further publication) even though the book was freely available outside the UK.

3. In 2008, Sarika Watkins-Singh won a case against her school when she challenged her exclusion for refusing to take off a silver bangle called a kara (a symbol of her Sikh religion).

4. In a 1996 case an Indian man was threatened with deportation from the UK. He claimed that he would be tortured if he was returned to India as he was a well-known supporter of Sikh separatism. However, the UK insisted that he should be returned as he was a suspected terrorist.

5. In 1984 the Thatcher government decided to ban membership of a union for workers at a high security 'listening station' in Cheltenham called GCHQ, which 'listened in' to international communications in the interests of British security.

## 10.4 Reasons for restricting freedoms

All of these freedoms (unlike certain human rights – see Chapter 11) are subject to possible restrictions. It is important to understand these restrictions because most freedoms are about a balance between competing interests. The ultimate test of a just legal system in a democracy such as ours is how well they strike that balance.

### Freedom of expression

Our rights to freedom of expression may be limited where:

- they incite others to violence, disorder or terrorism
- they incite others to commit crime
- it is necessary to protect health or morals
- they break the laws of defamation
- they break the laws of obscenity
- they give away state secrets and threaten national security
- they would undermine legal processes such as disclosing jury discussions
- they would incite racial hatred or are blasphemous.

**EXAMPLE**

A good example of the right to free expression being restricted because of national security interests is *Chandler v DPP* (1962). The case involved the CND (Campaign for Nuclear Disarmament) who were very active protestors against nuclear weapons. Some CND protestors got into an RAF station and held a 'sit-in' on the runway to prevent aircraft taking off or landing. They were convicted under the Official Secrets Act 1911 with 'entering a prohibited place for purposes prejudicial to the interests of the state' because their right to freedom of expression was outweighed by the risk to national security.

*From the case of Chandler v DPP (1962)*

## Freedom of the person

Freedom of the person may be restricted where a person is:

- lawfully stopped, searched or arrested with reasonable grounds of suspicion
- lawfully detained to prevent crime or disorder
- lawfully detained for questioning with reasonable grounds of suspicion
- being detained in connection with allegations under terrorism legislation
- lawful searches are being undertaken and/or samples are being taken
- lawfully detained under mental health legislation
- being deported to a country of origin where not at risk.

**EXAMPLE**

An example of a case where the right to freedom of the person was restricted to prevent crime or disorder was *Austin and Saxby v Metropolitan Police Commissioner* (2005). In this case the police penned in a large number of political protestors during a demonstration at Oxford Circus on May Day 2001 as some of them were threatening a potential breach of the peace. Austin (a peaceful protestor) and Saxby (an innocent shopper) were caught up in the demonstration and were

penned in for 7 hours in unacceptable conditions – they therefore brought a case against the police. However, the court said that it was justified to restrict their freedom because the police had taken the action in difficult operational circumstances to prevent violence.

*From the case of Austin and Saxby v Metropolitan Police Commissioner (2005)*

## Freedom of association and assembly

The freedom to associate freely and assemble may be restricted where:

- individuals are participating in an illegal strike or illegal picketing
- individuals are organising or participating in an unauthorised public march or demonstration
- individuals belong to a banned organisation (mostly terrorist organisations such as Al Qaeda or the Irish Republican Army)
- individuals are attending an unlawful public meeting
- individuals are participating in an unlawful assembly such as an illegal rave, illegal gathering at an ancient monument, demonstrating against lawful activities on private land (such as hunting) or have remained on land after lawful permission to be there has ended (such as a festival)
- free movement would spread disease
- individuals would be trespassing on private land.

**EXAMPLE**

In 1985 during the miners' strike, the police stopped a convoy of 25 cars on the M1 motorway. The car passengers were all striking miners who were on their way from the picket line at one mine to the picket line at another mine to reinforce picketing – known as 'flying pickets'. Some of them refused to obey an order from the police to turn back and they were convicted of obstructing the police. The court said that it was justified to restrict

## ACTIVITY

## Activity 3 Civil liberties crossword

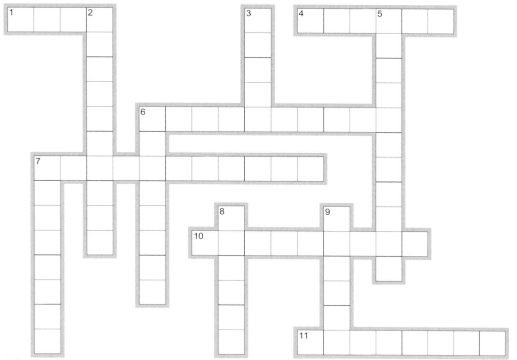

EclipseCrossword.com

Across

1. This treaty helps to outlaw discrimination under Article 141 (4)

4. A freedom you might feel strongly about – but not religious (6)

6. The name of a book written by Peter Wright (10)

7. This freedom is all about joining groups like unions and attending meetings (11)

10. The name of a druid?! (9)

11. This freedom allows you to follow your faith without interference (8)

Down

2. This freedom protects the communication of ideas and opinions through speech, writing and many other media (10)

3. The _ _ _ _ _ Carta (1215) contained an early recognition of the freedom of the person (5)

5. This freedom protects access to things like data on computers (11)

6. National _ _ _ _ _ _ _ _ is often given as a reason to restrict freedoms (8)

7. This freedom is all about people gathering together (8)

8. This freedom protects us from unwanted interference from things like unlawful stop, search and arrest (6)

9. An antiques dealer who had his phone tapped (6)

their right of assembly and association because of the possibility of a breach of the peace.

*From the case of Moss v McLachlan (1985)*

# Freedom of thought, belief and religion

Freedom of thought, belief or religion may be restricted where it is necessary to protect:

- public safety
- public order
- health or morals
- the rights and freedoms of other people.

 **EXAMPLE**

A druid called Pendragon claimed that the right to freedom of thought, religion and belief had been interfered with by not being allowed access to Stonehenge to celebrate the summer solstice. However, the court disagreed, saying that the freedom could be restricted on the grounds of public safety.

*From the case of Pendragon v United Kingdom (1998)*

# Freedom of information

Freedom of information rights may be withheld where there is suspicion of:

- involvement in crime, disorder or fraud
- involvement in terrorist activities
- a threat to national security
- other illegal activity such as grooming or downloading child pornography

or where there is a need to protect:

- the economy
- the morals of others (eg protecting children 'online')
- the rights or freedoms of others
- against obscenity.

 **EXAMPLE**

An example of the right to freedom of information being restricted in the interests of the rights and freedoms of others can be seen in Information Commissioner Decision Reference: FS50142320 29.02.09, where the Information Commissioner refused a request to release letters between the late Diana Princess of Wales and the Government on the basis that they were of a personal nature and not in the public interest. The request to view the correspondence was made by a member of the public in 2006 but the Commissioner said the correspondence is of a personal nature and does not comment on government or public policy stating also that the public interest in keeping them secret 'outweighed' the interest in making them public.

*From the case of Information Commissioner Decision Reference: FS50142320 29.02.09*

 **KEY FACTS**

- Fundamental freedoms are the cornerstone of a civilised democracy as they set out the relationship between citizens and the state by setting out the basic freedoms that should be protected by law.

- Most countries have these freedoms written down in their written constitution.

- The UK does not have a written constitution so these freedoms are found in the traditional sources of UK law: statute, common law and European law.

- Examples of fundamental freedoms in UK law include freedom of the person, freedom of expression, freedom of information, freedom of assembly and association and freedom of thought, religion and belief.

- These freedoms may be restricted for reasons such as national security, prevention of crime, terrorism and disorder, protection of health or morals, prevention of obscenity and various lawful interventions by the police and others.

# CHAPTER 11

# HUMAN RIGHTS

## Aims

This chapter aims to:

- introduce you to the idea of human rights
- draw a distinction between rights and liberties
- consider the historical development of human rights legislation and culture in the UK and
- examine some of the key human rights.

## 11.1 Introduction

In Chapter 10 we considered civil liberties. These are best summed up by saying that they represent all the things you are free to do provided there is no law against it. Civil liberties have been part of our legal system for hundreds of years and are constantly changing. They can be found in many sources as explained in section 10.2. However, there is a difference between a system which 'allows' certain freedoms and one which guarantees certain fundamental 'rights'.

## What are human rights?

Human rights are the collection of fundamental rights we all have just by virtue of being human. They exist regardless of race, sex, creed or religion. They refer to certain key rights that cannot be taken from you although, as you will see, they can be restricted or limited in certain circumstances.

## The idea of human rights

The idea of human rights can be traced back to ancient civilisations like the Greeks who thought that there were certain rights and values that were higher than man's laws as they had divine

 **ACTIVITY**

### Activity 1

LOST! This task is best done in small groups. Imagine you have survived a crash landing on a deserted island like the characters in the television series 'Lost' or the book by William Golding, *Lord of the Flies*. You have to decide on a set of rights everyone is going to be entitled to. Don't get confused with 'rules' like 'no murder' or 'no stealing' at this stage as you are just agreeing which fundamental rights everyone should expect. Think about words like equality, fairness, respect, dignity, autonomy and justice.

Agree and write down your top 10 fundamental rights and put them on the wall for other groups to compare and consider. How many of the same rights did all the groups come up with?

authority. Enlightenment writers thought that fundamental rights were necessary to participate wholly in society, to prosper as a human being and, as such, vital to democracy. These writers influenced the founders of some countries (such as the USA) who decided to make fundamental rights part of their constitution (a set of rules which say how a country is run and what the rights of its citizens are) and write a Bill of Rights into their constitution.

## Rights and responsibilities

One of the most important aspects of understanding 'rights' is the recognition that they come with 'responsibilities'. Put simply, this means that you cannot expect to have your rights respected unless you recognise the corresponding rights of others. For example, you might claim that you have a right to freedom of movement in order to move freely through the country you live in but this comes with the responsibility that you must respect other people's property rights and not trespass on private land. Similarly, you may wish to express an opinion you hold about something such as animal experimentation or the reasons we should not have gone to war in Iraq but having the right to express these views comes with the responsibility to allow others who disagree with you to express their views as well.

## Restricting rights

For the reasons explained above it is necessary to look again at human rights and decide whether or not they should be restricted and, if so, under what circumstances. The three main ways to categorise rights based on these restrictions are outlined in Figure 11.1.

### ACTIVITY

**Activity 2**

LOST! Part II: It would now be a good idea to return to your 'Lost' activity. Think again about the rights you agreed and make a second chart of restrictions. Try to think about the circumstances where you would restrict each of the rights you agreed on and why.

## 11.2 European Convention on Human Rights

The modern expression of human rights can be traced to the horrors of the Second World War. Under Hitler's Third Reich millions of Jews, gypsies, homosexuals and disabled people were murdered in the death camps and millions of other people were persecuted, tortured and displaced. After the war, in 1948, an international organisation called the United Nations sought to establish human rights in international law when its members adopted the Universal Declaration of Human Rights.

In 1950 the Council of Europe decided to use a similar approach and establish the same rights in regional law to establish stronger 'localised' recognition of human rights and created the European Convention on Human Rights (ECHR) and a European Court of Human Rights. The ECHR was written and adopted by countries that belonged to the Council of Europe which includes the UK.

## 11.3 Key rights

The examination will often feature case studies and application questions based on these rights

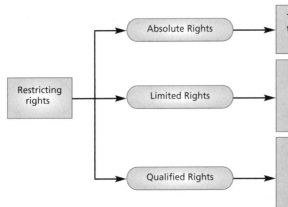

Figure 11.1 Restricting rights

and their corresponding restrictions; therefore, there is a key research case for each right. Students should research these cases and consider the moral arguments that surround them as they will often feature as AO3 discussion questions.

## 11.3.1 Article 2: Everyone's right to life shall be protected by law

This is probably the most fundamental right but it can be restricted:

- by the state for 'judicial execution' where the death penalty has been passed by a recognised court (the UK does not have the death penalty)
- during times of war within the rules of engagement
- during peacetime the army, police or prisons may use lethal force in certain circumstances.

### Examples to consider

- conjoined twins – where an operation involved the death of one twin in order to save the other – see the conjoined twins case *Re: A [Conjoined Twins]* (2001)
- euthanasia – how have the courts dealt with the argument that the right to life carries a corresponding right to death? *Pretty v UK* (2002)
- switching off a life-support-machine *Airedale NHS Trust v Bland* (1993)
- whether the right to life takes priority over an expulsion order from the UK to a destination where the individual's life may be threatened.

 **EXAMPLE**

Research Activity Case: *Pretty v UK* (2002)

## 11.3.2 Article 3: No one shall be subjected to torture or to inhuman or degrading treatment or punishment

Freedom from torture is an absolute right and cannot be taken away under any circumstance.

Inhuman treatment or punishment is less severe than torture. They may arise in circumstances such as:

- serious assaults and/or forceful arrest and restraint methods in police custody, prison, mental institutions or other custody
- the use of psychological interrogation techniques
- inhuman detention conditions or restraints
- failing to provide proper medical help to someone with a serious illness
- the threat of torture in some circumstances.

### Examples to consider

- corporal punishment of children at school and at home
- female genital mutilation
- deporting people to countries where they will be tortured
- child neglect
- leaving asylum seekers destitute without benefits or permission to work *R v Secretary of State for Home Department, ex parte Limbuela* (2005).

 **EXAMPLE**

Research Activity Case: *Z v UK* (2001)

## 11.3.3 Article 4: No one shall be held in slavery or servitude or be required to perform forced or compulsory labour

You have the right not to be treated like a slave or forced to perform certain kinds of labour. This right can be restricted where:

- working while in detention
- following orders in military service
- performing certain emergency work
- work is done under a civil obligation (such as tax collecting).

## Examples to consider

- not holding domestic staff by removing their passports
- sweatshops using forced labour
- child labour
- forced prostitution.

 **EXAMPLE**

Research Activity Case: *Siliadin v France* (2005)

## 11.3.4 Article 5: Everyone has the right to liberty and security of person

This right is more specific than the general right to freedom of movement as it protects the individual against unlawful arrest, detention and custody. Your right to liberty can be restricted:

- where a lawful arrest has taken place
- where you are detained during police investigations (where there are reasonable grounds)
- to ensure you attend court and bail is not appropriate
- where you have been lawfully sentenced by a criminal court
- to prevent your entry/exit to/from the UK
- where you have been detained because of your status as a refugee or asylum seeker or for deportation
- if you are under 18, lawful detention to ensure you are subject to certain educational supervision
- to prevent the spread of infectious diseases
- where you are of unsound mind, an alcoholic, drug addict or vagrant.

## Examples to consider

- delays in making quick decisions over asylum applications while in detention
- detention of foreign nationals without trial under terrorist legislation

- lawfulness of 'effective house arrest'
- reviewing detention under mental health legislation
- the power of the Home Secretary to set and/or change the length of sentences
- imposing mandatory life sentences and 'unduly harsh' custodial sentences
- escorting people away from demonstrations under police escort
- holding innocent people caught up in demonstrations.

 **EXAMPLE**

Research Activity Case: *Austin v Metropolitan Police Commissioner* (2005)

## 11.3.5 Article 6: Everyone is entitled to a fair and public hearing within a reasonable time by an independent and impartial tribunal established by law

This right includes:

- the right to a fair hearing
- a public hearing
- a hearing before an independent and impartial court
- a hearing held within a reasonable time.

There are extra rights in criminal cases like:

- the right to silence
- the right to be present in court
- the presumption of innocence
- a right to effective assistance
- the right, if necessary, to an interpreter.

## Examples to consider

- what kind of hearings are covered and what exactly a 'criminal case' is
- whether the article covers appeals, immigration cases, extradition cases, taxation and voting cases

- whether it guarantees a right to legal aid
- what constitutes a court or tribunal (eg planning tribunals and Courts Martial)
- rules on the status of disclosure of evidence
- status of evidence gained through 'entrapment' and covert surveillance
- whether children tried in an adult court amounts to a fair trial.

 **EXAMPLE**

Research Activity Case: *Thompson and Venables v UK* (1999)

## 11.3.6 Article 8: Everyone has the right to respect for his private and family life, his home and his correspondence

This article covers a broad range of rights which were not well protected in English law before the Act. Consequently, a lot of legislation has had to be put in place and/or updated to improve the situation. Examples include the Regulation of Investigatory Powers Act 2000, the Data Protection Act 1998 and the Freedom of Information Act 2000. The article protects the individual from interference with their privacy and may impose an obligation on some public bodies to promote privacy.

The article has four distinct parts:

- privacy which is your right to live your own life the way you choose and might include:
  - your sexuality
  - your appearance, for example the way you dress and look
  - your right not to be interfered with by the media.
- family life which might include:
  - the right to have a family relationship recognised by law (eg homosexual partnerships, unmarried mothers and foster families)
  - the right of a family to live together (eg where immigration status [or similar] threatens to separate a family).
- home life – the rights here extend to tenants as well as owners and could include business premises and might involve:
  - the right to have access to your home and occupation of your home without interference from public authorities (eg to prevent arbitrary eviction)
  - the right to peaceful enjoyment of your home (eg public authorities must do what they can to prevent noise and pollution, etc).

Correspondence could include mail, email, phone calls or faxes.

Article 8 is not an absolute right and may be restricted for reasons like:

- Lawful investigation of criminal activity where there is reasonable suspicion
- To protect the public from risks to national security especially the threat of terrorism
- To promote public safety
- To protect the economy
- To protect health and/or morals (eg monitoring of paedophiles)
- To protect the rights and freedoms of others.

### Examples to consider

- police searches of people, homes, cars, etc
- inappropriate use of covert surveillance like telephone tapping and being filmed secretly
- monitoring employees' calls, emails and correspondence at work
- misuse and exchange of personal data such as medical and financial histories
- prisons intercepting prisoners' mail
- risks of family separation subsequent to deportation
- privacy rights of celebrities subject to press intrusion.

**EXAMPLE**

Research Activity Case: *Campbell v MGN Ltd* (2004) or *Peck v United Kingdom* (2003)

 **EXAMPLE**

Research Activity Case: *R (on the application of Begum) v Denbigh High School* (2004)

## 11.3.7 Article 9: Everyone has the right to freedom of thought, conscience and religion; this right includes freedom to change his religion or belief

This article has two aspects. First, the freedom to 'hold' a particular belief; this is an absolute right which is very broad and covers a range of views, beliefs and thoughts as well as religious faiths. Second, the freedom to 'manifest' a belief; this right is a qualified right and can be restricted where necessary and proportionate in order to protect public safety, public order, health or morals or the rights and freedoms of others.

### Examples to consider

- employers accommodating the Art 9 rights of employees (such as the right to pray or have 'faith days' recognised)
- arrangements for prisoners to practise their religion in prison
- how far followers can go to persuade others to convert or 'punish' members of their own faith for converting or leaving
- being forced to work on holy days or wear a uniform contrary to religious convictions
- being refused access to employment or other opportunities because of religious commitments
- claims that the publication of certain books such as *The Satanic Verses* by Salman Rushdie is blasphemous
- claims that smoking marijuana or practising polygamy are part of a religion.

## 11.3.8 Article 10: Everyone has the right of freedom of expression

This is a freedom that exists to promote freedom to express ideas, views and opinions by individuals, religions, political groups, journalists, commercial organisations, governmental institutions and artistic expression. The right is essential in a democracy but by allowing wide freedom of expression it has to be accepted that unpopular and disturbing views will also be expressed, as there cannot be selective freedom of expression in a democracy.

Freedom of expression may be achieved through many means such as:

- speaking aloud
- publishing books, pamphlets or articles
- broadcasting on the television, radio or Internet
- producing works of art
- live performances.

Freedom of expression can be restricted where public authorities can show that their action is lawful, necessary and 'proportionate' in order to:

- protect national security, territorial integrity or public safety
- prevent disorder or crime
- protect health or morals
- protect the rights and reputations of other people
- prevent the disclosure of information received in confidence
- maintain the authority and impartiality of the judiciary.

## Examples to consider

- publication and censorship of:
  - shocking, corrupting and pornographic materials
  - racially and religiously offensive materials
  - extreme political views.
- promoting other extreme views such as animal liberation groups and anti-abortion extremists
- publication of defamatory material about individuals
- silencing the voice of those with certain political views such as the IRA
- banning publication of politically sensitive materials
- freedom of workers to 'whistle-blow' on employers.

 **EXAMPLE**

Research Activity Case: *Attorney-General v Guardian Newspapers Ltd* (1987)

## 11.3.9 Article 11: Everyone has the right to freedom of peaceful assembly and to freedom of association

This right allows you to assemble with other people for peaceful purposes. It is mainly associated with the right to protest and also includes the right to form a trade union or other society. Both aspects have a negative element in that there is a corresponding right not to join a trade union or take part in an assembly against your will. Because demonstrations can carry the potential for disorder the right can be restricted where it is lawful, necessary and 'proportionate' in order to:

- protect national security or public safety
- prevent disorder or crime
- protect health or morals

- protect the rights and freedoms of other people.

There are also extra restrictions on certain groups like the police and armed forces and civil servants who are necessary to maintain stability and national security.

## Examples to consider

- ramblers asserting their right to roam the countryside
- gypsies and new-age travellers challenging rules on trespass
- demonstrators with opposing views clashing (eg Anti-Nazi League and BNP)
- dealing with protests such as those by anti-vivisectionists, animal cruelty activists, anti-veal calf export groups, pro and anti-hunting campaigns and the anti-capitalist movement
- dealing with political rallies
- dealing with illegal assemblies such as raves, festivals and concerts
- confrontational strikes and associated picketing behaviour
- membership of terrorist organisations.

 **EXAMPLE**

Research Activity Case: *Applebey and others v UK* (2003)

## 11.3.10 Article 14: Freedom from discrimination

- Discrimination is treating people in similar situations differently or treating people in different situations the same way without justification. It is not a right in itself but acts in conjunction with the other rights so that it goes against Art 14 not to have equal access to the rights contained in the rest of the Human Rights Act 1998.
- Discrimination may be on the grounds of: sex, race, colour, language, religion, political (or other) opinion, property, birth, sexual

orientation, disability, national or social origin, membership of a trade union and age.

- Discrimination may be positive (eg in *favour* of the individual) or negative.
- Rights under Art 14 can be restricted if done in pursuance of a legitimate aim.

## Examples to consider

- schools only employing teachers who can speak a particular minority language (eg Welsh)
- leisure facilities insisting on a particular gender to work in intimate circumstances
- discriminating on basis of sexual orientation in relation to property (and other) rights
- discriminating on basis of gender re-assignment
- racist abuse within the armed forces and elsewhere
- being unfit for military service on basis of religion or sexual orientation
- refusal of access to benefits due to single parent status.

 **EXAMPLE**

Research Activity Case: *BB v United Kingdom* (2004)

## 11.4 Human Rights Act 1998

### 11.4.1 Introduction

The UK does not have a written constitution with a set of guaranteed rights and although the UK signed up to the ECHR in 1950 it was not possible for UK citizens to take cases to the Court of Human Rights until 1966 and, even then, the UK could not be forced to comply with the convention meaning that UK citizens had no effective means of enforcing their human rights. This was because we never made the convention part of our domestic law.

In 1997 the Labour Government wanted to bring about a fresh culture of respect for human rights and deal with the misuse of public power in the UK. Consequently, in 1998, they passed the Human Rights Act 1998. This Act effectively brought the ECHR into domestic law and says that all UK laws (past or future) must agree with the ECHR. Consequently, UK citizens may now protect their fundamental human rights in the UK courts.

### 11.4.2 How it works

The Human Rights Act brings the rights outlined in section 11.3 into domestic law (s 1) and works in four main ways:

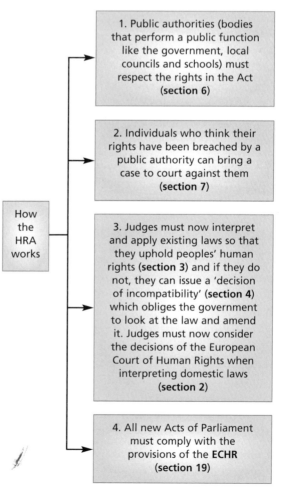

**Figure 11.2** How the Human Rights Act works

**KEY FACTS**

- Human rights are fundamental rights that we all have by virtue of being human.

- These rights cannot be taken away and allow individuals to live and prosper in a free democracy.

- Rights come with responsibilities which often involve recognising the rights of others.

- The UK has signed both the Universal and European Declarations of Human Rights but these were not part of domestic law and citizens had to go to the European Court in Strasbourg to claim their rights.

- In 1998 the Human Rights Act was passed which brings the rights in the ECHR into domestic law.

- Individuals can now pursue their fundamental human rights in UK courts which are now obliged to interpret all domestic law in line with the Human Rights Act and can declare contrary laws as incompatible.

- Most rights can be restricted in certain circumstances.

# EMPLOYMENT RIGHTS AND RESPONSIBILITIES

# CHAPTER 12

# EMPLOYMENT STATUS AND THE CONTRACT OF EMPLOYMENT

## Aims

The aims and objectives of this chapter are to show the basic aspects of employment, the different ways in which employment can occur and the principles that govern a contract of employment.

This is important because employment is a key part of life – people need to work to earn money to support themselves and provide for their families, as well as being a way in which they can contribute to society.

It is crucial that employment is regulated to offer protection to employers and employees, as well as giving them responsibilities they must fulfil and so the law relating to employment has evolved.

## 12.1 Differences between employment and self-employment

The difference between employment and self-employment is crucial as it can change the rights and duties of the parties to the contract of employment.

Here are some key differences:

Employees:

- have a contract of employment – an agreement setting out terms and conditions

- have deductions for income tax and national insurance contributions (NICs) made from salary or wages before payment
- have rights relating to:
  - maternity, adoption and paternity leave and pay
  - statutory redundancy pay
  - payment of the national minimum wage
  - statutory sick pay
  - rest breaks, paid holiday and limits on night work.
- have the right to be protected from:
  - unfair dismissal
  - unauthorised deductions from pay
  - less favourable treatment because of being part-time
  - less favourable treatment for making a disclosure in the public interest – this is often called 'whistleblowing'
  - unlawful discrimination.

Self-employed workers:

- have no contract of employment although they may have a contract to provide services for a fee and over a fixed time period
- have to pay their own income tax and NICs
- can decide how much to charge for their work and time
- can set their own holidays
- do not get the employment rights and protections listed above

- must not be discriminated against
- must be kept safe if they are working on someone else's property.

 **EXAMPLE**

Four musicians were self-employed players with an orchestra, but they wanted to be 'part-time players'. The musicians played with the orchestra when asked to do so but were entitled to reject any engagement offered. They were paid session fees and some expenses. They were not taxed as employed persons and paid national insurance as self-employed persons.

An Employment Appeal Tribunal decided that while the musicians were at work there was some degree of control by the orchestra but that fact was not a decisive pointer to there being a contract of employment. While playing for the orchestra each musician was still pursuing his own profession as an instrumentalist, with his own individual reputation and skills and so they were still self-employed.

*From the case of Addison v London Philharmonic Orchestra Ltd (1981)*

## 12.2 The tests of employment status

If a dispute arises, all the circumstances of the case will be taken into account to try and reach the best solution. There are four main tests:

- Control: this looks at the extent to which an employer decides on the tasks an employee has to do and how they are done:
  - If you have to do the work yourself you are likely to be an employee.
  - If you are told how to perform duties you are likely to be an employee but this is not the case if you are an expert such as a surgeon.
  - If you have to work set hours each day or week you are likely to be an employee although some flexibility may be possible.

- If you have the freedom to do work when and where you want you are likely to be self-employed.
- If you can send (substitute) someone in your place you are more likely to be self-employed.

 **EXAMPLE**

A hop merchant owned houses used for his business and a man who was the merchant's clerk lived in one of the houses with his family. The court held that the man was not 'a servant' but they also said that a servant is subject to the command of his master.

Although this is an old case it does make the point that control can be an important test of employment status.

*From the case of Yewens v Noakes (1880)*

- Integration: this looks at the extent to which an employee is part of the organisation:
  - If you are taken on to manage staff you are normally an integral part of the organisation and are likely to be an employee.
  - If you are entitled to benefits such as paid leave, canteen facilities and so on you are likely to be an employee.
  - If you have access to a grievance procedure and are subject to disciplinary procedures you are likely to be an employee.

 **EXAMPLE**

Dr Cassidy worked as a hospital doctor and the case concerned his employment status. As he had specialist skills which his employer could not directly control, the court held that the old 'servant'-based control test was inappropriate.

The Court of Appeal said that an employee was a worker whose work was integral to the business, rather than an independent contractor who would only be an accessory to the business.

*From the case of Cassidy v Ministry of Health (1951)*

• Mutuality of obligations: this is the extent to which your employer is required to offer you work and whether you are expected to do it:
  • If there is an obligation on you to do the work and on your employer to pay you for that work, you are likely to be an employee.
  • If your employer has to provide you with work for the life of your contract during your agreed working hours, you are likely to be an employee.

 **EXAMPLE**

Mr Carmichael worked at a power station operated by National Power on a 'casual as required basis'. Mr Carmichael worked part-time for several years and wanted written particulars of his terms of employment.

The House of Lords said there was no obligation on National Power to provide work, or on Mr Carmichael to undertake it so there was no mutuality of obligation and no contract of service. They also said that there needed to be enough control to create a contract of employment and that did not exist here.

*From the case of Carmichael v National Power plc (1999)*

• Economic reality: this is the extent to which an employee bears financial risk:
  • If you are provided with the equipment and materials you need, you are likely to be an employee.
  • If you have to provide your own equipment and materials, you are likely to be self-employed.
  • If you have to use your own money to buy equipment, pay for overheads and materials, or undertake training you can use later, you are likely to be self-employed.
  • If you have to put unsatisfactory work right in your own time for no extra payment, you are likely to be self-employed.
  • If you take the risk of quoting a fixed price for a job and then bear the additional costs if the job overruns, you are likely to be self-employed.

 **EXAMPLE**

L was the driver of a concrete mixer lorry. He had been employed on a contract of service and was then re-engaged as an independent contractor with different terms and conditions. L had to buy a vehicle in the company's colours on hire purchase from the company but he was responsible for running and maintaining it. L could only use the lorry to deliver company products; he had to wear their uniform; and was subject to their general control. Income tax and national insurance were not deducted from L's pay and if he was sick he had to hire someone else to drive the lorry.

The court held that L was an independent contractor because he carried his own risk of profit or loss and he could be viewed as running his own business.

There would have been a contract if L had agreed to provide his skill for a wage, if L had agreed to be subject to company control when he was doing his job, and if other provisions of the contract were consistent with it being a contract of service.

*From the case of Ready Mixed Concrete Ltd v Minister of Pensions (1968)*

All these factors have to be taken into account by the court and it makes an evaluation of the overall effect by looking at the picture as a whole.

## 12.3 Written particulars of the contract

Under the Employment Rights Act 1996 an employer must give an employee a 'written statement of employment particulars' within two months of starting work. This sets out the main terms of the employment contract and, if they change, the employer must issue a new statement within one month.

## ACTIVITY

### Activity 1

Tick the correct box in each of these examples to indicate whether the person concerned is an employee or self-employed.

| | Employee | Self-employed |
| --- | --- | --- |
| Claude is an actor. He has a small part in a film this week but next week he will be on stage at his local theatre and the week after that he will be making voice-overs for TV adverts. | | |
| Sarah works in an office. She has to work for 40 hours per week but she is allowed an hour off for lunch when she can eat at a reduced rate in the office canteen. | | |
| Kelvin works as a chauffeur. He owns a Rolls Royce and advertises in his local newspaper and on the Internet for business. | | |
| Aphrodite is a barrister. She is also a keen skier and every January she takes no cases so that she can pursue her hobby. | | |
| Farouq is an engineer. He enjoys his job but is always upset to see how much income tax and national insurance has been deducted when he receives his monthly pay slip. | | |

Table 12.1

Here is what the written statement must include:

- employee's name
- employer's name
- date employment began
- rate of pay and how payment will be made
- hours of work
- holiday entitlement
- entitlement to sick leave and pay
- details of pensions and pension schemes
- entitlement to notice of termination for both the employee and the employer
- job title or a brief job description
- period for which your employment is expected to continue or, if it is for a fixed term, the date when it will end
- place of work
- details of disciplinary and grievance procedures
- details of collective agreements
- specific details of overseas work.

**ACTIVITY**

## Activity 2

Working in groups, draw up some contracts of employment. Make some which will be lawful and some which will not. Swap with other groups and see if you can spot which contracts are lawful and why this is so.

Think about why contracts need to have certain information in them and make a presentation to explain why the law needs to be clear in this area.

## Written Statement of Employment Particulars

**P1**
Name of employee

began employment with (name of employer)

on (date)

**P2**
*a.  Your previous employment with

**does** count as part of your period of continuous employment which therefore began on

**or**
*b.  Your previous employment **does not** count as part of your period of continuous employment

**P3**
a.  You are employed as (job title)

**or**
*b.  A brief description of the work for which you are employed is:

**P4**
a.  Your place of work is (address)

b.  You are ***required/permitted** to work at the following places

and the address of your employer is

**P5**
Your pay will be

**P6**
You will be paid (weekly, monthly etc)

**P7**
Your hours of work are

**P8**
Your holiday entitlement is

**P9**
a.   In case of incapacity to work

**or**
b.  Particulars of any terms and conditions relating to incapacity to work due to sickness or injury, including any provision for sick pay, **can be found in**

**P10**
a.  Particulars of pensions and pension schemes are

**or**
b.  Particulars of terms and conditions relating to pensions and pension schemes, **can be found in**

**P11**
a.  The amount of notice of termination of your employment you are entitled to receive is

Figure 12.1 Written statement of employment particulars

The amount of notice you are required to give is

or

b. Particulars of the amount of notice of termination of your employment you are entitled to receive and are required to give **are given in**

### P12

a. Your employment is permanent – subject to 11 above, to general rights of termination under the law and to the following

or

b. Your employment is for a fixed term and expires on (date)

or

c. Your employment is temporary and is expected to continue for

*This should only be used as an indication of the likely duration*

### P13

The collective agreements which directly affect the terms and conditions of your employment are

### P14

*a. You are not expected to work outside the UK (for more than one month)

or

*b. You will be required to work in

For

You will be paid in (currency)

and will be entitled to

The terms relating to your return to the UK are

### P15

a. The disciplinary rules which apply to you are

or

b. The disciplinary rules which apply to you can be found in

### P16

a. The disciplinary and dismissal procedure which applies to you is

or

b. The disciplinary and dismissal procedure which applies to you can be found in:

### P17

If you are dissatisfied with any disciplinary or dismissal decision which affects you, you should apply in the first instance to (name of officer)

### P18

You should make your application by

### P19

If you have a grievance about your employment you should apply in the first instance to (name of officer)

### P20

You should make your application by

### P21

a. Subsequent steps in the firm's disciplinary, dismissal and grievance procedures are

or

b. Subsequent steps in the firm's disciplinary and grievance procedures are set out in

### P22

A contracting-out certificate under the Pensions Schemes Act 1993

***is/is not** in force for the employment this statement is being issued for

*delete as appropriate*

## 12.4 Terms of the contract

A contract of employment is an agreement between an employer and employee. It is the basis of the employment relationship and is made when an offer of employment is accepted. It creates rights and duties which are enforceable in the courts.

It is always best for an employment contract to be in writing to give certainty.

The terms in an employment contract should achieve three aims:

• maintain trust and confidence between an employer and employee through co-operation
• encourage the employer and employee to act in good faith towards each other

### ACTIVITY

**Activity 3**

Explain whether each of the following is an example of an express term or an implied term.

1. Adrian works for a computer software company and other employees tell Adrian they are always able to leave work early on Christmas Eve. This is an .......................... term because ...............................................

2. Betty is employed as a school cleaner and her contract states that she is to be paid every Friday. This is an ................................... term because ...........................................

3. Clive gets a job at a garden centre and his contract says the company will provide waterproof clothing. This is an ........................ term because ...................................

4. Dennis is employed as a check-out operator in a supermarket. He sees other employees take unsold food home at the end of the day and the store detective who all the employees have to pass never stops them, so Dennis does the same thing. This is an ........................... term because .............................................

• ensure that reasonable care is taken to guarantee health and safety in the workplace.

Express terms are specified in a contract of employment.

Implied terms become part of the contract because of the way the employer and employee behave or through custom and practice over time.

### KEY FACTS

■ In an employment relationship it is vital to distinguish between the employee or the self-employed.

■ An employee has a contract which gives clearly protected rights.

■ A worker who is self-employed has a choice as to how hard he works and when he does his job but he has no contract and his situation may not be so secure as he has less protection than an employee.

■ The courts have tried to establish tests to decide whether or not a worker is an employee – there are four different tests and the courts use a combination of these to try and achieve the fairest results.

■ Every employee has a contract of employment which must contain key information to protect both parties to the contract and it is important to be able to refer to specific examples.

■ Some contract terms are express and some are implied – it is important to know the difference but both can be enforceable.

■ The purpose behind the law is to be clear and fair.

# PROTECTION FROM DISCRIMINATION

The aims and objectives of this chapter are to show how important it is to protect against discrimination. This is in order that everyone has a fair chance of being employed and of being treated like other employees while they are at work. An employee should have the security of knowing that he has been treated fairly and appropriately.

It is not necessarily unlawful to treat people differently but it is discrimination for an employer to treat one employee less favourably than another.

Unlawful discrimination can be based on many issues and some are covered in this chapter.

## 13.1 Ways of discriminating

Unlawful discrimination can happen in different ways:

## Direct discrimination

This is when an employer treats an employee less favourably because of, for example, their gender or race.

Examples of direct discrimination would be:

- to make a driving job open only to male applicants
- to assume that a woman with young children will be an unreliable employee
- to dismiss a woman because she is pregnant or not employ her because she is, or might become, pregnant.

## Indirect discrimination

This is when a condition that disadvantages one group of people more than another is applied to a job.

Examples of indirect discrimination could be:

- stating that applicants for a job must be clean shaven
- a job advertisement stating that applicants must be over a certain height
- a job advertisement with very particular age restrictions.

Not every situation creates indirect discrimination, especially if an employer can show a good reason for a particular condition. Think about the example above asking for an applicant to be clean-shaven. Although this could indirectly discriminate against Sikhs, it might be justified if the job involves handling food, as having a beard or moustache is a genuine hygiene risk.

## Harassment

This means offensive or intimidating behaviour, sexist language or racial abuse which aims to humiliate, undermine or injure its target.

## Victimisation

This means treating somebody less favourably than others because they tried to make a discrimination complaint.

There are also other ways in which discrimination can occur and these include:

- being bullied as this is not acceptable in the workplace
- mistreatment after a request to be paid the national minimum wage
- not being given a written statement of employment particulars
- not being protected from unlawful deductions from wages
- not being given the correct paid holiday entitlement
- having unreasonable limits put on working hours
- being prevented from joining a trade union.

 **ACTIVITY**

### Activity 1

Fill in the gaps in each of the sentences below to indicate which type of discrimination is most appropriate in each of the following factual situations:

Anup, a Sikh, is told he must shave off his beard and not wear a turban to work as a police officer. This is ....................................................

Carmen is a typist. She has three children under five. Carmen goes for an interview for a job and has the best typing speed but the interviewer thinks that she will be absent a lot because her children are young, and he gives the job to someone who is not as good a typist as Carmen. This is ....................................................

Floella sees an advert for a job as Father Christmas which says that only men can apply. This is ....................................................

Sean, who is Irish, works in a hospital as a nurse. When he goes to his locker to change into his uniform he keeps finding notes stuck on the door which say 'Get lost, Paddy!' This is

....................................................

Glenda and Michael are school cleaners. Glenda was told she had to empty heavy rubbish bins and she complained to her employer that she thought Michael should do that job. Glenda no

longer has to empty the heavy bins but every day her employer tells her to clean the toilets and she is not given protective gloves to do the job. This is ....................................................

Sasha goes for a job as an art teacher in a school. She has impressive qualifications, a wide range of relevant experience and excellent references. She is 28 years old and has just got married. She does not get the job. This is

....................................................

Enrique gets a job making sandwiches for a supermarket. He has long hair, of which he is very proud, because he plays guitar in a rock group in his spare time. Enrique is told that he must wear a hairnet to cover his hair but he refuses and so he loses his job. This is ....................................................

Maria sees a job advertised for a bouncer at a night club. It says applicants must have a self defence qualification and be over 1.8 metres tall. Maria has a black belt in judo but she is only 1.6 metres tall. This is ....................................................

Choose from:
- direct discrimination
- indirect discrimination
- harassment
- victimisation
- not discrimination.

## 13.2 Equal pay

The law about equal pay comes from the Equal Pay Act 1970, the Sex Discrimination Act 1975 and the Employment Act 2002. It states that men and women are entitled to equal pay when they do:

- the same work
- broadly similar work
- different work but their jobs have been assessed as being the same
- work which is of equal value.

Pay includes wages, salaries and pensions and the law applies to all workers. Equal pay law does not give a right for people of the same gender to be paid equally for the same work.

Equal pay claims are dealt with by employment tribunals. A claim can be made up to six months after leaving employment. The person who makes the claim must show that, on the face of it, they are being paid less than a person of the opposite gender doing the same work – this person is known as a 'comparator'.

It is a problem that certain jobs are often thought of as either 'women's work' or 'men's work'. The Equal Pay Act deals with this by allowing a person to compare themselves with a person doing 'work of equal value'.

Another problem is that the person making the claim and the person with whom they compare themselves must work for the 'same employer'. It can be hard in big organisations, such as the NHS, to know exactly who the employer is.

If men and women are paid at different rates for the same, or similar, work, the employer must prove that there is a reason for it which is not gender-related.

In a successful case for equal pay, a tribunal can order a declaration of the claimant's rights; they can equalise their contractual terms for the future; and order arrears of pay for up to six years.

 **EXAMPLE**

Ms Lawton was employed as a cook in the Directors kitchen at Capper Pass Ltd where she cooked lunch for 10–20 people a day. She claimed equality with two male assistant chefs in the staff kitchens who were cooking 350 meals a day over six sittings.

The tribunal had to decide if Ms Lawton was doing 'like work'. They decided that the work was 'broadly similar' and so Ms Lawton was successful in her claim.

*From the case of Capper Pass Ltd v Lawton (1977)*

 **EXAMPLE**

Ms Bodman had been employed as an accountant at a manufacturing company. She was promoted to be a financial controller and when she questioned the salary and benefits offered to her male replacement, she discovered that he was paid £8,000 more and received an £8,640 car allowance as well as additional benefits.

The tribunal found that Ms Bodman had been employed to do comparable work to her successor as an accountant; the company had no genuine material factor defence for the differences in their salaries; and she received £25,000 compensation.

*From the case of Bodman v API Group (2007)*

 **EXAMPLE**

A Birmingham employment tribunal held that special 'anti-social hours' bonuses paid to police officers rostered to work at any time of the day or night were indirectly discriminatory as women with childcare responsibilities were not eligible for the bonuses.

The tribunal found that, while the requirement to work on a '24/7' basis could be a genuine material factor for equal pay purposes, and rewarding anti-social hours was a legitimate aim, it had not been carried out in a proportionate or reasonably necessary way.

*Adapted from Blackburn and Manley v West Midlands Police ET/1305651/2003http://employment.practicallaw.com/jsp/ binaryContent.jsp?item=:32435232*

 **ACTIVITY**

Activity 2

❝ Individual incomes for women were less than those for men across all age bands. Average total individual income was highest for women aged between 25 and 29 at £249 per week. This was 76 per cent of the average for men in the same age band. For men, average total individual income was highest between the ages of 35 and 49. Individual income for women relative to men was lowest for those aged 55 to 59, where the average for women was 42 per cent of that for men. **"**

This information comes from the National Statistics office. Go to their website, http://www.statistics.gov.uk, and investigate what they have to say about equal pay. Write a short report about what you find and discuss whether the current situation is acceptable.

## 13.3 Sex discrimination

The Sex Discrimination Act 1975 makes it unlawful for an employer to discriminate against an employee because of sex, gender or marital status.

It does not matter whether the discrimination is direct or indirect, deliberate or accidental.

 **EXAMPLE**

A Southampton Employment Tribunal has held that the rock star Sting and his wife Trudie Styler sexually discriminated against their pregnant cook, Jane Martin. Ms Martin was sacked after becoming pregnant after eight years of service to the couple, who are high-profile champions of human rights and ecological causes.

The 41-year-old cook was unlawfully dismissed from her £28,000-a-year job by the couple's management company, Lake House Estate. In passing judgment, the tribunal panel accused Ms Styler, referred to under her married name of Sumner, of manipulating staff and then failing to take responsibility for her actions.

It said: "Although Mrs Sumner tried to distance herself from various unlawful acts and have them carried out by minions, when the evidence is looked at holistically, her involvement is clear.

She is without doubt the driving force manipulating others to perform her dirty work."

During the hearing Ms Martin claimed that despite being pregnant she was required to work 14-hour days. On one occasion, when she was towards the end of her pregnancy she was ordered to travel from the couple's 800-acre estate near Salisbury to their London home overlooking St James' Park just to make soup and salad for Styler, she said.

Ms Martin has since been awarded in £24,944 in compensation. Ms Styler appealed. In the appeal the tone of the tribunal was criticised but the overall decision stood, as did the compensation.

*Adapted from 'Sting's wife guilty of treating cook shamefully' by Jonathan Brown, The Independent, 11th May 2007 © The Independent*

The law covers almost all workers, all types of organisation and all parts of employment from recruitment through to dismissal.

 **EXAMPLE**

A male student nurse who quitted the profession because hospital bosses banned him from performing 'intimate procedures' on female patients today won a landmark sex case.

Andrew Moyhing, 29, was awarded £750 compensation after winning his case against Barts and the London NHS trust. He successfully challenged an earlier employment tribunal ruling, which found that it was acceptable for the trust to have a different policy for male nurses than for female nurses when intimate procedures were carried out on patients.

He told the Employment Appeal Tribunal that his training was undermined because he was only allowed to perform many procedures on male patients while female colleagues were taught how to treat both male and female patients. He also said that a female member of staff would have to chaperone him while he carried out an electrocardiogram, which records the electrical activity of the heart, because one or both of the patient's breasts might be exposed.

Mr Justice Patrick Elias ruled that the chaperoning policy, which the trust said was a safeguard against assaults on female patients and false accusations against male nurses, was unlawful. Mr Moyhing said he hoped the ruling would encourage more men to become or remain nurses.

Under Royal College of Nursing guidelines, nurses must first explain how and why an examination is carried out and then ask the patient's permission. If the patient objects the examination must be stopped immediately. Patients of either sex undergoing intimate examinations must always be offered a chaperone and given privacy to undress and dress.

*Adapted from http://www.guardian.co.uk/society/*
*2006/jun/09/health.genderissues*

Sometimes 'positive action' is allowed – for example, an employer who has no women managers might offer management training only to women or encourage them to apply for management jobs. This only applies to training and encouragement to apply for posts – when choosing who gets the job all candidates must be considered equally on their suitability.

However, 'positive action' is not always acceptable.

 **EXAMPLE**

To try and increase the number of female MPs the Labour Party tried to have selection lists for candidates in several constituencies open to women only.

An industrial tribunal held that discrimination in favour of one group meant discriminating against another group and so positive discrimination in favour of women was unlawful.

*Adapted from Jepson and Dyas-Elliot v*
*the Labour Party (1996)*

There is no minimum period of employment to qualify to bring a claim.

When advertising a job an employer should use gender neutral terms when advertising for staff and avoid terms such as 'policeman', 'barman', 'waitress'. However, sometimes there could be a 'genuine occupational qualification' such as some jobs in single-sex schools, jobs in some welfare services and acting jobs that need a man or a woman – perhaps advertising for a man to be Father Christmas!

 **EXAMPLE**

**Housemaster wanted!**

From September 2009, we seek an outstanding Housemaster to lead the development of a 13–18 boys' boarding house. Energy, leadership ability and excellent teaching skills in any suitable subject are essential for the post, as is commitment to boarding school life.

Interviews will take place on Tuesday 27th January.

*Adapted from http://www.tes.co.uk/JobDetails*

If an employee makes a request to be considered in the same way as a person of a different gender an employer must consider the request and facilitate it if they possibly can.

 **EXAMPLE**

A vehicle technician whose employer refused to let him work part-time so that he could help look after his son won his sex discrimination case against a former employer. Neil Walkingshaw had worked full-time for a company for over eight years when his son was born and his wife also worked full-time. During her maternity leave the couple decided that Mr Walkingshaw should be the one to go part-time at the end of her maternity leave. When Mr Walkingshaw discussed this with his managers, he was told that the proposal was 'too messy'. He considered that they had dismissed his idea without really considering it – despite allowing four women workers in the same company to reduce their hours after having children. He handed in his resignation shortly afterwards.

Finding that Mr Walkingshaw had been discriminated against because of his sex, the tribunal awarded him £3,700 compensation. It concluded that Mr Walkingshaw's employers 'gave no meaningful consideration' to his request and that they would probably have agreed to a similar request from a woman.

*Adapted from http://www.hrmguide.co.uk/diversity/male_mechanic.htm*

 **ACTIVITY**

### Activity 3

Using your local newspaper or a national newspaper see how many articles you can collect which deal with sex discrimination. For each case, see if you can identify the sex discrimination, explain why a particular result was reached and discuss whether the decision is good or bad.

## 13.4 Racial discrimination

The Race Relations Act 1976 makes it unlawful for an employer to discriminate because of race – this means colour, nationality, ethnic or national origin.

It is irrelevant whether or not the discrimination is done on purpose and the law covers every part of employment.

It is also unlawful to treat someone less favourably on the grounds of another person's race; so, for example, it is discriminatory to treat a white employee less favourably because he or she has a black partner.

Examples of different kinds of racial discrimination:

- Racist name-calling or abuse is direct discrimination.
- Segregation on racial grounds by providing separate washing facilities, even if the facilities are of the same standard, is direct discrimination.
- A pub or club operating quotas to prevent black members or customers from exceeding a specific number or proportion is direct discrimination.
- A policy that requires all employees to be clean-shaven, as this would put Sikhs in general at a disadvantage, is indirect discrimination.
- A practice of excluding job applicants who live in a certain area of a city which is occupied by a higher proportion of ethnic minority people, as this would put ethnic minority candidates at a disadvantage, is indirect discrimination.
- Making racist jokes at work is harassment as it is participating in, allowing or encouraging behaviour that offends someone or creates a hostile atmosphere.
- Taking disciplinary action against someone for complaining about discrimination against themselves or another person is victimisation as it is treating someone less favourably because they've complained or been involved in a complaint.

 **ACTIVITY**

### Activity 4

Quiz

See if you can identify the most relevant type of discrimination in each of the following cases:

Jerome is an electrician from the West Indies. He is interviewed for a job at Sparks Electric by the boss, Shane. Shane has heard friends say that West Indians are always lazy. Jerome has excellent qualifications and a reference from his previous employer who praises his hard-working attitude. Shane does not give Jerome the job. This is ........................................................

Svetlana has a job in a call centre. She likes her job but several of the other workers make remarks about her Russian accent. One man does a strange Russian dance every time she comes into the room which makes the others laugh. Svetlana is upset and tells her boss who tells her it is just a bit of fun. This is

........................................................

Southwood High School is trying to improve its image and so it introduces a new uniform. All the boy pupils have to war caps and the girls have to wear berets. The school has many Sikh and Muslim pupils and they are told they must wear a hat or a cap. This is

........................................................

Frank is an English waiter who loves Indian food. He goes for an interview at the Star of India Restaurant. The owner of the Star of India thinks his customers will want to be served by Indian waiters and so he does not give Frank the job even though he has excellent qualifications. This is ........................................................

Choose from:
- direct discrimination
- indirect discrimination
- harassment
- victimisation
- no discrimination.

A job may be restricted to people of a particular racial or ethnic group if there is a 'Genuine Occupational Requirement' (GOR). An example is where a black actor is needed for a particular role. It is not always easy to prove that a GOR exists.

 **EXAMPLE**

'Prospects' was a Christian charity and non-Christians could be recruited for some jobs if they acknowledged sympathy for the Christian faith. Over time the workforce ceased to be exclusively Christian. 'Prospects' reviewed their employment policy and decided, as a genuine occupational requirement, that it needed to employ only Christians. 'Prospects' told existing non-Christian employees that they would not be promoted. Mr Sheridan was a manager with 'Prospects'. He was pessimistic about his future and resigned when he was required only to employ Christians and not to promote non-Christians.

Mr Sheridan brought a claim for discrimination on the grounds of religion or belief. The tribunal held that 'Prospects' had directly discriminated against him. It had not made out its 'genuine occupational reason' (GOR) defence as it had not carried out a job evaluation for every post and it was not proportionate to require all its employees to be Christians.

*Sheridan v Prospects for People with Learning Disabilities (2006)*

Positive action can be used to support or encourage a particular racial group when a group is badly under-represented or to fill particular posts in an employer's workforce. An employer can provide special training to members of the group and encourage them to do the work or fill the posts but cannot discriminate in favour of them when it comes to choosing people to do the work or fill the posts, as that is unlawful discrimination.

Race does not need to be the only reason for discrimination and it is enough if race is a contributing cause as it is a 'significant influence' on the way that person is treated.

## 13.5 Disability discrimination

Disabled workers have the same employment rights as other workers with extra provisions under the Disability Discrimination Act 1995. The law covers all aspects of employment from application forms through to dismissal or redundancy.

There is a duty on an employer to make 'reasonable adjustments' so that a disabled person is not at a substantial disadvantage because of how they have to work or where they work. 'Reasonable adjustments' might include:

- allocating some work to another employee
- transferring an employee to another post or another place of work
- making adjustments to the buildings
- being flexible about hours if time away is needed for assessment, treatment or rehabilitation
- providing training or retraining if the current job can no longer be done
- providing modified equipment
- making instructions and manuals more accessible
- providing a reader or interpreter.

It is important to remember that the employer only needs to act 'reasonably'. To decide this the employer might ask themselves about any adjustments:

- how effective will it be?
- will it significantly reduce the disadvantage of a disability?
- is it practical?
- will it cause a lot of disruption?
- will it help other people in the workplace?
- is it very expensive?

The only type of discrimination an employer can justify is disability related discrimination if, in the circumstances, it is for a 'material' and 'substantial' reason.

If an employee feels they have been discriminated against, they can go to an employment tribunal within three months of the act of discrimination. In most circumstances there is a legal requirement to use a grievance or disciplinary procedure first; and then there is an extra three months in which to bring a claim. If the procedure is not used when it should have been, the tribunal will reject a claim.

 **EXAMPLE**

Iain Smith, who has lumbar spondylosis (osteoarthritis in the lower spine), applied for a sales job with Churchill's Stairlifts, which makes mobility aids and radiator covers. He was offered the job, but between the job offer and starting his training, the company made the decision that salespeople would have to carry full-size models of the radiator covers they would be selling and Mr Smith's job offer was withdrawn.

This was despite Mr Smith suggesting various alternatives, including a trial period without using the sales aids.

This was the first disability discrimination case concerning recruitment to be heard by the Court of Appeal and Mr Smith won.

A Churchill's Stairlifts spokesperson commented: 'We acted in good faith, accept the court's ruling and have implemented new rules so this issue cannot re-occur.'

Martin Jones, senior campaigns manager at Arthritis Care (at time of publication) said: 'This is a crucial case because discrimination at recruitment stage has typically been so hard to prove, particularly for people with arthritis.'

*Amended and reproduced with the permission of Arthritis Care (UK) and originally published on their website www.arthritiscare.co.uk*

 **EXAMPLE**

**Long-serving police officer wins disability discrimination claim**

PC Weaver joined Lincolnshire Constabulary in 1976 and during 31 years of service had an excellent attendance record. In 2000 he was diagnosed as suffering from a debilitating condition, which amounted to a disability under the Disability Discrimination Act. Mr Weaver was placed on restricted duties and in June 2001 became an Enquiry Officer at Police Headquarters. He had no sick leave due to his disability and no sick leave at all in the last six years of his employment.

In 2006 he achieved 30 years' service. This entitled him to join the '30 plus Scheme' which gave him an option to keep working beyond the normal retirement age. He applied but was refused because he was on 'restricted duties' and was likely to remain so.

Mr Weaver believed this was discriminatory. He challenged the decision by internal appeal and then went to an employment tribunal.

The tribunal found that Mr Weaver ought to have been allowed to access the Scheme to remove the substantial disadvantage he faced in comparison with non-disabled persons so he won his case and was awarded compensation.

*Adapted from news feed on Russell Jones & Walker website, http://www.rjw.co.uk/news-events/press/ long-serving-police-officer-wins-disability-discrimination-claim*

 **ACTIVITY**

## Activity 5

In each of the following situations identify whether there has been disability discrimination or whether reasonable adjustments have been made:

Sharona works for an IT company and she is blind. The company provides a computer handbook but they do not have one in Braille. Sharona asks if there is an audio copy of the handbook she can listen to. The company tells her she will have to find someone to read the handbook to her in her own time. This is

...........................................................

Tim is a teacher at a school in an old country house with lots of stairs. Tim is a keen mountaineer and breaks his back in a fall which means he has to use a wheelchair for the rest of his life. Tim asks the school to install a disabled lift so he can get to his classroom. The headmaster says the cost is too much because the building is so old but offers to move Tim to a small and rather dark classroom on the ground floor. This is ...........................................................

Khalid has been diagnosed with cancer. He has to visit the hospital on a regular basis for treatment. He is an accountant and Khalid's boss gives him a laptop he can use at home to do his work when he feels well enough. This is

...........................................................

Mina is an artist who works for a company which makes hand-painted plates. Mina suffers from arthritis and it becomes so bad that she cannot hold a paintbrush for very long. She asks her boss if she can move to a job where paint is sprayed onto plates using a gun which she can hold. Her boss says he has enough staff to use the paint guns and if Mina cannot use the brush, she needs to find work elsewhere. This is

...........................................................

## 13.6 Recent developments – sexual orientation, transsexuals, age, religion and belief

### 13.6.1 Sexual orientation

It is against the law for an employer to discriminate against an employee because of sexual orientation or 'perceived' sexual orientation.

The law covers all stages of employment from recruitment through to redundancy and dismissal. Since December 2005, same-sex couples can register a civil partnership and a civil partner is entitled to the same benefits as a married person.

Discrimination on grounds of sexual orientation can happen in different ways:

- If an employer allows the unmarried opposite sex partner of an employee to drive the employee's company car but refuses the same benefits to same-sex partners, this is direct discrimination.
- If a company arranges a conference in a country where homosexuality is illegal and there is no good reason for it to be held there, this is indirect discrimination.
- If there is a general culture of disrespect by telling homophobic jokes at work or in a work-related setting like an office party this is harassment.
- If an employee is treated less favourably because of a complaint, or involvement in a complaint, about sexual orientation discrimination this is victimisation.

 **EXAMPLE**

Issac Blake, who played a character in the CBBC television programme, *In the Night Garden*, brought a claim for unfair dismissal after he said he could not work because he was injured while playing one of the Tombliboo characters. He said he was dismissed after complaining of a 'faulty' animatronics suit that he was forced to wear, despite not being able to see out of it. Blake claimed he was also discriminated against and verbally abused for being homosexual.

The tribunal did not find that he had been unfairly dismissed but they did find that he suffered harassment when he was called a 'faggot' twice, and awarded him £2,000 compensation.

*Adapted from http://www.personneltoday.com/articles/ 2008/01/18/44013/cbeebies-night-garden-actor-loses-unfair- dismissal-case-against-ragdoll-productions.html*

It is not discrimination if an employer can show that a job has to be done by someone of a particular sexual orientation.

### 13.6.2 Transsexuals

It is lawful to undergo gender reassignment (sex change) surgery. It is covered by the European Convention on Human Rights, and the Gender Recognition Act 2004.

The Gender Reassignment Regulations 1999, which amend the Sex Discrimination Act 1995, prohibit discrimination in employment and vocational training. Public authorities are under a general equality duty to eliminate discrimination and harassment against transsexuals.

✓ **EXAMPLE**

A transsexual trucker won a sex discrimination claim after he was forced out of his job just weeks after arriving at work dressed as a woman. Former soldier Mike Gaynor was well liked and respected in his trucking job in Liverpool but trouble began when the twice-married father arrived for his shift as Vikki-Marie, wearing make-up and jewellery.

The former scout leader, who obtained his HGV licence with the Royal Corps of Transport, told bosses in February last year that he intended to become a woman. He claimed that bosses began cancelling his shifts and he was subjected to cruel jibes from colleagues. A colleague made offensive gestures at him at traffic lights, and belongings and make-up were removed from his lorry and dumped in a bin liner in a disabled toilet.

An employment tribunal ruled that Vikki-Marie Gaynor, who was born a man, was wrongly forced out of a job after cross-dressing and was discriminated against by his employer in the way it dealt with his two grievance complaints.

*Adapted from http://www.dailymail.co.uk/news/ article-557868/Transsexual-trucker-wins-sex-discrimination-case-turning-work-dressed-woman-called-Vikki-Marie.html*

## 13.6.3 Age

A person cannot be denied a job, an equal chance of training or a promotion because of age under the Employment Equality (Age) Regulations 2006. These also protect against age-based harassment or victimisation. This affects almost all types of employment, all employees and workers of any age.

Age discrimination can occur in different ways and sometimes an age-based practice may be reasonable if it is 'proportionate' and in pursuit of a 'legitimate aim'. This can cover economic factors, such as business needs and efficiency, but expense is not a valid justification. Here are some examples:

- George has been teaching Economics at Middleton School for 30 years. He has a good record of examination results and the students enjoy his lessons. He is at the top of his pay scale and the school is trying to save money. The school wants to make George redundant and give his job to Samantha who has been teaching for only five years – this could be direct discrimination unless an age requirement can be objectively justified.
- Middleton School also employs a number of part-time teachers, most of whom are older and have a great deal of teaching experience. In its quest to cut costs the school selects only part-time workers for redundancy – this could be indirect discrimination unless an age requirement can be objectively justified.
- Ben, aged 23, sees an advertisement in which Middleton School wants to employ a residential tutor in their sixth form boarding-house and the applicant has to be over 25 years of age. This may not be direct or indirect discrimination because there might be a minimum age requirement which is both reasonable and proportionate.
- Farouk, aged 52, sees an advertisement for workers on a building site which says applicants must have a good level of physical fitness and be under 50 years old. This may not be direct or indirect discrimination because there might be a maximum age for workers for health and safety reasons.

The national retirement age is 65, although this is not compulsory. An employer can only retire an employee below 65 if they can show that it is appropriate and necessary.

An employer must give at least six months notice of a retirement date and an employee has the right to request to keep working. An employer does not have to agree to a request or give a reason for turning it down, but they must meet the employee to consider their request.

## Activity 6

Go to http://www.ageconcern.org.uk/ AgeConcern/ageism_advisers_case1.asp. Here you will find some case studies you can work through to decide whether people have been discriminated against on the basis of age. When you have completed these, write a report on what you found and try to make some comment on the current state of the law.

### UNISON wins back job for UK's first Age Discrimination Case – 12 April 2007

Ann Southcott (66), a clerical worker at Treliske Hospital in Truro, was dismissed on the last day before the Employment Equality (Age) Regulations 2006 came into force. That meant that she received just 11 weeks' pay instead of being entitled to 11 months' pay (one for each year of her service).

UNISON instructed Thompsons solicitors to represent her. As a result of the claim the Hospital Trust has agreed to re-instate Mrs Southcott with back pay from October and with no loss of service.

Mike Jackson, UNISON Senior National Officer for Health, said,

66 This is a fair and just outcome to a sorry chapter in the hospital's history. There is no doubt that the decision to dismiss Ann Southcott was fuelled by the debt crisis at the Royal Cornwall Hospitals NHS Trust. However, after the appointment of a new chief executive a new policy on age discrimination has been agreed and Ann is able to return to the hospital to a job she clearly did well and enjoyed. 99

Mrs Southcott said,

66 I'm delighted with this result as I was clearly discriminated against on the grounds of my age which was grossly unfair. I cannot afford to give up work at this time and why should I when I was doing a job I loved. I am looking forward to the challenge of my new job back in the therapies department. 99

*Adapted from http://www.thompsons.law.co.uk/ ntext/first-age-discrimination-case.htm*

## 13.6.4 Religion or belief

It is against the law for an employer to discriminate on the grounds of religion or certain beliefs. The law defines religion or belief as any religion, religious belief or similar philosophical belief. It includes all major religions, and less widely practised ones. It covers several things:

- a person's religion or belief
- their perceived religion or belief
- the religion or belief of people with whom they associate.

Discrimination on the grounds of religion or belief can happen in different ways:

- An employer will not promote an employee who is married to a person with religious views the employer does not like – this is direct discrimination.
- A head-covering policy for all employees which could discriminate against a devout Muslim or Sikh – this is indirect discrimination.
- Office events where an employee is always made fun of because their religion forbids alcohol and they will not take part in drinking games – this is harassment.
- An employee feels they have suffered after they complained that their request for time off on a religious holiday was refused – this may be victimization.

An employer should try to be helpful within the boundaries of reasonableness:

- An employee does not have to tell an employer about their religious beliefs but such information should be treated confidentially.
- An employer does not have to provide time and facilities for religious observance (eg a prayer room), but they should try to do so where possible.
- An employee should be allowed to follow their religious observances, provided that it does not disrupt others or the employee's ability to do their job properly.
- An employee who wants time off for religious holidays must ask in advance. An employer should consider a request sympathetically but can refuse if it will affect their business.
- An employee who wears clothing or jewellery for religious reasons should normally be allowed to do so as long as there is no health and safety risk.
- An employee who does not want to eat or handle certain foods must tell his employer and the request should be accepted as long as it does not affect the business.

 **EXAMPLE**

**A devout Christian has become the first driver to refuse to get behind the wheel of a bus bearing an atheist poster declaring God probably does not exist**

Ron Heather, 62, walked out in protest after seeing the advert declaring: 'There's probably no God. Now stop worrying and enjoy your life.'

He told his managers that he could not drive the bus because the slogan, placed on the side of 800 buses across the country last week after a fundraising campaign raised £140,000, went against his faith.

They have now agreed to accommodate his religious beliefs by letting him drive buses in Southampton that do not bear the controversial message, which has been supported by atheists including Professor Richard Dawkins, the evolutionary biologist.

More than 200 people complained to the Advertising Standards Agency about the posters, which were created by Ariane Sherine, a comedy writer, as an antidote to religious adverts on public transport that 'threaten eternal damnation' to passengers. The watchdog is now considering whether to investigate the campaign on the grounds that it is offensive, or that its central claim about God's existence cannot be substantiated.

Mr Heather, who served in the Royal Navy for 25 years before becoming a bus driver four years ago, said:

66 When I first saw the bus last Saturday I was shocked. My first reaction was horror. I was in a dilemma but I felt strongly I couldn't drive that bus and so I went up to my inspectors and told them there was no way I could drive it. They said they didn't have another one, so I thought I'd better go home. To be fair the company have been very good and have agreed to do everything they can to keep me off those buses. 99

He added:

66 There would be no way buses would be able to drive around with an anti-Muslim message like that on the side mentioning Allah. There would be uproar. I'm not the only one who has mentioned it – some of the passengers don't like the adverts at all. 99

A spokesman for First Bus said:

66 As a company we understand Mr Heather's views regarding the atheist bus advert and we are doing what we can to accommodate his request not to drive the buses concerned. Mr Heather accepts though that he may need to drive one of these buses if no other vehicle is available for him. The content of this advert has been approved by the Advertising Standards Agency and therefore it is capable of being posted on static sites or anywhere else. 99

Hanne Stinson, chief executive of the British Humanist Association, which is running the campaign, said: 'I have difficulty understanding why people with particular religious beliefs find the expression of a different sort of beliefs to be offensive.'

*http://www.telegraph.co.uk/news/newstopics/howaboutthat/4270238/Atheist-bus-adverts-Christian-refuses-to-drive-bus-declaring-theres-probably-no-God.html*

Discrimination is allowed if religious belief is a necessary requirement for the job.

## EXAMPLE

### Faculty leader of Religious Education

**Required from April or September 2009**

We are looking for an enthusiastic and committed, suitably qualified and experienced practising Catholic teacher to lead and manage the development and delivery of Religious Education.

A team of both experienced and newly qualified teachers of RE deliver the subject curriculum. At GCSE we study Catholic Christianity and The Gospel of Mark; at GCE AS/A2 level Christian Theology is a popular and very successful Sixth Form course.

Many more staff, coordinated by our Lay Chaplain, work with RE teachers, and a large team of chaplains, to deliver a wide-ranging liturgical programme and we have recently opened a new school chapel.

This school is committed to safeguarding and promoting the welfare of children and young people and expects all staff and volunteers to share this commitment.

*Adapted from http://www.tes.co.uk/JobDetails*

## ACTIVITY

### Activity 7

In the following situations, decide whether or not there has been discrimination based on religion or belief:

Sancha is a humanist who works in a bank. She tells her boss about her faith but also tells him she does not want her colleagues to know because she thinks they might be unpleasant to her. Sancha's boss tells some of his friends who are also Sancha's colleagues and soon they make unpleasant remarks every time she comes into the office. This is ..................................................
..............................................................................

Sukhy is a key player in his school's rugby team. He wears a prayer bangle which is a key part of his religion. The rugby coach says Sukhy cannot wear his bangle to play rugby. Sukhy offers to wear tape over the bangle but the coach says if he wears the bangle he cannot play for the team. This is ...............................................

Saif is a Muslim and he asks his employer if he can be excused from work when it is time to pray. His employer agrees to his request and tells him he can use a room which will be empty at prayer time. This is .................................

Ebiye works on fishing boat. He is a Muslim and asks the captain if he can be excused when it is time to pray. The captain agrees but other members of the crew complain that landing the fish is dangerous if Ebiye is not there. The captain tells Ebiye he can only pray when his shift has finished. This is ......................................

Derek is a member of the Church of England who strongly believes women should not be priests. He runs an art gallery and interviews Patrick for a job. Patrick is a world-renowned expert on modern art and Derek really likes him but in the course of the interview Patrick tells Derek that his wife is training to become a priest. Derek gives the job to someone who is not as well qualified as Derek. This is ................
..............................................................................

## Comment

The whole area of discrimination is very complex. There are many laws and they can be difficult to understand. It is very important to have laws which prevent discrimination of any kind at work as people spend much of their time doing their job and it should be a situation in which they feel comfortable as well as being able to do their best. Here are some reasons why it is important to have these laws:

- They are needed so there is fairness and justice for everyone in the workplace.
- They are essential to preserve equality so that everyone has the same chance of procuring a job and doing it well.
- They are essential to prevent any kind of stereotyping or prejudice from employers or other employees.
- They ensure that employees are appointed to jobs because they are the best applicant.
- They ensure that promotion is based on merit.
- They protect against bullying and harassment which can make a worker's life a misery.
- They make the workplace a productive environment where everyone is able to work with a sense of common purpose.
- They give an employer a good reputation so that they can attract the best workers.
- They save an employer money as employees will not need to make claims against them.

## KEY FACTS

- Discrimination has been the object of a great deal of legal activity, both by the courts and by Parliament.

- It is important that employees are protected from discrimination which can happen in many different ways – knowing each of these is important.

- Discrimination can happen in different ways – it can be direct or indirect; it can be by harassment or victimisation – being able to give a simple definition of each is important.

- The most important areas deal with issues relating to pay, sex, marital status, race and disability – it is important to be able to give examples of each kind of discrimination and be able to recognise when it has taken place.

- New important areas include age, sexual orientation, transsexuals and religion and belief and it is important to be able to recognise these types of discrimination.

 **EXAM QUESTION**

This question shows the range of information you need to cover in your study and the different skills you will be tested on in the examination.

Read each of the following three situations and complete activity (a), activity (b) and activity (c) which follow them:

(i) Ann, a woman, and Brian, a man, are employed in the same restaurant by the same employer. Ann is a waitress and Brian is a waiter. They both work exactly the same hours and do exactly the same work but Ann is paid only half the wage that Brian is paid.

(ii) Claude is employed by Derek who hates all gay people. Recently Claude has been dismissed by Derek who has found out that Claude is gay.

(iii) Fatima, a clerical worker, has developed severe arthritis in her knees and now has to use a wheelchair. Fatima used to work on the second floor and has requested an office on the ground floor as the controls in the only lift in the building are too high for Fatima to reach from her wheelchair. Her employers have refused.

(a) Identify which area of discrimination law is involved in each situation.

[3 marks]

Situation (i)

..............................................................................

Situation (ii)

..............................................................................

Situation (iii)

..............................................................................

(b) Give reasons why the party in each situation (i), (ii), and (iii) will be able to show that they have in fact been discriminated against.

Situation (i)

..................................................................

..................................................................

..................................................................

..................................................................

..................................................................

..................................................................

Situation (ii)

..................................................................

..................................................................

..................................................................

..................................................................

..................................................................

..................................................................

Situation (iii)

..................................................................

..................................................................

..................................................................

..................................................................

..................................................................

..................................................................

[9 marks]

..................................................................

..................................................................

..................................................................

..................................................................

..................................................................

..................................................................

..................................................................

..................................................................

..................................................................

..................................................................

..................................................................

..................................................................

..................................................................

..................................................................

..................................................................

..................................................................

..................................................................

..................................................................

[6 marks]

(c) Without anti-discrimination laws in (b)(i) above Ann would be doing the same job as a man for half the pay, in (b)(ii) Claude would lose his job just because he is gay, and in (b)(iii) Fatima would not be able to carry on with her job.

Discuss three other reasons why it is important to have laws preventing discrimination at work.

..................................................................

..................................................................

..................................................................

..................................................................

# CHAPTER 14

# HEALTH AND SAFETY AT WORK

The aims and objectives of this chapter are to show how important health and safety issues are at work. Accidents are common and they range from minor incidents to those where a person is unable to work for a period of time or even not able to work again. This can have severe implications for the individual and for their family as well as affecting the reputation of an employer.

As a result employers and employees have legal rights and responsibilities in this important area. These obligations have evolved in different ways – by the judges when they decide cases, by Parliament and by the European Union (EU). This chapter will look at these different types of obligations and their effectiveness.

## ✎ ACTIVITY

### Activity 1

Make a list of all the things which appear to be health and safety risks in this cartoon.

Figure 14.1

## 14.1 Common law protections

The common law is the law made in cases. This can be a very good method as it is done by judges who work in this area all the time; it allows the law to evolve to meet changing needs and to react quickly if the law is not doing its job.

 **EXAMPLE**

Mr English was employed by Clyde Coal and injured at work by machinery. His employer said they employed an agent to make sure the mine was safe and so the agent, rather than Clyde Coal, should be liable. The House of Lords held that Clyde Coal could delegate the performance of the duty but not the responsibility to take reasonable care of employees' health and safety and so they were still liable.

*From the case of Wilsons and Clyde Coal Co Ltd v English (1938)*

This case was very important as it set out the common law duty of care an employer owes to an employee and this is to provide:

- a safe place of work
- a safe system of work
- safe plant and appliances
- competent fellow employees.

 **EXAMPLE**

An employee was forced to make a round trip of 400 miles in a company van that had no heater and cracked windows. The employee suffered frostbite and sued his employer. The court held that the employer was liable as the employee did not have safe equipment or a safe place of work.

*From the case of Bradford v Robinson Rentals (1967)*

Although this duty is important an employer can only do what is reasonable in terms of taking precautions to prevent harm occurring.

 **EXAMPLE**

After a storm the floor in a factory flooded and water mixed with oil used in the factory, making the floor very slippery. The employer had sawdust laid on the floor but Latimer slipped on an area of floor which had no sawdust on it and was injured. The House of Lords held that AEC was not liable. They had taken reasonable precautions and the danger was not so bad that they should have closed the factory down.

*From the case of Latimer v AEC Ltd (1953)*

More recently another duty has been added and this is one to protect against psychiatric injury.

 **EXAMPLE**

Mr Walker worked as a social services manager for a County Council. His workload grew bigger and contained many upsetting cases. He asked the Council to recruit extra staff but they did not do so and Mr Walker suffered a nervous breakdown. When he went back to work the Council provided extra staff but soon moved them to other jobs. Mr Walker had another nervous breakdown and was dismissed on the grounds of permanent ill health.

A court held that the duty for an employee's safety covered physical and psychiatric injury and the Council was liable as Mr Walker's second nervous breakdown was foreseeable since they did not do enough to help him.

*From the case of Walker v Northumberland County Council (1995)*

In later cases the courts have made the law clearer. Stress-related illness or injury is covered if this kind of injury was reasonably foreseeable by the employer on the basis of what the employer knew or ought to have known. The test applies to all occupations. An employer needs to take notice of any indications of problems on the part of the employee. However, an employer can only take what an employee says at face value and do what is reasonable in an effort to help, such as provision of, or access to, confidential support services.

## 14.2 Statutory regulation

The key piece of statute law is the Health and Safety at Work Act 1974. This builds on the common law duties considered above and incorporates them into the statute.

### 14.2.1 Employer rights and responsibilities

Under the Act every employer, whatever the size of their business, has a general duty 'so far as is reasonably practicable' to protect the health, safety and welfare at work of all employees.

To do this an employer must provide:

• safe plant and systems of work
• safe methods for the use, handling, storage and transport of articles and substances
• necessary information, instruction, training and supervision
• a safe and well-maintained workplace, including safe access and exits
• a safe working environment with adequate welfare facilities.

 **EXAMPLE**

Mr Berry worked in an area of a factory which was very noisy. His employer provided ear defenders but did not check whether Mr Berry wore them. A court decided that if the employer knew about the risk of injury, even if it was not apparent to the employee, then the employer had to take steps to make sure that employees used the equipment. They could even dismiss an employee who would not use the equipment.

*From the case of Berry v Stone Manganese Co Ltd (1972)*

An employer must prepare, and keep up-to-date, a policy statement on safety and put arrangements in place to ensure the general policy is carried out. The employer must ensure that all employees know the policy. Any safety representatives must be consulted, along with employees, in making health and safety arrangements.

Employers must also ensure that other people, such as the general public and contractors, do not have their health and safety adversely affected. Where necessary, an employer must give these people information about hazards.

Although the 1974 Act creates wide-ranging duties there are some limits as an employer can only act 'so far as is reasonably practicable'. This means that an employer can argue that the costs of a particular safety measure far outweigh any potential reduction in risk. An employer can also expect an employee to behave reasonably.

 **EXAMPLE**

A lift in a Gateway store was regularly maintained by lift contractors but it kept jamming. The contractors showed some of the store staff how to free the lift manually. It often happened that a member of staff would free the lift manually when it jammed although Gateway head office did not know this was happening. One day a store manager went to free the lift, fell through a trapdoor which had been left open and was killed.

The Court of Appeal held that the company was liable as a failure at the store or at head office to take reasonable precautions to protect the health and safety of employees was a breach of the 1974 Act.

*From the case of R v Gateway Foodmarkets Ltd (1997)*

### 14.2.2 Employee rights and responsibilities

Under the 1974 Act every employee has a duty to:

• take reasonable care of their own health and safety

 **ACTIVITY**

## Activity 2

Tick the relevant box to indicate if there is a health and safety risk in each of the following situations.

|  | Health and safety risk | No health and safety risk |
|---|---|---|
| Graham is told to change a light bulb in the factory where he works. The only ladder he can find has two broken rungs so Graham stands on a chair to change the bulb. |  |  |
| Sandra works as a kennel maid. She is given gloves to wear when she feeds the dogs. Sandra does not wear the gloves as she says they smell funny. Sandra is bitten by a dog and the bite becomes infected. |  |  |
| Tariq works in a chemical factory. He is given strict instructions on how to store the chemicals and protective clothing. His boss checks every week that Tariq is following the correct procedures. |  |  |
| Kendra works at a computer all day. She gets headaches and asks her employer for a better screen. Kendra's employer tells her that if she wants a better screen, she will need to buy it herself. |  |  |
| Roberto delivers tomatoes to an Italian restaurant. He carries several boxes down a corridor and trips over a chair which has been left in the corridor. Roberto breaks his leg. |  |  |

Table 14.1

- take reasonable care of the health and safety of anyone who could be adversely affected by their 'acts or omissions at work'
- cooperate with their employer to meet legal requirements.

The 1974 Act set up the Health and Safety Commission (HSC). This has a Chairman and six to nine members who represent employers, employees, local authorities and professional bodies.

The Act also set up an inspectorate called the Health and Safety Executive (HSE). This is led by a Director General and two Deputies. The HSC and HSE work closely to recommend legislation, develop guidance and Codes of Practice.

The HSE and local authorities appoint inspectors to enforce the law. When inspectors believe that legal requirements are being breached, they can issue an Improvement Notice. This states the breach and gives a time limit in which it must be put right. Inspectors normally give employers at least two weeks' written notice of an intention to issue an Improvement Notice to give them a chance to put things right. If an Improvement Notice is issued, the employer can appeal to a tribunal.

When an inspector believes that there is a risk of serious personal injury, they can issue a Prohibition Notice. This does not require any actual breach of the law, and it can take immediate effect. This can close a business until the problem is resolved.

## 14.3 EU regulation

Regulations came into effect in 1993 to create common health and safety standards. The EU believes these are important to achieve a 'Single European market' and prevent unfair competition by any particular member state. They are known as the 'Six Pack' and are very detailed. Although you would not need to remember every one of the provisions, you need to appreciate just how thorough they are. Some of the matters that each of the six headings cover include:

1.  Management of Health and Safety at Work Regulations
    - Conduct and keep assessments of all significant risks to employees or other persons and identify measures to control them.
    - Pay attention to risks to new and expectant mothers.
    - Pay attention to risks to young people.
    - Plan, organise, control, maintain and review health and safety effectively.
    - Appoint and train competent staff to ensure health and safety compliance.
    - Devise procedures to deal with serious or imminent danger, including evacuation.
    - Limit access to dangerous areas to trained workers.
    - Provide thorough health and safety training for all employees.

2.  Manual Handling Operations Regulations
    - Where reasonably practical to do so avoid workers doing manual handling tasks which involve risk of injury, or assess and reduce the risk to the lowest reasonably practicable level.
    - Provide workers with a general indication of risks and specific information where possible.
    - Ensure employees make proper use of systems provided by the employer.

 **EXAMPLE**

While unloading materials from a lorry and throwing them into a skip Mr Cullen tripped on some of the materials. He fell off the lorry and was injured.

He brought an action under this part of the 'Six Pack'. At the original trial the court held that the regulations only applied to injuries from lifting but on appeal it was stated that injury could come from tripping too.

*From the case of Cullen v North Lanarkshire Council (1998)*

3.  Display Screen Equipment (DSE) Regulations
    - Make a risk assessment of all workstations and reduce risks to the lowest reasonably practicable level.
    - Daily use of DSE must be broken up by rest breaks or other types of work.
    - Allow users of DSE to have regular eye and eyesight tests and pay for them.
    - Pay for any special spectacles or lenses needed for DSE work.
    - Provide health and safety training on use of workstations and information on the risks and measures to control them.

4.  Workplace (Health, Safety and Welfare) Regulations
    - Workplaces and equipment must be maintained in good condition.
    - Enclosed workplaces must have fresh or purified air.
    - A reasonable temperature must be maintained during working hours and thermometers provided.
    - There must be suitable and sufficient lighting. Emergency lighting must be provided where necessary.
    - Workplaces and equipment must be kept clean.
    - Any workspace must be big enough for the health, safety and welfare of staff.
    - Workstations must be suitable for workers and their work.

- If work can be done sitting down, suitable seats must be provided.
- Floors should be suitable and not uneven, holed or slippery. They should be kept free from obstruction and staircases should normally have a handrail.
- Windows and transparent or translucent doors or walls must be made of safety material or protected against breakage and be clearly marked. Windows and skylights must be safe to open and clean.
- Pedestrians, vehicles and traffic must be able to move safely.
- Doors which can be pushed from either side should have panes to provide a clear view of the space around the door.
- Escalators and moving walkways must be safe to use and have emergency stop controls.
- Suitable and sufficient toilets must be readily accessible. They must be well ventilated and lit and kept clean.
- Washing facilities, including showers if needed, with hot and cold water, soap and hygienic means of drying must be provided.
- A supply of drinking water must be readily accessible for all workers.
- Storage and changing facilties for clothes must be provided where necessary.
- Suitable rest facilities must be conveniently accessible, including for pregnant women and nursing mothers.
- Facilities for eating meals must be provided where meals are normally taken at work.

5. Provision and Use of Work Equipment Regulations
   - Work equipment must be suitable for its intended purpose.
   - Equipment must be properly maintained and a 'maintenance log' kept.
   - Users of equipment and their supervisors must be provided with information, instruction and training on correct use of equipment and on foreseeable abnormal situations which might occur.

- Use of equipment with a specific risk should be restricted to trained workers.
- Measures must be taken to prevent access to dangerous parts of machinery and to protect against substances, gases, liquids, dusts, overheating, fire or explosion, disintegration of parts of equipment, extremely hot or cold surfaces.
- Ensure all controls are safe to use and clearly identifiable. Start and stop controls must be designed to ensure health and safety. Where appropriate, it must be possible to isolate machinery from its energy source.
- Where necessary, clearly visible markings or other warning devices must be fitted.

 **EXAMPLE**

Mr Stark was a postman provided with a bicycle to do his round. He was riding the bicycle when the front brake broke; he was thrown to the ground and suffered injury.

It was accepted that an inspection of the brake would not have shown up the defect but Mr Stark argued there was an absolute obligation on his employer to provide safe work equipment and the Court of Appeal agreed with him.

*From the case of Stark v The Post Office (2000)*

6. Personal Protective Equipment (PPE) Regulations
   - An employer must provide PPE which is appropriate to the risk involved and the work done. It must be ergonomic and fit the user.
   - If more than one item of PPE is needed, they must be compatible and effective when worn together.
   - Before buying PPE an employer must do a risk assessment to identify the risk and make sure that the PPE protects against it.
   - An employer must ensure that PPE is maintained in good repair and cleaned or replaced as often as necessary.

- There must be storage for PPE when it is not in use.
- Staff must be given information, instruction and training on the risks PPE is intended to avoid, how to use it and how the employee should maintain it.
- The employer must take steps to ensure that PPE provided is properly used.
- Employees must use PPE as directed and report loss or any obvious defect to the employer.

 **ACTIVITY**

### Activity 3

Using the website http://www.hse.gov.uk/ Prosecutions identify one case example which shows a breach of each of the types of regulation found in the 'Six Pack'. Analyse why each of the examples you chose was bad enough to breach the Regulations. Write a report on whether you think the Regulations do a good job.

According to statistics for the Health and Safety Executive (HSE) in 2007–08, 34 million working days were lost. This is equivalent to 1.4 days for every worker, at a total cost to the economy of around £30 billion. Of these days, 28 million were due to work-related ill-health and 6 million due to workplace injury. Some 229 workers were killed at work and 2.1 million people were suffering from an illness they believed was caused or made worse by their current or past work. HSE research has also shown that failure to manage health and safety is the main cause of 80 per cent of accidents (http://www.hse.gov.uk/statistics/index.htm).

 **ACTIVITY**

### Activity 4

Quiz

True or false?

1. Temporary workers have the same right to safety information as other employees.

2. Ladders should always be inspected prior to use.

3. An employee who uses a computer has his eyes tested and is told that he needs to wear glasses for his job. The employee says that the employer must pay for them.

4. Proper lifting techniques can injure spinal tissues.

5. Swapping personal protective clothing or equipment between employees is prohibited unless it has been properly cleaned.

6. Try to carry all loads by yourself to save time.

7. Approved hard hats must be worn where the danger of falling objects exists and they should be inspected periodically for damage.

8. People who work in offices do not have to worry about workplace health and safety.

9. Appropriate foot protection is required where there is a risk of injury from hot or corrosive substances, falling objects, or crushing or penetrating actions.

10. Office falls are frequently caused by using makeshift ladders.

11. Health and safety failures cost the UK up to £18 billion each year.

12. Aisles and passageways must be kept clear of obstruction.

 **EXAMPLE**

**Town left without Christmas tree over health and safety row**

A town has been left without a Christmas tree after organisers were told they would have to pay £2,000 for a concrete slab to anchor it down under health and safety rules.

Under the regulations, they were told they would need a 20-ton concrete slab to secure the 26ft Scots pine.

But members of Walton Forum in Essex, who are organising the decorations, said the tree itself only cost £400.

Chairman of the forum John Halls called it 'health and safety gone mad'.

He explained the group had wanted to make a permanent hole in the ground where the tree could be installed, fixed to a metal pole, each year.

But Tendring District Council turned down the request because they feared the tree would topple over.

Mr Halls said: 'All we want to do is put a steel tube into the ground to put the Christmas tree in, but the structural engineers want a concrete, two metres by two metres, 20-ton foundation.

'We just don't have the money to do it.'

He added: 'We have been talking about it for about four months and we thought we were home and dry but there's all this bureaucracy.'

The row has led to a delay in putting up the Christmas tree in the town's Millennium Square.

Nigel Brown, Tendring Council communications manager, said the council felt the proposals were not safe and put forward an alternative.

He said: 'Officers have made every effort to try to help them come up with an acceptable solution and accommodate their requirements.

'However, the council is the landowner of Millennium Square and, as such, must ensure that whatever is put up on the site is both suitable and safe.'

*Adapted from an article in the Daily Telegraph, 4th December 2008*

 **EXAMPLE**

## The Gloucestershire health and safety officers who love danger

As health and safety officers, Roger Garbett and his Forest of Dean District Council colleagues should probably be more cautious than most when it comes to diving into sub-zero water.

But they enthusiastically took the plunge in the icy waters of a disused quarry.

Dubbing themselves 'Health And Safety Gone Mad', they are on a mission to convince us the nanny state is not stopping us being adventurous.

Roger and fellow officers from the council's environmental health department Keith Leslie, Haydn Brookes and Rhys Thomas say they are fed-up of taking the blame for bosses who do not want to put up Christmas decorations in the office or poor organisers who cannot be bothered to arrange a pancake race.

After hearing health and safety officials were blamed for ending a traditional Christmas Day swim in Southwold, Suffolk, Roger and Keith took a New Year dip at the national diving centre in Tidenham, near Chepstow, to prove to people they can still do it.

Admittedly it wasn't an impromptu dip, and they made sure there were people on hand with blankets and hot drinks in case they got into trouble, but they say there is nothing wrong with a few precautions.

'We want to show people by example that health and safety is about saving lives, not stopping lives,' said Roger, 49, the council's group manager of environmental services.

'We are not suggesting an 89-year-old who has never swum before should suddenly dive in an outdoor pool in January.

'But people should stop using health and safety as an excuse.

'If you believe some of the stories you hear, health and safety is all about stopping any activity that might possibly lead to harm.

'This is not our vision of sensible health and safety. Our approach is to seek a balance between the unachievable aim of absolute safety and the kind of poor management of risk that damages lives and the economy.'

*Adapted from an article in the Western Daily Press, 7th January 2009*

**ACTIVITY**

## Activity 5

Quiz

Follow the link: http://www.rsc-sw-scotland.ac.uk/project_pages/health_safety.htm – and there is an interactive health and safety quiz you can try.

The pictures below are common health and safety signs. Can you identify what they mean?

 **KEY FACTS**

There is a lot of information on this area – you do not need to spend hours learning lists of facts but it is worth knowing the basic duties and several examples of the kind of things which will be health and safety risks.

■ Common law duties – you need to know that there are several things an employer must provide – safe place of work, a safe system of work, safe plant and appliances and competent fellow employees.

■ Statutory duties – there is a need to know an outline of the duties and responsibilities

created by the Health and Safety at Work Act. It is best to try and remember them from the point of view of the employer and the employee. It is especially important to think about how they would be applied in real-life situations.

■ EU duties – there is a lot of information here and it is not necessary to learn it all. It is a good idea to know the key areas with which the 'Six Pack' deals and a few examples of each kind of protection they offer.

# CHAPTER 15

# RULES ON TERMINATION OF EMPLOYMENT

The aims and objectives of this chapter are to show how important it is to have clear rules when employment comes to an end. Employees need protection to make sure that they do not lose their jobs unfairly or are put in situations where they feel forced to takes steps that can expose them, and their families, to financial pressure. However, employers need to be able to run their businesses and they may have to end a contract of employment with an employee if there are good reasons for doing so.

There are different ways a contract of employment can end and the main ones are covered in this chapter. There is a lot of detailed regulation in this area of the law but you do not need to know all the complex provisions – there are many lawyers who spend all their professional lives dealing with the intricacies of these regulations!

## 15.1 Summary dismissal

Summary, or instant, dismissal is the dismissal of an employee on the spot. Normally this means that the employee has behaved in a way which is so bad that it could be classed as gross misconduct and so there is an exemption from any need to give notice.

The definition of gross misconduct can change but some things are nearly always included. These include:

- fighting
- stealing

- arson
- deliberate falsification of time-sheets
- accessing and/or distributing pornographic emails or websites
- serious bullying or harassment
- serious infringement of health and safety rules.

It is not always easy to be so clear. Here are two examples:

- Smoking – some employers are flexible about where employees smoke so long as it is outside, but on an oil rig, smoking anywhere other than in a specified area is likely to be gross misconduct
- Alcohol – if an airline pilot or a surgeon works under the influence of alcohol this will almost certainly be gross misconduct. For other employees, alcohol may not be taken seriously unless it affects performance. If an employee is expected to spend time entertaining clients, *not* drinking might be more of a problem!

 **EXAMPLE**

### Swearing in the workplace

The sacking of Ian Millward, the St Helens Rugby League Head Coach, in May 2005, brought to the fore the employment law consequences of swearing.

The use of foul and abusive language can, in certain circumstances, justify the dismissal of employees for gross misconduct. Furthermore, if foul and abusive language is used by an employer or a senior employee in a supervisory position, then this could expose the employer to claims for constructive dismissal or discrimination.

There is no general legal principle that the use of swearing by employees is an act of gross misconduct that would justify instant dismissal. The use of foul and abusive language in certain workshop and factory floor environments may be commonplace between employees and would not ordinarily justify dismissal. However, where foul and abusive language is used by an employee against his boss, particularly in circumstances where an employee is refusing to carry out a reasonable order, has been held to justify instant dismissal. Similarly, where an employee uses foul and abusive language in order to intimidate or humiliate a more junior employee, this is likely to expose an employer to a claim in the employment tribunal and may also justify the instant dismissal of the employee who used such language. There has been one case, however, where an employment tribunal held that where an employee used abusive language in a sudden explosion of temper and under the influence of drink, it was unfair to dismiss that employee without first giving him the opportunity to apologise.

There have been a number of recent cases where the courts have emphasised that employers who swear at their employees do so at their own peril. In one case, a director who said of his secretary that she was an 'intolerable bitch on a Monday morning' was held to have constructively dismissed her.

There is a suggestion in the case of Mr Millward that he also used sexist language in a foul-mouthed tirade against a female employee. Employers need to be particularly careful to prevent such conduct as it will expose them to claims in the employment tribunal for discrimination where there is no limit to the amount of compensation that an employment tribunal can award.

*Adpated from*
*http://www.lindermyers.co.uk/article.asp?id=129*

 **EXAMPLE**

Graham works as a security guard at a bank and in his contract it states that he must not drink alcohol when he is on duty. Graham's wife has left him for another man. He is on duty alone and in the middle of the night he starts feeling depressed so he drinks some brandy from the bottle the bank manager keeps in his office. Next morning the bank manager finds Graham asleep and smelling of brandy when he arrives for work.

Is this gross misconduct? Yes, because Graham knows that drinking on duty is not acceptable. He is asleep on duty, so he is not doing his job. Drinking the bank manager's brandy could also be theft.

Nico works in a fashion store in the middle of London. The company handbook states that fighting, stealing and gross insubordination all constitute gross misconduct. Nico arrives for work late three times in two weeks and his boss tells him not to bother coming to work the next day.

Is this gross misconduct? Probably not because although Nico ought to be on time, being late is not identified as being gross misconduct and he should have had some warnings before being told he has lost his job.

Andy is a trumpet teacher who gives one-hour lessons to children at a local school. The school handbook states that punctuality is essential, as parents pay privately for these lessons, and that lateness will be treated as gross misconduct. Andy is late for lessons three times in two weeks and the school tells him not to bother coming to work the next day.

Is this gross misconduct? Yes, because Andy knows that this is a key condition of his employment and so by being late he is not doing his job properly and he is not giving value for money. Then, instant dismissal for lateness is acceptable.

If an employer wants to set high standards, they need to make the limits clear and explain them clearly to their employees.

If an employer summarily dismisses an employee, they need to be able to show that:

- Their decision was one that a reasonable employer would have made.
- The decision was fair and reasonable in the circumstances.
- The offence was so wrong that dismissal was an appropriate sanction.

Once an employee has been summarily dismissed the employer must:

- write to the employee, detailing the alleged misconduct with evidence that leads the employer to believe the employee is responsible, and explaining their rights to appeal against dismissal
- invite the employee to an appeal meeting if the employee asks for one.

To give some protection to the employer and allow him to run his business, summary or instant dismissal may be acceptable where:

- the gross misconduct is very serious
- it has been established that the gross misconduct took place
- the employer dismissed the employee when they became aware of the conduct or immediately afterwards
- alternative sanctions were considered
- mitigating factors such as the employee's past history, their age, position, length of service and any previous warnings were taken into account.

## 15.2 Redundancy

### Reasons

If an employee is going to be made redundant, he should be treated fairly and certain steps should be followed under the Employment Rights Act 1996. Redundancy is a form of dismissal. Reasons for redundancy include:

- New technology or a new system makes a job unnecessary.
- The job an employee was hired for no longer exists.
- The need to cut costs means staff numbers must be reduced.

If an employer moves the location of their business, some contracts of employment include a mobility clause which means an employer can normally force an employee to move unless it is completely unreasonable. An employee may not want to move because of increased travel costs and time, the cost of moving house or disruption to a child's education. If there is no

 **ACTIVITY**

**Activity 1**

Would summary dismissal be suitable in the following situations? Explain the reasons for your answer.

Frankie has worked at Plug-it Plumbers for two weeks. His reference from his previous employer says Frankie was a good worker but he had 'a bit of a temper'. Frankie is sent to do a job that should take an hour but he returns three hours later. His supervisor, Terry, asks Frankie where he has been. Frankie says, 'None of your business' and hits Terry so hard that he breaks Terry's jaw.

Steve has worked at Woody's Timberyard for 15 years and he is well known for being a hard worker. On a Friday lunchtime he goes to the pub and comes back so drunk that he can hardly walk. It turns out later that he had just become a grandfather for the first time.

Owen works as a driver for Hank's Haulage Company. Owen's supervisor rings up to tell Owen that the lorry has been scratched and the money will be deducted from Owen's pay. Owen shouts abuse at his supervisor and slams down the phone. When Owen arrives for work the next day, he is told he has been summarily dismissed.

mobility clause and an employee decides not to move, they can be made redundant on the grounds that their job no longer exists or the alternative job is refused as it is unsuitable.

## Procedure

If redundancy is necessary there are several things an employer should do:
- Select those to be made redundant fairly.
- Consult with those employees.
- Make any redundancy payments due.
- Give the correct amount of notice.
- Consider any alternatives to redundancy.

## Pay

Redundancy pay depends on factors such as how long the employee has been employed. An employee is entitled to a redundancy payment if he has at least two years' continuous service with the employer and it can be claimed if an employee is temporarily laid off for more than four weeks in a row (or six weeks in a 13-week period). The contract of employment may specify how the amount will be worked out. If it does not, there is a statutory formula. The first £30,000 of any payment is tax-free.

 **ACTIVITY**

### Activity 2

Go to http://www.berr.gov.uk/whatwedo/ employment/employment-legislation/ employment-guidance/page33157.html. This is a reckoner for redundancy pay and you can see how the figures are reached.

An employer must make the payment when, or soon after, the employee is dismissed. If the employer does not pay or says they do not have to pay, an employee must write to the employer asking for payment. If this does not work the employee can take the matter to an employment tribunal within six months of the date the employment ended. The tribunal will decide if an employee is to receive any money.

The actual amount is also affected by age and pay up to a limit of £350 per week from 1st February 2009:
- An employee receives 0.5 week's pay for each full year of service if they are less than 22 years old.
- An employee receives one week's pay for each full year of service if they are over 22 but less than 41 years old.
- An employee receives 1.5 weeks' pay for each full year of service if they are over 41 years old.

## Does redundancy pay cover everyone?

No – some types of employee have no right to a redundancy payment under the Act. These include:
- members of the Armed Forces
- members of the police services
- House of Lords and House of Commons staff
- apprentices whose service ends at the end of the apprenticeship contract
- Crown servants or employees in a public office
- merchant seamen.

## Notice

An employer should also give proper notice of termination of employment (or pay in lieu of notice). Details of the notice period will be in the contract of employment.

An employee who is being made redundant is entitled to reasonable time off with pay during working hours to look for another job or make arrangements for training for future employment.

## Collective redundancy

If there are fewer than 20 employees being made redundant, then the statutory minimum dismissal procedure above should be followed. If there are 20 or more, then the collective consultation procedure applies instead.

**ACTIVITY**

## Activity 3

Tick the appropriate box in each of the following factual situations to indicate whether a redundancy is fair or unfair.

| | Fair | Unfair |
|---|---|---|
| Stephanie has been employed as a company telephonist. The company changes to an automated telephone system and Stephanie is made redundant. | | |
| Federico is a social worker. He is called for jury service and the trial lasts for six weeks. Federico's work has to be given to other social workers and at the end of his jury service his employer makes him redundant. | | |
| Hannah is a newly qualified drama teacher who has worked at a stage school for a term. The poor financial situation means that the stage school needs to save money and they make Hannah redundant as she is the member of staff most recently appointed. | | |
| Craig is an estate agent. He works hard and has a good record of selling houses. Craig receives a letter from his boss telling him he is being made redundant. Craig had no idea this was going to happen. | | |

Table 15.1

If a method for deciding redundancies has been agreed with a trade union, the employer should follow it. They can decide what reasons to use as long as they can be shown to be fair. The most common ones are:

- last in, first out
- asking for volunteers
- disciplinary records
- staff appraisal markings
- skills, qualifications and experience.

An employer can use a combination of criteria, perhaps using some kind of points system to get an overall score. If an employee feels they have been selected unfairly they can appeal in writing, explaining what they want the employer to do to put the situation right.

## Can redundancy be unfair?

It is unfair if to be chosen for redundancy for discriminatory reasons. Some unfair reasons for

redundancy include:

- maternity leave
- being a part-time worker
- membership or non-membership of a trade union
- taking part in lawful industrial action lasting 12 weeks or less
- taking action on health and safety grounds
- doing jury service.

If an employer uses redundancy to cover up the real reason for ending employment, or if they do not carry out the redundancy procedure properly, it may amount to unfair dismissal.

## 15.3 Constructive dismissal

Constructive dismissal is when an employee is forced to quit his job against his will because of his employer's conduct. It can make an employee feel that their life is very difficult and that they cannot remain in the job. Although there is no actual dismissal by the employer, the end result is the same as being sacked and it amounts to a fundamental breach of the contract of employment.

Therefore, the reason for leaving must be very serious and examples include:

- a serious breach of contract such as non-payment or a sudden demotion
- being forced to accept unreasonable changes to employment conditions without agreement such as being moved to another town, or changing a contract for day shifts to night-work
- bullying, harassment or violence by work colleagues
- working in dangerous conditions.

If an employee feels they have to leave, they should do so immediately or the employer may argue that, by staying, they accepted the conduct or treatment. However, they must avoid resigning before the actual breach of contract occurs because the employer could then claim that there was no dismissal.

The employer's breach of contract may be one serious incident or the last in a series of less important incidents that are serious when taken together. A claim can be brought in the employment tribunal.

 **EXAMPLE**

Ms Morrow was employed in a supermarket as a bakery production controller. She had a bad working relationship with the store manager who, she felt, unreasonably harassed her. The store manager had a special promotion on a certain kind of loaf and found that insufficient loaves were on the shelves. The manager told off Ms Morrow in front of staff and a customer, saying, 'If you cannot do the job I pay you to do, then I will get someone who can'. Two hours later he told her off again. Ms Morrow was

extremely distressed and resigned, claiming constructive and unfair dismissal.

An employment tribunal said that although public criticism was a breach of trust and confidence, it was not serious enough to entitle her to resign and claim constructive dismissal. On appeal this was held to be wrong and conduct which amounts to a breach of the implied term of trust and confidence is a fundamental breach which goes to the root of the contract.

*Adapted from Morrow v Safeway Stores plc (2002)*

Wrongful dismissal is based on contract law. Any claim means looking at the employee's employment contract to see if the employer has broken the contract. A wrongful dismissal claim is made in the same way as a breach of contract claim and compensation for wrongful dismissal usually only covers pay for the notice period.

Examples of breaches include:

- An employee is dismissed without notice.
- The notice given is too short.
- Failure by the employer to follow a contractual disciplinary procedure.

Wrongful dismissal claims can be brought in the employment tribunal, County Court or High Court, depending on the value of the claim.

 **EXAMPLE**

Mr Wilson was a head gardener. His boss, Mr Racher, set impossibly high standards and Mr Wilson believed that Mr Racher wanted 'to get rid of him'. One day the two men argued. Mr Racher accused Mr Wilson of not doing certain things he had been asked to do and of being lazy on a particular day. Mr Wilson answered, 'If you remember it was pissing with rain on Friday. Do you expect me to get ****ing wet?' The argument went on and Mr Racher summarily dismissed Mr Wilson.

The Court of Appeal held that this was not a case of willful disobedience by Mr Wilson.

Although he had a duty of obedience, courtesy and respect toward his employer Mr Racher had goaded and provoked him so much that the dismissal was wrongful.

*Adapted from Wilson v Racher (1974)*

## ACTIVITY

### Activity 4

Quiz

Decide in each of the following situations whether constructive or wrongful dismissal is the most appropriate basis of a claim.

Abdullah has worked for his boss for five years. He has always worked from 9 am to 5 pm on Monday to Friday. Abdullah receives a letter from his boss telling him he now has to work from 11 am till 9 pm on Saturdays and Sundays. This would give rise to a claim for ................................ dismissal.

Grace has worked at Superdeal Foodstore for two years. She complained to her boss about her bad back from lifting heavy boxes. Now, Grace's boss has moved her to a job chopping vegetables for the sandwiches which Superdeal sells. This job pays less money and Grace's boss keeps asking her, in front of her colleagues, whether she is well enough to be at work. This would give rise to a claim for ................................ dismissal.

Hugo works for Sparks Electrics as an electrician. He is supposed to be paid every Friday but for the last two weeks he has not been paid and his boss has not told him why. This would give rise to a claim for ................................ dismissal.

Diego works in a coffee shop. His boss accuses him of stealing from the till. Diego says that someone is stealing but it is not him. The boss says he has heard that it is Diego and tells him not to come to work anymore. This would give rise to a claim for ................................ dismissal.

Veronica is a lawyer in a big London solicitor's firm which also has offices in Dubai and Hong Kong. Veronica is told that she must go and work in Dubai but Veronica does not want to as she has young children who like their school in London. Veronica is told that if she does not move she will have to take a job which pays less money. This would give rise to a claim for ................................ dismissal.

## 15.4 Unfair dismissal

Unfair dismissal is when an employee is dismissed from his job and the law is found in the Employment Rights Act 1996. Unfair dismissal can happen in several ways:

- The employer does not have a valid reason for dismissal and/or has acted unreasonably.
- A fixed-term contract is not renewed.
- An employer forces someone to retire.

### 15.4.1 Fair or unfair?

There are some reasons for dismissal which are potentially fair:

- Conduct: this covers a very wide range of behaviour and there are examples in the earlier section on summary dismissal. The relevant conduct must normally occur at work. Occasionally, however, conduct outside work might be enough if it was relevant.
- Capability: this covers incompetence and an inability to do a job because of illness or injury. Sickness can justify dismissal but an employer should first consult with the employee concerning the nature and likely length of the illness, seek medical advice relating to the employee's condition, and consider whether there might be a suitable alternative job which could be offered to the employee. If dismissal is based on incompetence, an employer should normally have warned the employee about the standard of his work, given him the opportunity to improve and possibly offered further training.

**ACTIVITY**

## Activity 5

Tick the box which you think indicates the kind of reason that lies behind the dismissal in each of the following situations:

| | Potentially fair | Automatically unfair |
|---|---|---|
| Keira has a job as a secretary and she tells her employer that she is pregnant. Keira's boss dismisses her. | | |
| Phillip has a job as a solicitor. His hobby is going to football matches and getting into fights. His boss tells Phillip he is bad for the solicitor's firm and Phillip loses his job. | | |
| Ameer is a footballer and he is suffering from cancer. He has to miss three months for medical treatment and when he returns, the club says he is being transferred. | | |
| Bertie is married to Jolinda. Jolinda has given birth to twins and one of the babies is very sick. Bertie wants to take his parental leave entitlement but his boss says that if he takes time off, he will lose his job. Berite takes time off and his boss dismisses him. | | |
| Ariadne is a waitress. She drops plates on a regular basis and several customers have complained that she added up their bills incorrectly. Ariadne's boss has shown her how to carry plates safely but Ariadne still carries them the old way and drops them. Her boss dismisses her. | | |
| Leon has a job as a lorry driver. He has been caught drink driving and has lost his licence. He says he will work as a labourer loading the lorries but his employer dismisses him. | | |

- Redundancy: this is covered in more detail earlier in the chapter.
- Retirement: this is covered earlier in the chapter.
- Illegality: this means that the employee cannot do his job without breaking the law and an employer should consider whether it's possible to find the employee another job.
- Another substantial reason: this can be very wide ranging! Reasons which have been held to justify a dismissal within this final permitted reason include refusing to accept the employer's reorganisation affecting working hours and dismissing an employee because of a personality clash between employees.

However, some reasons for dismissal are automatically unfair, including:

- use, or attempted use, of a statutory employment right (for example, taking parental leave)
- pregnancy
- membership/non-membership of a trade union.

## 15.4.2 Procedure

If there is to be a dismissal certain steps need to be followed:

- The employee must show that they have been dismissed.
- The employer must show a valid reason for dismissal.
- The employer must show that they acted reasonably.
- The employer must investigate the situation.
- The employer must normally have followed the statutory minimum dismissal procedure.

To avoid an automatically unfair dismissal the employer must:

- Send the employee a written statement explaining why there is a need to dismiss
- Hold a meeting with the employee to discuss the matter
- Hold an appeal meeting with the employee if asked to do so
- Make a final decision and inform the employee of this and the notice period in writing

 **EXAMPLE**

Ms Swanson was a housing officer who alleged that she had been automatically unfairly dismissed because Yorkshire Housing delayed in notifying her of the reason to dismiss her for gross misconduct.

A meeting had been held between Ms Swanson and Yorkshire Housing but notification of the outcome was only given to Ms Swanson several months later. The question was whether Ms Swanson was unfairly dismissed if the standard procedure had not been completed in a timely fashion. The Employment Appeal Tribunal held that unreasonable delay meant Ms Swanson was unfairly dismissed.

*Adapted from Yorkshire Housing v Swanson UKEAT 0057/07*

After the normal procedures have been used, if an employee still feels that they have been unfairly dismissed, they can go to an Employment Tribunal. This should happen within three months of being dismissed and normally the employee must have worked for the employer for a year. The tribunal looks at a range of factors to decide if what the employer has done is acceptable because it is reasonable. These include:

- Did the employer have a genuine belief in the employee's guilt?
- Was it a reasonable belief based on a thorough investigation?
- Was the employee given all the information gathered in the investigation?
- Did the employee have a chance to put his case and have someone with him?
- Was there a disciplinary hearing, chaired by someone who was impartial?
- Was the employee warned that there would be a disciplinary hearing and given time to prepare?
- Was the offence gross misconduct, as set out in company policy, and did the employee know the penalty for gross misconduct?
- Were there mitigating facts that should have been taken into account?
- Were alternatives to dismissal considered?
- Was the employee informed of his right to appeal and given an opportunity to appeal against the decision to dismiss?

If there is a tribunal hearing and it finds in the employee's favour, he is entitled to have his job back or receive compensation. Although the employee does not have to return to his job the amount payable in compensation can be reduced if they refuse. A tribunal may reduce compensation if it decides that the employee's conduct played a part in his dismissal, or if he did not comply with the statutory minimum disciplinary procedures.

### EXAMPLE

Funeral director Scott Ralston lost his job for 'speeding' at 6 mph. He had been working for Cooperative Funeral Care for 16 years prior to his dismissal.

His bosses claimed that, in October last year, he left the company's garage in a hearse loaded with four sets of remains, used the vehicle's horn, let the tyres squeal and drove too fast. This, they said, showed a lack of respect for the dead.

An employment tribunal found that it was not unusual for employees to drive faster than 5 mph. In addition, the garage had signs at the exits and entrances warning drivers to use their horns. They upheld Mr Ralston's claim for unfair dismissal and awarded him compensation of £30,000.

*Adapted from news feed on Russell Jones & Walker website, http://www.rjw.co.uk/news-events/directnews/employee-secures-a330k-payout-in-unfair-dismissal-case_786*

Compensation is meant to put the employee back to their financial position if they had not been sacked. This means that it does not pay out for hurt feelings. There is a basic award and the calculation of this amount is done in much the same way as it is for redundancy. There is also a compensatory award which covers loss of earnings up to a maximum level of £66,200 (on or after 1st February 2009).

### EXAMPLE

Ms Hope had been employed for 11 years as a payroll accounts supervisor. In 2006 her employer decided that only one part-time administrator was required. Another employee also worked part-time in that role. Ms Hope was put in a selection pool with another full-time employee and the part-time employee. During consultation Ms Hope made it clear that she did not want to accept the part-time role. The post was offered to the part-time employee who accepted it; no alternative position was made available to Ms

Hope; and there was no further consultation as Ms Hope was then absent for sickness. As Ms Hope had confirmed that she did not want the part-time role, the management decided to dismiss her. She was not required to work her notice but received her entitlement of 10 weeks' pay in lieu of notice together with a redundancy payment. She was not advised of any right to appeal.

Ms Hope commenced proceedings for unfair dismissal. The tribunal decided that the reason for the dismissal had been redundancy and her dismissal for that reason had been both procedurally and substantially fair. However, the Tribunal took the view that in not offering an appeal against the decision to dismiss the company breached statutory dismissal and discipline. This made the dismissal automatically unfair but Ms Hope was not awarded any compensation.

*Adapted from Hope v Jordan Engineering Limited (2008)*

### EXAMPLE

Three truck drivers were employed to transport parts to and from a Land Rover factory. Their original employer was taken over by another company and when the three men turned up for work they were told by the new company that there was no job for them to do.

The three drivers said their original employer had promised them a transfer to the new company but their original employer said they had been offered alternative jobs and had not accepted them.

An employment tribunal found that all three drivers had been unfairly dismissed and that the new company, rather then the original employer, was responsible for the job losses. Between them they were awarded £68,000 in compensation.

*http://www.personneltoday.com/articles/2008/02/08/44351/truck-drivers-awarded-68000-in-unfair-dismissal-case.html*

Some employees can never claim unfair dismissal. They are:

- police officers
- members of the Armed Forces
- share fishermen
- people who work outside Great Britain
- registered dock workers.

### ACTIVITY

### Activity 6

Explain what an employer could do in each of the following situations to make sure they do not become liable for an unfair dismissal claim:

Carlos is a Spanish teacher in a school. The Headmaster asks Carlos to teach some extra lessons. Carlos says he is busy. The Headmaster asks again and Carlos shouts, 'Not bloody likely; I hate kids!' The Headmaster writes to Carlos, telling him his is dismissed but offering him a meeting at school to discuss the matter. This is ...................................... dismissal.

Pablo has a job delivering furniture. He is pulled over by the police when he is driving his car erratically. Pablo is over the drink-drive limit and he loses his licence. Pablo tells his boss what has happened and his boss tells him he no longer has a job. This is ...................................... dismissal.

Vanessa works in a bank as a secretary. She finds out that she is pregnant and tells her boss. Next day Vanessa receives a letter telling her she has lost her job. This is ...................................... dismissal.

Derek is a policeman and he is very slow in completing forms after he has arrested criminals. His boss has met with him and told him he needs to do better but Derek continues to be very slow and he receives a letter from the Chief Constable telling him he has no future in the police force. This is ...................................... dismissal.

Delia is a cook at Firstclass United Football club. She has worked for her employer for 10 years. She is elected to be the union representative and then receives a letter saying she has lost her job. This is ...................................... dismissal.

## 15.4.3 Comment

This chapter has shown some of the ways in which the employment relationship can be ended. If an employer is to be able to run a business successfully, it is important that they can dismiss an employee if necessary. Here are some reasons why:

- An employee might have lied about his qualifications and so he did not get the job fairly.
- Even with training and support the employee might be incapable of doing the job he was appointed to do.
- An employee might become ill and if this continues for a long period it is not fair to expect the employer to pay the sick employee and another worker to do the job the employee can no longer do.
- An employee might be a danger to himself or to other workers because he will not comply with the safety procedures he is told to follow.
- The employee may be found to be dishonest.
- The employee may be violent towards other workers.
- The employee may have been warned about rudeness and continue to be rude.
- The employee may have been disciplined many times for repeated misconduct.
- The employer's business may be in financial difficulties and cuts may be needed to save the business.
- The employer may have gone out of business.
- The business may be restructured and so some of the original employees are no longer required.
- The employee has completed their fixed-term contract and there is no reason to renew it.
- Changes in the law may mean that an employer is no longer allowed to employ certain staff.

However, it is also essential that an employee is protected because:

- The employee and their family may well be dependent on that salary or wage.

- The ending of employment needs to be clear and structured to give an employee time to plan.
- No employee should be at an unfair disadvantage to any other employee.
- Employees need to be protected against unscrupulous employers.
- Employees deserve the chance to be good at their job.
- Employees need to have the opportunity for training and support to prove they can do their job.

 **KEY FACTS**

- There is a great deal of factual information in this area of law and you certainly need to know the key types of dismissal.

- It is a good idea to be able to define the different types of dismissal and to have an understanding of the differences between them.

- You need to know the kinds of issue which give rise to each of the different types of dismissal.

- It is certainly worth knowing what factors are counted as potentially fair and unfair dismissal.

 **EXAM QUESTION**

**Question 4**

a) There are different types of dismissal:
   - summary dismissal
   - wrongful dismissal
   - unfair dismissal
   - constructive dismissal.

   (i) Outline the ways in which constructive dismissal is different from the other types of dismissal.

   ..................................................................
   ..................................................................
   ..................................................................
   ..................................................................
   ..................................................................
   ..................................................................
   ..................................................................
   ..................................................................
   ..................................................................

   [3 marks]

   (ii) Chris has been dismissed half-way through his working day, escorted from the premises and told never to return (summary dismissal). His employer told Chris that this was because Chris refused to obey an instruction from his manager to stop reading the newspaper when he should be working, and when the manager repeated the instruction, Chris punched the manager in the face.

   Explain three reasons why summary dismissal may have been appropriate.

   Reason 1

   ..................................................................

   Reason 2

   ..................................................................

   Reason 3

   ..................................................................

   [3 marks]

b) (i) In any claim for unfair dismissal some types of dismissal are automatically unfair.

   In the following chart identify the THREE situations that are automatically unfair dismissals. Show your answer with a tick next to the appropriate situations.

|  | Tick |
|---|---|
| A genuine redundancy |  |
| Dismissal of a pregnant employee purely because she is pregnant |  |
| Dismissal of a person who has stolen from his employer |  |
| Dismissal of a person who is too ill ever to return to work |  |
| Dismissal of a person working on a building site who insisted on being given a hard hat |  |
| Dismissal of an employee because he joined a trade union |  |

Table 15.2

[3 marks]

(ii) Discuss some reasons why it is important for employers to have the right to dismiss employees, giving examples of situations in which dismissal would be necessary.

[9 marks]

.......................................................................
.......................................................................
.......................................................................
.......................................................................
.......................................................................
.......................................................................
.......................................................................
.......................................................................
.......................................................................
.......................................................................
.......................................................................

# UNIT 4

# CONSUMER RIGHTS AND RESPONSIBILITIES

# CHAPTER 16

# THE BASIC CHARACTER OF CONTRACTS AND BASIC PRINCIPLES OF NEGLIGENCE

## Aims and objectives

After reading this chapter you should be able to:

- understand the essential requirements for making basic contracts
- understand that the terms of contracts are what the parties are bound by law to do
- understand that false statements made in advance of a contract to induce the other party to contract can make the contract invalid
- understand the essential elements of a claim in negligence
- apply knowledge of contract or negligence to factual situations
- respond to sources or arguments concerning contracts and negligence.

## 16.1 Basic rules of formation of contracts

### 16.1.1 What a contract is

Each of us makes contracts every day, often without even realising that we are doing so. The bus ride to school or college in the morning involves a contract. Buying a ticket involves forming a contract with the bus company. Buying a newspaper or some sweets from the shop before going to school or college or work involves a contract with the shop, even though there is only an exchange of goods and no written agreement. Even our favourite pastimes involve contracts, whether it is going to a professional football match, or to the cinema or even just getting on a bus to go to a friend's house. Even when we are sending text messages to each other on our mobile phones we are still in a contractual relationship with the network provider.

The significance of all these things involving contracts is that they mean that we have rights under those contracts and those rights can be enforced in a court of law. If those rights are interfered with, then we might also be able to gain compensation.

A contract is completed when both parties to a contract carry out what they have each agreed to do under the contract. It is a breach of contract when one of the parties then fails to do what he was supposed to or does not do it in the way that he should have.

The sales of goods contracts in section 17.2 are an example. A person may breach his contract by failing to deliver the goods that he has agreed to. Alternatively a shopkeeper may be selling the goods to the customer, as he is supposed to, but if he sells goods that are inferior, then this may still be a breach of contract.

Because of the enforceable nature of contractual agreements, we cannot identify a breach of contract where we may feel that we have not received what we paid for or 'bargained' for, without first showing that the agreement was indeed a contract as opposed to some kind of arrangement which is not enforceable.

## 16.1.2 Forming a contractual agreement

Therefore, our first objective in a contract case may be to prove that there is actually a contract in existence. We can tell if it is a contract because to be so it must have been formed according to certain standard rules.

There are generally three main ones:

• Agreement: the parties must have reached an agreement (this is one where one person makes a legitimate offer and the other person accepts the offer unconditionally).
• Consideration: they must give something known as consideration (this is in effect the price that each is prepared to pay for what is being given by the other side).
• Legal intent: they must intend that the agreement they reach will be enforceable in a court of law (obviously many arrangements we make are not contractual, so we would not be allowed to enforce them).

A contractual agreement exists when a valid offer is followed by an unconditional acceptance. This seems straightforward enough, and where one person offers to sell something to another party who accepts the price and agrees to buy, then there is no difficulty at all. In business contracts often negotiations can be much more complex than this and on the other hand agreements can be identified that appear to have no formal negotiating steps: purchasing goods from a vending machine being a classic example of that.

Obviously there are also some basic rules in relation to each of the three aspects of formation. It is not necessary to look at them all in detail but some are worth knowing.

### Agreement

Clearly, for an agreement an offer has to be communicated and so does acceptance. If the one party does not know of the existence of the offer, how can he accept it? Similarly, if the person supposedly accepting does not say so to the person making the offer then it would be unfair to allow him to enforce it.

On this basis the person making the offer does not have to keep the offer open indefinitely. He is able to withdraw his offer any time before the other person accepts it. Once it is accepted, then the contract is made.

Clearly, these rules are important for knowing when the contract is made and for knowing when it has been breached.

✔ **EXAMPLE**

Shops have not always been self-service in the way that they are now, with customers selecting the shopping they want from shelves out in the shop and then taking it to a checkout to pay. Traditionally, goods were kept behind a counter

 **ACTIVITY**

## Activity 1

Read the statements 1 to 3 in the left-hand column below and the rules of formation of contract in the right-hand column. Then complete the activity below.

| | | | | |
|---|---|---|---|---|
| 1 | Something that is given by a contracting party in return for what he is receiving from the other party to the contract | | AGREEMENT | A |
| 2 | An intention by both parties that what they have agreed on, they should be able to enforce in a court if necessary | | CONSIDERATION | B |
| 3 | An offer which one party is prepared to be legally bound by which is then unconditionally accepted by the other party | | LEGAL INTENT | C |

Table 16.1

In the chart below insert the correct letter A–C next to the number 1–3 for the rule for formation of a contract which accurately represents the statement in the left-hand column above.

| | |
|---|---|
| 1 | |
| 2 | |
| 3 | |

Table 16.2

and passed to the customers by assistants. Boots the Chemists was one of the earliest examples of self-service. It altered one of their shops to self-service. Because of a provision in the Pharmacy and Poisons Act 1933 a registered pharmacist had to be present at the sale of certain drugs and poisons. It was important to know where the contract was formed. If it was formed when the customer selected the goods, then Boots would be breaking the law. The court held that the contract was formed when the goods were actually taken to the cash desk where a pharmacist was present, not when taken from the shelf.

*From the case of Pharmaceutical Society of GB v Boots Cash Chemists Ltd (1953)*

This was very important as it helped to preserve freedom of contract. In general, we have a choice to whom we sell. Again this could be important, for instance when a person under the age of 18 picks an alcoholic drink from a shelf in an off-licence. If the contract was formed at that point, then the shopkeeper would either be in breach of contract for refusing to sell the drink or breaking the law by doing so to an under-age person.

## Consideration

Almost anything can be consideration. You do not have to pay the value of the goods; so the law does not interfere with bargains freely made. If you get goods at a really good price, that is fair enough. The law simply wants to know that there has been some consideration.

In general the law only recognises something as consideration if it is real, tangible and has some economic value.

## Legal intent

Generally the law operates two presumptions, both of which could be rebutted if there was evidence:

- The law presumes that in the case of domestic agreements the parties have no intention for the agreement to be enforceable in a court of law. (This is sensible since otherwise it would mean that the courts could be overwhelmed with silly domestic disputes. Therefore, if I promise my children pocket money and do not pay it, they would not be able to sue me for the amount.)
- The law presumes that in any business agreement there is an intention that the agreement will be legally enforceable. (Again this is very useful because it stops businesses from trying to avoid their obligations.)

## 16.2 Basic character of terms

The terms of a contract can be what the parties have expressly agreed upon, but they can also be

| Type of statement | Contractual significance | Reasoning |
| --- | --- | --- |
| Terms | You can rely on these and can sue for a breach of contract | because they are actually incorporated into the contract. |
| Mere representations | You cannot rely on these | because they are not part of the contract. They are not important enough. |
| Misrepresentations | You may be able to get out of the contract or sue for compensation | because if false they may have wrongly induced you to contract when you would not have done if you had known the truth. |
| Opinions | You cannot rely on these | because the other party's opinion is no more valid than our own. |
| Expert opinions | You can rely on these because they will often be terms | because we do rely, and should be entitled to rely, on the opinion of experts. |
| Trade puffs | You cannot rely on these | because they are usually advertising boasts that we should not take seriously. |

Table 16.3 The legal consequences of different representations made when contracting

what the law has said should be included in the contract and therefore is implied into the contract.

## 16.2.1 Express and implied terms

Therefore, there are two types of terms, or to put it another way there are two ways in which something can become a term of a contract:

* Express terms: those terms that are agreed by the parties when the contract is made (this does not always mean that a consumer had any control over the terms in the contract because these are usually dictated by the seller anyway)
* Implied terms: these are not in the contract itself but they are things that are inserted into all contracts by law, most usually following an Act of Parliament (a classic example of these are the implied terms in the Sale of Goods Act 1979; see section 17.2).

## 16.2.2 The difference between terms and mere representations

Any statement made by one of the parties at the time when they contract might be significant to the contract, but not all will. Statements made during negotiation of a contract are generally called representations. The effect of representations is usually that the information contained in the statement is true. A further aspect of this is that it should also represent the intention of the party making it.

The law rightly has to distinguish between different representations according to the significance they have for the contract and its enforcement. Where a contract is in writing, then the terms are easily identified in the contract itself. Otherwise the following distinctions can be drawn:

* A statement made by a contracting party which may be intended to induce the other party to enter the contract, but was not intended to form part of the contract is a representation. If it is false then in certain circumstances the party affected by it might have some remedy. However, it is not a term because it is not incorporated into the contract.
* A statement made by a contracting party by which he intends to be bound will be incorporated and form part of the contract and is therefore a term. It will have legal consequences, although these may differ according to what type of term it is.

## 16.2.3 The importance of different types of term

Just as some representations are more important than others and so become terms, some terms are also more important than others. Some terms are vital to the contract and without them the contract could not be completed. On the other hand some terms are of lesser importance. They may, for instance, be purely descriptive and even if they are breached, this will not mean that the contract cannot be carried out.

The consequence is that, depending on the type of term, a person who is the victim of a breach of contract may have different remedies available to him. The law refers to two different types of term in this way:

* conditions
* warranties.

### Conditions

A condition is a term of a contract which is so important to the contract that failing to carry out a condition would make the contract meaningless and destroy the whole purpose of the contract.

As a result the law refers to a condition 'going to the root of a contract'. Because of the importance of these terms as well as being able to sue for compensation in the event of a breach

**ACTIVITY**

## Activity 2

Write TRUE next to the THREE statements below which are accurate descriptions of some basic rules on contract and FALSE next to the THREE that are inaccurate.

| i) | All contracts have to be in writing and signed to be enforceable. | |
|---|---|---|
| ii) | Consideration is the price a party pays for what he is getting in return from the other party. | |
| iii) | The law will usually not interfere in agreements made between family members because they are presumed not to wish those agreements to be enforceable. | |
| iv) | The terms of a contract are all what the parties to the contract have agreed to. | |
| v) | In general whether a term of a contract is described as a condition or as a warranty does not matter because if a term is breached the victim of the breach always has the same remedy. | |
| vi) | Terms are often implied into contracts by an Act of Parliament and this is sometimes so as to protect consumers. | |

Table 16.4

of contract, the victim of the breach can also avoid carrying out his own obligations, or indeed he could do both. This can be really good for the consumer as it may mean that he can contract with an alternative party and treat himself as relieved of his obligations under the contract, without fear of the defendant alleging a breach of contract by him.

You will see in section 17.2 that the Sale of Goods Act implied terms are conditions. This is very useful to a consumer who does not then have to accept an exchange of goods that are not satisfactory or as they were described, but instead can have his money back and buy alternative goods elsewhere.

## Warranties

Warranties are generally all terms that are not conditions and that do not go to the root of the contract. They are often seen as minor terms of the contract or those where in general the contract could continue despite them being breached. As a result the remedy for a breach of warranty is only to sue for compensation for the effect of the breach but not to back out of the contract.

Therefore, you can see that the way in which the terms are classified is critical in determining the outcome of the contract and the remedies available in the case of a breach of the terms.

## 16.3 False and misleading statements

Sometimes something is said to the consumer to try to make him enter the contract. A misrepresentation occurs as we have already said when a representation made at or before the time of the contract is also falsely stated. A misrepresentation can therefore be defined as a statement of material fact, made by one party to a contract to the other party to the contract, during the negotiations leading up to the formation of the contract, which was intended to operate and did operate as an inducement to the other party to enter the contract, but which was not intended to be a binding obligation under the contract, and which was untrue or incorrectly stated.

If a person has entered a contract because of a misrepresentation by the other party then it may be possible either to back out of the contract in some circumstances or to get compensation.

## 16.4 Basic principles of negligence

The law of negligence covers many different situations from badly manufactured products to car crashes to operations performed carelessly by surgeons. It is part of the law of torts – which simply means wrongs. It aims to protect people against wrongdoing and to compensate them for the wrongs suffered that are the fault of the defendant.

For consumer rights this means that people are protected against products that cause them harm.

 **EXAMPLE**

A lady claimed to suffer shock and gastroenteritis after drinking ginger beer from an opaque bottle out of which a decomposing snail had fallen when the dregs were poured. A friend had bought her the drink and so she could not sue in contract law because she was not a party to the contract. She claimed £500 from the manufacturer for his negligence and was successful. The manufacturer should have realised in advance that if he allowed his ginger beer to become contaminated then it would most likely cause some illness or injury to someone who drank it.

*From the case of Donoghue v Stevenson (1932)*

From this we can see that a manufacturer owes a duty of care towards consumers or users of his products not to cause them harm.

In order to claim successfully for negligence a person needs to prove three things:

- that he is owed a duty of care by the defendant
- that the defendant breached this duty
- that the person claiming negligence suffered damage which was caused by the defendant's breach and which is a foreseeable consequence of the breach.

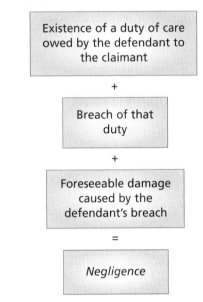

**Figure 16.1** The key elements for a successful claim in negligence

### 16.4.1 Duty of care

This means that the defendant has to behave in a way that will not cause foreseeable harm to the claimant.

There is no general duty of care owed. There are many situations like the one above where duties have been identified – manufacturers owe a duty not to harm consumers of their products because of defects in the products that could have been reasonably avoided. In the same way a motorist owes a duty to drive carefully and be aware that his careless acts might injure other road users or damage their vehicles. Similarly, a doctor has to behave reasonably in his treatment of a patient because again careless treatment could result in injury to the patient.

However, there will be no duty owed where damage is unforeseeable, where the defendant could not have been aware of the claimant, and where it would generally be unfair to make the defendant liable to compensate the claimant.

 **EXAMPLE**

The mother of the 13th victim of the Yorkshire Ripper, Peter Sutcliffe, argued that her daughter would not have been murdered but for the negligence of the police. They had interviewed him several times and spotted his car in the locality of the murders on several occasions. He also looked very much like a 'photofit' picture made from descriptions of women who had been attacked and harmed but not killed by Sutcliffe. However, the police would be unable to tell in advance who was going to be a victim and it would be unfair to make the police responsible for the crimes of a mass murderer. As it would be almost impossible for the police to give us all absolute protection, there was no negligence.

*From the case of Hill v Chief Constable of West Yorkshire (1988)*

## 16.4.2 Breach of the duty of care

Once a claimant has proved that he is owed a duty of care in the circumstances, then he must next prove that the defendant breached that duty. This simply means that the defendant fell below the standard of care that was appropriate in the circumstances.

In the first example above, this means that the manufacturer of the ginger beer had not taken sufficient steps to ensure that it was free from defects.

Breach of duty is measured objectively by something we call the 'reasonable man test'. In other words a reasonable manufacturer would have processes to ensure that decomposing snails

or any foreign bodies do not get into their foodstuffs. The fact that the snail was in the drink indicates that the manufacturer in the example had not taken the care that a reasonable manufacturer would. What if the ginger beer had contained something much more poisonous than the snail and the lady had died?

Many different factors can be looked at to decide whether the defendant has fallen below the appropriate standard and breached his duty of care:

- whether some harm is foreseeable – we cannot be expected to guard against risks of which we would be completely unaware
- the magnitude of the risk – so the degree of care expected depends on the likelihood of the risk
- the practicability of precautions – the reasonable man only has to do what is reasonable to avoid harm. We do not expect someone to go to extraordinary lengths
- social utility of the activity – if the defendant's act is to avoid greater harm, then there is no liability. An example would be when a motorist hits a street lamp to avoid a pedestrian who has walked out in front of him.

There are other factors also.

## 16.4.3 Foreseeable damage caused by the defendant

The defendant must have *caused* the damage suffered by the claimant or (s)he is not liable. *Causation* is measured by the '*but for test*'. Therefore, if but for the defendant's negligent act or omission the claimant would not have suffered loss or damage, then the defendant is liable. However, if the defendant would have suffered damage or loss despite the defendant's negligence, then the defendant has not caused the damage and the defendant is not liable.

**EXAMPLE**

Three nightwatchmen from a college went to the casualty ward of the hospital at around 5.00 am on the morning of New Year's Day complaining of vomiting and stomach pains after drinking tea. The doctor on duty refused to attend to them and told them to call on their own doctors. One of the men died a few hours later. It was discovered later that this was because of arsenic poisoning. The hospital was not liable for the failure to treat the man. Even though this was a clear breach of its duty, it was shown that the man would not have recovered even with treatment.

*From the case of Barnett v Chelsea & Kensington Hospital Management Committee (1969)*

The damage must also be '*reasonably foreseeable*'.

The precise extent of damage need not be foreseen as long as the defendant could have foreseen damage of the general type suffered by the claimant.

 **EXAMPLE**

A council failed to move an abandoned boat from its land for two years. It was well known that children played in the boat and it was a clear danger. A boy of 14 was hurt when he and a friend tried to repair the boat. It was argued that it was rare for boys of this age to act in this way, so that the circumstances in which the boy was injured and the type of injury was not foreseeable. However, the boat was clearly dangerous and it was quite foreseeable that children coming into contact with the boat might suffer some kind of harm, so the Council was liable.

*From the case of Jolley v London Borough of Sutton (2000)*

 **ACTIVITY**

## Activity 3

Fill in the gaps in the statements below from the list that follows:

1. In negligence first of all you must prove that you are owed a ........................................ of care by the defendant.

2. To prove negligence you must also show that the defendant fell below the ........................................ appropriate in the circumstances.

3. You must also have suffered ............................. damage caused by the defendant's breach.

Choose from the following list:

debt

duty

standard

reasonable

foreseeable

serious.

**ACTIVITY**

## Activity 4

Negligence can only be claimed when the defendant owes a duty of care to the claimant; the defendant has breached that duty; and the breach of the duty has caused the claimant foreseeable damage.

Write TRUE next to the THREE statements below which are accurate descriptions of these rules on claiming in negligence and FALSE next to the THREE that are inaccurate.

| i) | A defendant owes a duty of care to someone he could foresee would be harmed by his negligent acts. | |
|---|---|---|
| ii) | A defendant only owes a duty of care to a person whom he knows. | |
| iii) | As long as a defendant has breached his duty of care he will always be liable for the damage caused to the claimant. | |
| iv) | Breach of duty usually means falling below the standard of 'a reasonable man' in the same circumstances. | |
| v) | A claimant does not have to suffer any damage to claim for negligence. | |
| vi) | A claimant can only recover compensation for foreseeable damage. | |

Table 16.5

 **KEY FACTS**

- A contract does not have to be in writing to be enforceable.
- A contract does need to have been properly formed to be enforceable – there must be:
    - an agreement between the two parties where one party has unconditionally accepted a valid offer made by the other party
    - both parties have given some consideration – this is the promise made by one party in return for the promise made by the other party
    - both parties must have intended that the agreement should be enforceable.
- Terms in a contract can come about in two main ways
    - they can be EXPRESS (what the parties have agreed to)
    - they can be IMPLIED (usually by Parliament in Acts).
- Terms are classed according to their importance into two types:
    - CONDITIONS – these go to the root of the contract so if they are breached the victim of the breach can avoid his own obligations under the contract as well as, or instead of, getting compensation
    - WARRANTIES – these are only minor terms; the contract can still be carried out so the victim of the breach can only get compensation.
- Other things may or may not have contractual consequences:
    - mere representations will have none
    - misrepresentations may lead to a remedy because they are false and the victim might not have entered the contract if he had known the truth.

# CHAPTER 17

# BUYING GOODS AND BUYING SERVICES

## Aims and objectives

After reading this chapter you should be able to:

- understand the essential elements of a consumer contract
- understand the terms implied into a contract when purchasing goods under the Sale of Goods Act 1979
- understand the terms implied into a contract when purchasing services under the Supply of Goods and Services Act 1979
- apply knowledge of these implied terms to factual situations
- respond to sources or arguments concerning the implied terms.

## 17.1 The nature of consumer contracts

Consumers have many legal protections when they buy goods or services. Therefore, it is important to remember what a consumer sale is because different rights might apply in a contract where a party is not buying as a consumer.

Buying as a 'consumer' has been defined by statute. A consumer purchase is one where:

- the person buying the goods or service is doing so as a consumer (This is because consumers have unequal bargaining strength with the person from whom they buy. If a business buys from another business, then it has equal bargaining strength and can negotiate terms with the seller. Therefore, the law does not give the same protection as it does to a consumer.)
- the person selling the goods or service is doing so in the course of a business (so a consumer will have fewer protections and should take greater care when buying in a private sale.)
- the goods or service are of a type that are commonly sold in a consumer contract. (If the consumer was buying types of goods or, for instance, enormous quantities of goods that would only normally be bought by a business, then they may have less protection.)

Whether a consumer buys goods or services, they have rights and protections given to them by law which help to stop them being taken advantage of by unscrupulous businesses.

Goods obviously could include everything from something as cheap as a packet of chewing gum to something very expensive like a car. Either would involve a contract and would be subject to the same type of protection. Many of these protections are found in the Sale of Goods Act 1979.

Services again could range from something quite inexpensive such as a haircut to something very expensive such as having an extension built onto a house. Again, there would still be a contract and the consumer would enjoy similar protections. Many of the protections are found in the Supply of Goods and Services Act 1982.

Sometimes a service will also include a sale of goods. For instance where a hairdresser dyes a

## ACTIVITY

### Activity 1

In the chart below, in the right-hand column write either GOODS (if you think it is a sale of goods) or SERVICE (if you think it is supplying a service) next to the scenario in the left-hand column.

| | | |
|---|---|---|
| i) | Amy buys some chewing gum from the corner shop on her way to school. | |
| ii) | Baljinder had his hair cut at the barbers on the way home from college. | |
| iii) | Chelsea had her hair styled and shampooed at the hairdressers. | |
| iv) | Darcus had a new fence erected in his garden. | |
| v) | Euan bought a new car from a car dealer. Before he took the car the garage serviced it and washed it . | |
| vi) | Folia bought some flowers for her mum on the way back from school. | |

Table 17.1

customer's hair or gives the customer a perm, then the customer has to pay for the dye and the perm solution as well as for the service being carried out. For this reason similar protections to those in the Sale of Goods Act are contained in the Supply of Goods and Services Act.

The way in which the law protects consumers in these Acts is by inserting implied terms into consumer contracts. These terms apply, and the seller is bound by them, even though they may not appear in the contract. This is the case even if the seller of the goods or the provider of the service would prefer them not to be included. So they are terms that the law insists should be in contracts in order to protect consumers from unscrupulous trading practices.

## 17.2 Sale of Goods implied terms

### 17.2.1 The Sale of Goods Act 1979 implied terms

When a consumer buys goods from somebody who is selling them in the course of a business, then this is a consumer contract and the Sale of Goods Act terms apply.

The Act states that the goods a consumer buys must satisfy three requirements:

- The goods must correspond with any description given them by the seller (s 13 Sale of Goods Act 1979). (If a second-hand car salesman says to a potential purchaser that a car is mechanically perfect and it is not, then this would be a breach of the implied term. The term applies to packaging and advertising also.)
- The goods must be of satisfactory quality (s 14(2) Sale of Goods Act 1979). (The goods must be fit for all the purposes that the type of goods would normally be used for. This obviously means that the goods are free from defects and are durable. A pair of trainers that fell apart the first time they were worn would not be of satisfactory quality.)
- The goods must be fit for the purpose for which they were bought (s 14(3) Sale of Goods Act 1979). (This means that if the buyer states a particular purpose for which he wants the goods, then he is entitled to rely on the skill and judgement of the seller when buying the

goods that the goods are fit for the purpose stated. If the buyer says to the seller that he wants boots for climbing mountains with then they must be fit for that purpose. If the boots sold were only normal walking boots and could not be used for climbing mountains, then the seller has breached the contract.)

These implied terms are also conditions. What this means for the consumer is that if the seller breaches the term, then the buyer is entitled to compensation for any damage or loss associated with the goods, but also can return the goods and have his money back. This is a very good potential remedy for the consumer.

## 17.2.2 The requirement that the goods fit any description given to them by the seller

The goods must be as they were described by the seller and if they are not, then there is a breach of contract and the buyer is entitled to a remedy, which would include getting his money back. The term applies to inter-business purchases as well as to consumer purchases.

The rule applies to precise descriptions given to the goods. If the seller states that the goods are of a particular size or quantity or include specific ingredients, then these descriptions must be accurate or the consumer can reject the goods.

 **EXAMPLE**

One party bought wooden staves which had been described as half-an-inch thick. When they were delivered they were a 16th-of-an-inch narrower and so they were not exactly as they were described in the contract. The buyer rejected the goods and when the seller sued, the court accepted that the buyer was entitled to reject the staves even though the buyer could still have used them for the purpose for which he had wanted them. Nevertheless, as the judge said,

'. . . a ton does not mean about a ton, or a yard about a yard. If a seller wants a margin he must, and in my experience does, stipulate for it . . .'

*From the case of Arcos Ltd v E A Ronaasen & Son (1933)*

The rule can also even apply to things like the packaging that the goods come in.

 **EXAMPLE**

Here the buyer bought a consignment of tinned fruit which was described as being in cartons of 30 tins. On delivery, even though the correct number of tins was delivered, half of the cartons contained 24 tins rather than 30. The court, taking a broad view, decided that the goods were not as they were described in the contract and the buyer was able to reject the goods.

*From the case of Re Moore & Co and Landauer & Co's Arbitration (1921)*

Sometimes, even though no actual description has been given by the seller, judges say that certain things describe themselves and a breach of contract occurs when the goods are not as they should be.

 **EXAMPLE**

A man bought woollen underpants which contained traces of chemicals which then caused him to develop a very painful skin disease. Underpants should not cause such a reaction and so there was a breach of the implied term.

*From the case of Grant v Australian Knitting Mills Ltd (1936)*

## 17.2.3 The requirement that the goods are of satisfactory quality

This implied term only applies in consumer contracts. The original provision in s 14(2) of the Sale of Goods Act has since been amended to be fairer to consumers and to give them more effective rights.

The meaning of satisfactory quality is explained in s 14(2)(A):

> ❝ goods are of satisfactory quality if they meet the standard that a reasonable person would regard as satisfactory, taking account of any description of the goods, the price (if relevant) and all other relevant circumstances. ❞

Obviously price could be relevant if for example the price had been reduced from the usual price to reflect some defect or inferior quality in the goods.

Section 14(2)(b) also identifies the factors that can be taken into account in deciding whether or not the goods are in fact of satisfactory quality. The definition includes:

a) fitness for all purposes for which goods of the kind in question are commonly supplied
b) appearance and finish
c) freedom from minor defects
d) safety and durability.

It is easy from this to think of examples of defects in goods which relate to each of these four types that will mean that the goods are not of satisfactory quality:

- 'Walking boots' that cannot be used in rough terrain are an example of a failure to match (a).
- Scratches on the bodywork of a brand new car are an example of a failure to match (b).
- Clothes where the stitching in the seams comes undone are an example of a failure to match (c).
- Electrical goods that are not properly earthed are an example of a failure to match (d).

Obviously defects in the goods may make them unsatisfactory. Sometimes even slight blemishes in the goods might also mean that the goods are not satisfactory. This will particularly be the case where the goods have been described as luxury goods or deluxe model or something similar and where a high price has been paid for them.

 **EXAMPLE**

The consumer bought a brand new Range Rover for £16,000. When it was delivered the car misfired, had an oil leak, and there were also scratches on the paintwork. It was not of satisfactory quality. The car had defects and the appearance and finish was unacceptable for such high-value goods.

*From the case of Rogers v Parish (Scarborough) Ltd (1987)*

Therefore, the higher the price of the goods then the greater the expectation of quality and it is more likely that defects in the goods mean that they do not match up to the standards that should be expected of them and they may not be of satisfactory quality.

 **EXAMPLE**

The consumer bought a second-hand sports car, a Fiat X-19, an enthusiast's car. He then discovered that the car had been submerged in water for some time before he bought it and as a result the manufacturer's anti-corrosion guarantee was no longer valid. The car was clearly not satisfactory as the buyer could expect that it would rust.

*From the case of Shine v General Guarantee Corporation (1988)*

Wherever the safety of the goods is in question, the goods are unlikely to be of satisfactory quality.

 **EXAMPLE**

A consumer bought a new car. When he had only had the car for three weeks and had only done 140 miles the engine seized while he was driving on the motorway. The car dealer offered to repair the car free of charge but the consumer was able to return the car and have his money back because the defect was potentially dangerous.

*From the case of Bernstein v Pamsons Motors (Golders Green) Ltd (1987)*

There are, however, two circumstances where the buyer may lose his right to claim that the goods are not of satisfactory quality:

a)   where the seller specifically tells the buyer of a particular defect in the goods

b)   where the buyer has himself examined the goods and an examination should have revealed the defect.

This is because in both situations the buyer is already aware of the defect in the goods before the contract was made, so must have been prepared to accept the defect. Often with goods described as 'seconds', for instance, while there are minor defects, the buyer will usually have been able to buy the goods for a much lower than usual price.

## 17.2.4 The requirement that the goods are fit for the purpose for which they were bought

Section 14(3) of the Sale of Goods Act inserts an implied condition into sale of goods contracts that the goods should be fit for the purposes for which they are required. The provision applies where the buyer

❝ either expressly or impliedly makes known to the seller any particular purpose for which goods are being bought regardless of whether or not that is a purpose for which goods of that kind are commonly supplied. ❞

If the buyer has stated a particular purpose for which he is buying the goods and the seller accepts the sale, then the buyer is entitled to expect the goods to be fit for that purpose. The buyer is entitled to rely on the skill and judgement of the seller.

 **ACTIVITY**

### Activity 2

In the right-hand column below, put a tick against the THREE points that are examples of factors to be taken into account when deciding whether or not goods are of satisfactory quality, as identified in s 14(2)(b) Sale of Goods Act 1979.

| i)   | the safety of the goods                    |  |
|------|--------------------------------------------|--|
| ii)  | the quantity of the goods                  |  |
| iii) | the durability of the goods                |  |
| iv)  | the finish of the goods                    |  |
| v)   | the age of the person buying the goods     |  |
| vi)  | the usefulness of the goods.               |  |

Table 17.2

## EXAMPLE

A buyer asked the seller to supply him with 'a fast, flexible and easily managed car that would be comfortable and suitable for ordinary touring purposes'. The seller sold him a Bugatti car which did not conform to these requirements that the buyer had set under the contract and that had been agreed to by the seller. The buyer was entitled to rely on the skill and judgement of the seller who had breached s 14(3) by not supplying goods which were fit for the purpose stated by the buyer.

*From the case of Baldry v Marshall (1925)*

It is also possible that the purposes for which the goods are bought are implied rather than being expressly stated by the buyer. In other words the courts will accept that some purposes should be obvious to the seller and the buyer can still claim that the goods are not fit for the purpose for which he bought them.

## EXAMPLE

A buyer bought a hot water bottle, obviously to warm a bed. The hot water bottle was continuously filled and refilled over a period of time because it was used to keep an ill person warm. The hot water bottle burst. The buyer was able to argue that the hot water bottle was not fit for the purpose even though it had been used excessively over a short period of time.

*From the case of Priest v Last (1903)*

Sometimes a purpose is so obvious that it goes without saying and the seller is assumed to know the purpose for which the buyer bought the goods.

## EXAMPLE

Here the buyer contracted a painful skin disease from chemicals in underpants that he had bought. The court accepted that the buyer would have impliedly made known the purpose

for which he was buying the underpants even if he had not actually stated it to the seller.

*From the case of Grant v Australian Knitting Mills Ltd (1936)*

Another point worth noting is that where the goods are accompanied by some instructions, then the instructions are also said to be part of the goods. If the instructions are misleading the seller may find that he is liable for goods that are neither fit for the purpose nor of satisfactory quality.

## ACTIVITY

### Activity 3

Read each of the following three situations and in the space below identify which implied term from the Sale of Goods Act 1979 is involved.

1. Rosie buys a brand new settee and armchair from a furniture shop which the salesman assures her is 'absolutely stainproof'. Rosie's husband, Darrell, spills red wine on the settee and the stain is impossible to remove.

2. Sally buys a new television. When she plugs in the television and switches it on, the television explodes.

3. Tom buys a mountain bike from a bicycle shop. Tom tells the shopkeeper that he intends to use the bike for cross-country bike races. In fact, the gears on the bike are inadequate for cycling up and down hills and Tom is unable to use it.

Answer in the spaces below.

........................................................................

........................................................................

........................................................................

........................................................................

........................................................................

........................................................................

........................................................................

........................................................................

## ACTIVITY

### Activity 4

In the spaces below see if you can give reasons to suggest whether Rosie, Sally and Tom have remedies against the businesses from which they bought the goods in the scenarios above.

..............................................................

..............................................................

..............................................................

..............................................................

..............................................................

..............................................................

..............................................................

..............................................................

..............................................................

..............................................................

## 17.3 Supply of Goods and Services implied terms

## 17.3.1 The Supply of Goods and Services Act 1982 implied terms

This Act covers those situations where the consumer buys a service. Sometimes this will only involve labour, for instance a person hired to do gardening work or cleaning work. More often, providing a service also involves providing goods. For example where a plumber repairs a leak and as well as doing the repair he has to use new pipe, the customer has to pay for the pipe as well as the repair, but both are covered by the Act.

For this reason the Supply of Goods and Services Act 1982 includes similar implied terms to those in the Sale of Goods Act 1979. The Act obviously offers consumer protection in the case of the provision of services rather than for merely the sale of goods.

These are:

- an implied term covering description in s 3
- an implied term covering satisfactory quality in s 4
- an implied term covering fitness for the purpose again in s 4.

Again these are conditions which mean that the consumer has as a remedy the right to reject the goods and have his money back.

Because of the nature of a service there are also three further and very significant implied terms that are particularly relevant to the supply of services:

- In a contract for the supply of a service where the supplier is acting in the course of a business, there is an implied term that the supplier will carry out the service with reasonable care and skill (s 13 Supply of Goods and Services Act 1982). (This means that the service must be carried out in a professional manner and if it requires specific skills, then these must be carried out in the manner appropriate to the particular trade. For example, if a builder erected a wall that then fell down, it is unlikely that he has shown appropriate skill in building it.)
- Where the time for the service to be carried out is not mentioned in the contract, there is an implied term that the supplier will carry out the service within a reasonable time (s 14 Supply of Goods and Services Act 1982). (This means that a person buying a service should be able to expect it to be carried out in a reasonable time and not to have to wait indefinitely for its completion. For example, if a house of a particular size would normally take no more than two weeks for complete internal redecoration, then it would be a breach of this term if a decorator was still working on the house after a month or two months. Obviously this is to avoid the potential inconvenience to the purchaser.

• Where the actual price of the service has not been stated in the contract there is an implied term that the party contracting with the supplier only has to pay a reasonable charge (s 15 Supply of Goods and Services Act 1982). (This is aimed at preventing unscrupulous business practices where the provider of the service fails to give an accurate estimate of the work before the contract and then charges an excessive price once it is completed.)

## 17.3.2 The requirement that the service is carried out with reasonable care and skill

Clearly a person paying for a service is entitled to expect not only that the person providing the service is competent to undertake the work but also that the person behaves professionally in carrying out the service.

If the work is not done with the appropriate care and skill, then there will be a breach of the implied term.

 **EXAMPLE**

A person contracted with a professional to design, supply and install a fitted kitchen for £1,200. Plans were drawn up which were approved by the client but then the professional failed actually to follow them and the work itself was not up to standard. The client was able to recover his money because of the shoddy workmanship.

*From the case of Lawson v Supasink Ltd (1984)*

Obviously one way of identifying whether work is carried out with appropriate care and skill is to see if it complies with any professional or legal standards set for the particular work.

 **EXAMPLE**

A person contracted with a package holiday firm for a holiday in Greece. While on holiday he fell through glass patio doors in the hotel and was badly injured. He sued the package holiday company and argued that the glass door was not of the thickness required by United Kingdom safety standards and that the company had therefore not shown care and skill in selecting the hotel in question. In fact the glass door did comply with Greek safety standards and the company was not bound to do other than check that local safety standards were complied with, which it had done.

*From the case of Wilson v Best Travel Ltd (1993)*

## 17.3.3 The requirement that the service is carried out within a reasonable time

In many contracts only an estimate can be given as to how long it will take to complete the service and this might also affect what the eventual bill is. Clearly the person providing the service must have some leeway; for instance where building work is being done, the builders may find aspects of the work more complex than at first thought.

Nevertheless, the buyer is entitled to the work being carried out in a reasonable time. It would be against common sense and completely unfair to the purchaser to allow the provider of a service an unlimited time to carry it out.

 **EXAMPLE**

In a contract to repair a car, the party providing the service took eight weeks to repair the car. It was shown that a competent repair should have taken no more than five weeks at the most and so was in breach of the implied term. The owner of the car was caused serious inconvenience by the unnecessary delay and was able to recover compensation.

*From the case of Charnock v Liverpool Corporation (1968)*

# 17.3.4 The requirement that, where no price is agreed in advance, the purchaser only has to pay a reasonable amount for the service

It is a feature of contract law that courts are unwilling to interfere with the actual bargain made by the parties. The parties are free to make their own bargain and if one party is prepared to pay an excessive price for goods or services, then the courts accept this as the bargain. (As a result if the parties freely agree to buy and sell, for example a car in working order for £1, this would seem like a very bad bargain. However, if the seller freely agreed to the purchase and was happy with the price, then the agreement would be enforceable. It is much more likely, of course, that it would be a seller asking an excessive price for providing a service, for example a plumber asking £300 to change a tap washer that could be done in moments. Nevertheless, again as long as the purchaser has freely agreed and is happy to pay the price, then the agreement is enforceable.)

However, it is when no price has been set at the time of contracting that unscrupulous behaviour might occur in demanding a very high price after the event. The law is then that the purchaser is entitled to expect that the actual price is a reasonable figure. (If the usual price in the trade for example for repairing a leaking tap is £30, and the plumber has not given the customer an estimate in advance and tries to charge £300, then a court would only expect the customer to pay a reasonable price, £30.)

Of course if the person providing the service wants a price that is unreasonable, then there is no reason why they should not ask for it. However, this should be indicated at the time of contracting. This would then allow the purchaser to consider the price and find a cheaper provider.

## ACTIVITY

### Activity 5

The grid below contains three scenarios involving possible breaches of the implied terms in the Supply of Goods and Services Act 1982. In the right-hand column indicate which implied term is involved in the scenario on the left by writing the section number, either 13, 14 or 15.

| | | |
|---|---|---|
| i) | Jez contracts with landscape gardeners to lay turf in his small back garden, which is about 6 metres wide and 10 metres long. Jez is not told how long the job will take but after six weeks the job is not yet finished. | |
| ii) | Mick contracts with a garage to carry out an annual service on his car. Mick is not told the price beforehand but after the service is complete the garage demands £1,800. Mick has never paid more than £300 with other garages that have serviced his car. | |
| iii) | Neera contracts with a plumber to install a new shower in her bathroom. When the shower is installed, the shower itself has hardly any pressure and water constantly leaks from underneath the shower tray. | |

Table 17.3

**ACTIVITY**

## Activity 6

In the spaces below try to give reasons to suggest whether Jez, Mick and Neera have remedies against the businesses which provided the services in the scenarios above.

..............................................................................

..............................................................................

..............................................................................

..............................................................................

..............................................................................

..............................................................................

..............................................................................

..............................................................................

..............................................................................

..............................................................................

 **ACTIVITY**

## Activity 7

In the spaces below try to explain three ways in which the implied terms in the Sale of Goods Act and the Supply of Goods and Services Act help to protect consumers.

1. ..................................................................

......................................................................

......................................................................

......................................................................

2. ..................................................................

......................................................................

......................................................................

......................................................................

3. ..................................................................

......................................................................

......................................................................

......................................................................

 **KEY FACTS**

- A consumer contract is one where:
  - the buyer is not buying in the course of a business
  - the seller is selling in the course of a business
  - the goods are of a type or quantity consistent with a consumer purchase.

- Consumers are protected by the insertion of implied terms into their contracts by which the sellers are bound.

- There are three significant implied terms in the Sale of Goods Act 1979:
  - the goods must correspond with the description given to them by the seller
  - the goods must be of satisfactory quality
  - the goods must be fit for the purpose which the buyer stated that they were being bought for.

- These terms are conditions, so it means that if they are breached by the seller, the buyer can end the contract and have his money back.

- Because providing services often involves providing goods as well, the Supply of Goods and Services Act 1982 includes almost identical terms.

- The Supply of Goods and Services Act also includes three other significant implied terms:
  - that the service is carried out with care and skill
  - that if the price is not agreed in advance, the buyer only has to pay a reasonable price
  - that if the time for completing the service is not stated in advance, then it should only take a reasonable time.

# CHAPTER 18

# UNFAIR CONTRACT TERMS

## Aims and objectives

After reading this chapter you should be able to:

- understand what exclusion clauses are and why the law controls when they can be used and the ways in which they can be used
- understand the controls on exclusion clauses that have been developed by the judges in the courts
- understand the controls placed on exclusion clauses by the Unfair Contract Terms Act 1977
- understand the controls placed on unfair contract terms in the Unfair Terms in Consumer Contracts Regulations 1999
- apply knowledge of all of these various controls to factual situations
- respond to sources or arguments concerning controls on unfair contract terms.

## 18.1 Reasons for regulating unfair contract terms

Sometimes businesses insert clauses in contracts which limit or exclude liability for breaches of a term of the contract and sometimes even for negligence. A typical term of this sort would read:

66 The company accepts no liability for damage to goods while on the premises, however caused. 99

Inevitably terms like this can be particularly harsh on consumers and also allow businesses to engage in unscrupulous trading. All a business needs to do is state in the contract that they accept no liability and they can get away with poor or even no service and the consumer has no remedy.

It was for this reason first that judges developed controls to prevent sellers from having absolute discretion to avoid liability for their contractual breaches and even for negligence.

More recently Parliament has also developed consumer protection, often because the United Kingdom has had to introduce controls that have been created by the European Union.

### ACTIVITY

#### Activity 1

In the spaces below try to explain THREE ways in which the use of exclusion clauses in contracts could be harmful to consumers

i) ................................................................
................................................................
................................................................
................................................................

ii) ................................................................
................................................................
................................................................
................................................................

iii) ................................................................
................................................................
................................................................
................................................................

## 18.2 Controls developed by the courts

Using exclusion clauses in contracts is inevitably harsh on consumers. Judges recognised this a long time ago and developed strict rules of incorporation of such clauses. They will not allow a seller to rely on an exclusion clause to avoid liability unless it conforms with these rules.

Incorporation of the clause means that the clause is actually accepted as being a part of the contract. In written contracts it is obviously easy to see which clauses (terms) form part of the contract because they are already written down. It is less obvious when the contract has not been made in writing. This is where the judges want to be absolutely sure of what is in the contract and what is not, and this is why they developed these rules.

The rules can easily be used as a way of deciding whether all other types of terms do form part of the contract, but they are particularly appropriate when we are looking at exclusion clauses.

## 18.2.1 Signed agreement

It is a general rule of all written contracts that are signed that, where a person signs a written agreement, then he is bound by the terms of the agreement. It is very important for consumers always to read written contracts.

 **EXAMPLE**

A woman bought a vending machine which was defective. She tried to return it but she was bound by a clause in the contract excluding liability for the defect. It did not matter that she had not read the written agreement. She had signed it which was proof that she agreed to its terms. This was in fact a business contract but the same point could apply to a consumer.

*From the case of L'Estrange v Graucob (1934)*

## 18.2.2 Knowledge of the existence of the clause at the time the contract is formed

One of the first principles that was developed by judges in court cases is that an exclusion clause

will only be incorporated into a contract where the person who is going to be subject to the clause had actual knowledge of its existence at the time when the contract was made.

 **EXAMPLE**

A married couple, Mr and Mrs Olley, booked into a hotel to stay overnight. As they registered at the desk this was the point at which a contract was formed between the couple and the hotel. A rule of the hotel was that guests should leave their room key at reception when they went out of the hotel. The couple did go out and they left the key at reception as required. While they were out a thief took the key to their room, and went into it and stole Mrs Olley's fur coat. When Mrs Olley tried to claim from the hotel for the loss of the coat it pointed to a notice on the back of each hotel room door which stated that *'the proprietors will not hold themselves liable for articles lost or stolen unless handed to the manageress for safe custody'*. The court was not prepared to allow the hotel to rely on this to avoid liability. Since the clause was on a notice inside the Olley's room, they would not have known about it at the time they made the contract at reception. Therefore it could not possibly form part of the contract.

*From the case of Olley v Marlborough Court Hotel (1949)*

Of course sometimes people will contract with each other regularly on the same terms. In this situation it would be hard for the consumer to argue that he was unaware of the exclusion clause. However, for the clause to be incorporated it still depends on the person subject to it knowing of it. Therefore, unless the parties have dealt consistently on the same terms in the past, then a clause cannot be relied on by the seller to avoid liability, because it cannot genuinely be shown that the consumer knew the terms that he was contracting on.

**EXAMPLE**

The consumer, Mr McCutcheon, lived on the Isle of Islay in Scotland, He was a wealthy man and owned an expensive car which he liked to use when he went to mainland Scotland. He had taken his car on the defendants' ferries from Islay to the mainland on many occasions. Sometimes when he boarded the ferry he was asked to sign a risk note which included an exclusion clause, but on other occasions he was not given any risk note. On this particular occasion the consumer's relative, McSporran, took the car to the ferry for him. He received a receipt on which was printed the exclusion clause, but he did not read it, and he was not asked to sign a risk note. Owing to negligence by the ferry owners, the ferry sank. Mr McCutcheon's expensive car sank too and was a write-off. Mr McCutcheon asked for compensation from the ferry company but it tried to avoid liability by pointing to the exclusion clause in the risk note and on the receipt. The company inevitably failed because there was not a consistent course of action that entitled them to assume that the consumer knew of the existence of the exclusion clause. It was not therefore incorporated into the contract. As the judge summed up the position very clearly in the case '. . . *previous dealings are only relevant if they prove knowledge of the terms actual and not constructive and assent to them.*'

*From the case of McCutcheon v David MacBrayne Ltd (1964)*

## 18.2.3 Doing enough to make the other party aware of the exclusion clause

Another way in which judges have been strict on businesses trying to avoid liability through exclusion clauses concerns the lengths that the business has to go to in order to make the consumer aware of the clause at the time the contract is formed.

The person inserting the clause into the contract and trying to rely on it to avoid liability has the burden of bringing it to the attention of the other party before the contract is formed.

 **EXAMPLE**

A consumer, Mr Parker, left his luggage in the cloakroom of a station for a fee. He was given a small ticket once he had paid. Mr Parker's luggage was then stolen so he tried to claim compensation from the railway company. He was told that on the back of the ticket that he had been given in tiny writing was a clause stating that the railway company would not be liable for any luggage that was worth more than £10 in value. Mr Parker's luggage was worth more than that. He was able to get compensation because the railway company was not allowed to rely on the clause. It was unable to show that it had informed Mr Parker of the clause or told him to read the back of the ticket. The clause had not been brought to Mr Parker's attention so it was not incorporated as part of the contract.

*From the case of Parker v South Eastern Railway Co (1877)*

In fact we would not expect things like small tickets when we are given them to contain contractual terms. We would usually see them merely as receipts. The judges have taken the same view and will not usually accept that such things have contractual significance.

 **EXAMPLE**

The consumer, Mr Chapelton, went to Barry Island and hired deckchairs on the beach. He was given two tickets by the council's beach attendant once he paid. The canvas on one chair was defective and worn and it collapsed injuring Mr Chapelton who then tried to claim compensation for his injuries. The council, which was responsible for the beach and owned the deckchairs, tried to rely on an exclusion clause written on the back of the small tickets. This said '*The council will not be liable for any accident or damage arising from the hire of the chair*'. Mr Chapelton had not read the back of the ticket which he thought was just a receipt. The court would not allow the council to avoid liability by using the clause. It had done nothing to bring it to the attention of Mr Chapelton and it was unreasonable to assume that he would know that the ticket had any kind of contractual significance.

*From the case of Chapelton v Barry Urban District Council (1940)*

It is also no good for the business to try and rely on an exclusion clause which is in another document given later to the consumer, even though this is before the contract is performed but where insufficient has been done to bring the consumer's attention to the existence of the clause in the other document.

 **EXAMPLE**

A woman and her daughter booked to go on a cruise. In the booking form it stated that the contract was ' . . . subject to conditions and regulations printed on the tickets'. In fact the tickets would only then be issued at a later date. The cruise ship sank and the woman was injured so she tried to claim compensation. The shipping company tried to avoid liability pointing to an exclusion clause in the tickets. The court held that there was insufficient notice given to the woman in the booking form.

*From the case of Dillon v Baltic Shipping Co Ltd (The Mikhail Lermontov ) (1991)*

Another interesting situation that has been considered by judges is where consumers are making purchases from things such as vending machines, ticket machines or indeed any other situations where there is no real negotiation and no chance to communicate at the effective time of contracting with the party trying to rely on an exclusion clause. In such situations it would be extremely unfair to allow the business to avoid liability, and the judges have realised this.

 **EXAMPLE**

Mr Thornton was injured when he used a car park owned by the defendants. In many multi-storey car parks like the one here, a person using the car park takes a ticket from a machine at a barrier which then raises once the ticket is taken. The person using the car park will then pay on exiting the car park, either by paying at a pay station or sometimes to an attendant at an exit barrier. At the entrance to this car park there was a notice that identified the charges by the number of hours cars were parked in the car park. It also stated that parking was at the owner's risk. The tickets received from the machine at the barrier by motorists such as Mr Thornton had printed on them the words 'This ticket is issued subject to the conditions of issue as displayed on the premises'. Notices inside the car park then listed the conditions of the contract including a clause excluding any liability for both damage to property and also for personal injury. When Mr Thornton tried to claim compensation, the car park owner argued that the exclusion clause meant that it did not have to pay. The court disagreed. The judge identified that in such situations the consumer has no chance to negotiate. As the judge said, the consumer ' . . . pays his money and gets a ticket. He cannot refuse it. He cannot get his money back. He may protest to the machine, even swear at it. But it will remain unmoved. He is committed beyond recall . . . The contract was concluded at that time.' In conclusion the judge stated that the consumer would only be bound by the terms of the contract '. . . as long as they are sufficiently brought to his notice before-hand, but not otherwise'. In explaining what the business would have to do to effectively bring the consumer's notice to its exclusion clause he also said, 'Some clauses which I have seen would need to be printed in red ink with a red hand pointing to it before the notice could be held to be sufficient.' In other words, this provides a lot of protection to the consumer.

*From the case of Thornton v Shoe Lane Parking Ltd (1971)*

## ACTIVITY

### Activity 2

In the right-hand column in the grid below put a tick against those scenarios in the left-hand column where the exclusion clause would NOT have been incorporated in the contract.

| | | |
|---|---|---|
| 1 | an exclusion clause in a form pasted onto the side of a till. The assistants do not ask customers to read the form | |
| 2 | an exclusion clause that is contained in a signed agreement that the salesman has asked the buyer to read before signing it | |
| 3 | an exclusion clause in a receipt where the parties have regularly dealt on the same terms and the receipt has always been handed to the consumer | |
| 4 | an exclusion clause in a notice pasted to the inside of a door to a hotel bedroom | |
| 5 | an exclusion clause contained in a risk note that the consumer is asked to read before contracting | |
| 6 | an exclusion clause on the back of a small cloakroom ticket. | |

Table 18.1

It is also of course fair to say that judges apply this strict approach to incorporation not only to exclusion clauses but to other unfair terms also.

## 18.2.4 Promises and misrepresentations made by the seller about the scope of the clause

Sometimes, even where a person has signed a written agreement containing a clause excluding liability, he may in some circumstances not be bound by it and will still be able to claim compensation. This happens when the person who is subject to the clause has enquired about the existence of the clause or about the consequences of the clause and the seller has misrepresented what is covered by the clause.

## EXAMPLE

A lady took her wedding dress to a dry cleaners to be cleaned. She was asked to sign a form which sensibly she read before she signed it. A clause in the form exempted the defendants from liability for any damage '. . . howsoever arising'. The lady, again very sensibly, queried the nature of the form that she was being asked to sign and what was meant by it. The assistant in the dry cleaners then told the lady that it only meant that the dry cleaners would not accept liability for damaging things like beads or sequins attached to the dress if they had not been removed. Reassured, the lady signed the form. When she went to collect the dress it was ruined. It had a chemical stain and so the lady tried to claim for the cost of the ruined dress. The dry cleaners pointed to the form that the lady had signed but it was still liable for the damage because of the oral assurances that had been made to the customer by the assistant.

*From the case of Curtis v Chemical Cleaning and*
*Dyeing Co Ltd (1951)*

# Ambiguity in the contract

Even though the court accepts that an exclusion clause satisfies the above tests and so it appears that it may have been successfully incorporated into a contract, this does not always mean that the court will allow the seller of the goods or service to rely on the clause to avoid liability in all cases. This will generally be because the clause is not absolutely clear on its meaning.

In this way judges will not allow a seller to avoid liability when the wording of the contract, particularly the exclusion clause, is ambiguous. There is a well-established principle of law that ambiguity in a contract works against the person who drafted it. It works like this: if a seller wants to avoid liability for contractual breaches or for negligence by using an exclusion clause in the contract, then the clause must be specific as to the circumstances in which liability is avoided otherwise the clause will fail.

 **EXAMPLE**

A man bought a new car. The contract for 'new Singer cars' contained a clause that excluded '. . . all conditions, warranties and liabilities implied by statute, common law or otherwise . . .'. One car delivered under the contract was, strictly speaking, a used car because a potential buyer had used the car and then returned it. The court held that supplying 'new Singer cars' amounted to an express term of the contract. Since the exclusion clause applied to 'implied terms', the clause was ambiguous in its wording and could not be relied upon by the seller to try to avoid liability.

*From the case of Andrews Bros (Bournemouth) Ltd v Singer & Co (1934)*

It is very important for businesses that want to avoid liability by using exclusion clauses that they phrase their terms very clearly and precisely, otherwise they run the risk that the courts will not enforce the clause and they will be liable. This

of course is a very good protection for consumers against unscrupulous business practices.

 **EXAMPLE**

A man took his car to a garage for servicing, as he had done many times in the past. The usual conditions of his contract with the garage were in a form that the man had signed on previous occasions, but he had not been asked to do so on this occasion. This form contained a term which stated that 'The company is not responsible for damage caused by fire to customers' cars on the premises'. The man's car was damaged in a fire which had been caused because of negligence by the garage. The court said that just because the man had previously contracted with the garage did not mean that the exclusion clause had been incorporated into the contract on this occasion when he had not been asked to sign the form. Besides this, it also concluded that in order for the garage to rely on the exclusion clause, it must have been phrased without any ambiguity. It would have had to say that it would not be liable even when the damage was caused by its own negligence. This would then have given the man the chance to accept that risk or go to another garage which did not try to avoid liability in the same way.

*From the case of Hollier v Rambler Motors (AMC) Ltd (1972)*

It is also worth remembering that this rule on ambiguity does not only apply to exclusion clauses. It has also been used in the case of other terms that may work unfairly.

 **EXAMPLE**

A person was buying a Ferrari car (a very expensive luxury make of car). The contract for the supply of the car included a price variation clause. The cars had to be imported and sometimes prices did go up between ordering and receiving the cars. However, the price variation could only actually apply in certain limited circumstances identified in the contract. When the supplier tried to increase the cost of the car to the purchaser for a reason that was not one of those identified in the contract, he was not able to enforce the price variation clause and the buyer could not be made to pay the increased price. Again, the use of this rule on ambiguous wording provided a very good protection for the consumer against a business which in effect was trying to cheat him out of extra money that it had no right to.

*From the case of Vaswani v Italian Motor Cars Ltd (1996)*

## 18.3 EU controls

Provisions created by Parliament either through statute or in regulations have proved very effective in controlling the abuses that a consumer might suffer because of an exclusion clause or similar unfair term in a contract.

There are two principal provisions provided by Parliament: the Unfair Contract Terms Act 1977 and the Unfair Terms in Consumer Contract

 **ACTIVITY**

### Activity 3

Read the following scenarios and then complete the questions below.

1. Jim drove into Westybury to attend an exam board meeting. He parked in a multi-storey car park. At the barrier Jim took his ticket from the machine, and when the barrier lifted, he drove in and parked. When Jim returned to his car he paid at the pay station and when he reached his car he found that it had been crashed into by another car, causing £2,000 for repairs to the damage caused. Jim straightaway reported the damage to the car park attendant. When Jim tried to claim the £2,000 from the car park he was told that he should have looked at his ticket which said 'See conditions of use of the car park'. The conditions of use of the car park, which were kept in the attendant's kiosk included a clause 'The management accept no liability for any damage to cars or other property of users of the car park'.

   In the spaces below explain whether the car park can rely on the clause and avoid paying compensation to Jim for the damage to his car.

   ..................................................................
   ..................................................................
   ..................................................................
   ..................................................................
   ..................................................................
   ..................................................................
   ..................................................................

2. Hassan left his suitcase at the left luggage department in Bruboro station and paid a £5 fee. He was asked to sign a document which, when he read it, stated 'The management will not accept liability for damage to goods left in the left luggage department.' Hassan signed the document. When Hassan returned to the station to collect his suitcase he found that the left luggage department had burned down in a fire when an attendant negligently dropped a lit cigarette into a bin full of waste paper. Hassan's suitcase was destroyed in the fire. The fire could have been put out if the station manager had rung the fire brigade immediately.

   In the spaces below, explain whether the station can rely on the clause and avoid paying compensation to Hassan for the loss of his suitcase.

   ..................................................................
   ..................................................................
   ..................................................................
   ..................................................................
   ..................................................................
   ..................................................................
   ..................................................................

Regulations 1999. These were both enacted in order to comply with EC Directive 93/13.

The 1999 Regulations are based on the directive which is aimed at harmonising rules on consumer protection throughout the European Union so that EU citizens can expect similar protections in all member states. The regulations are actually narrower in scope than the Act. This is because existing UK law already provided many of the features of the directive. Nevertheless, in some ways the regulations are actually broader than the Act because they apply in a much wider range of circumstances, not just exclusion clauses, and they often impose stricter duties.

## 18.4 Statutory controls

### 18.4.1 The Unfair Contract Terms Act 1977

The Unfair Contract Terms Act 1977 was introduced to comply with EU law. It is an effective limitation on the operation of exclusion clauses. The Act applies to exclusions for tort damage as well as contractual breaches.

It protects consumers in a number of ways:

- It distinguishes between consumer purchases and inter-business deals.
- It makes certain types of exclusion invalid so that they cannot be enforced against the consumer.
- It makes other types of exclusion clause enforceable only if they are reasonable.
- It creates tests of what is reasonable for guidance.

### 18.4.2 The essential features of a consumer contract

In order to protect consumers effectively, it distinguishes between consumer contracts and inter-business contracts.

The definition of a consumer contract is in

s 12(1). This states that a consumer contract is where:

a)  The one person (the consumer) does not make the contract in the course of a business

b)  The other party does make the contract in the course of a business

c)  The goods passing under the contract are of a type ordinarily supplied for private use or consumption.

Whether a particular contract involves a consumer can often be a question of fact for the courts to decide. This is because there can be complications where a person is buying in bulk or buying goods that would only usually be used in the course of a business.

### 18.4.3 Types of exclusion clause that are invalid against a consumer under the Act

One way that the Act helps consumers is by making certain types of exclusion clause unenforceable against the consumer, even though they might actually be contained in the contract.

These include the following important ones to consumers:

- In a consumer contract there can be no exclusion of liability for death or personal injury caused by the seller's negligence (s 2(1)). (This is important because a consumer is always then able to get a remedy where he is injured by a defective product or service.)
- In a consumer contract there can be no exclusion of liability by reference to the terms of a guarantee in respect of defects which have been caused by negligence in the manufacture or distribution of the goods (s 5(1)). (This obviously makes guarantees more secure.)
- In a consumer contract there can be no exclusion of liability for breaches of the implied conditions of description (s 13),

## ACTIVITY

### Activity 4

In the column on the right write CONSUMER next to the contracts on the left that are a consumer contract.

| | |
|---|---|
| A hotel chain buys 20 million square metres of carpet sufficient to carpet all of its hotels. | |
| Ahmed buys 20 million square metres of carpet because he is getting a discount for buying in bulk. He is buying carpet for all his family, friends and neighbours and will collect the individual cost of their carpets from them. | |
| Beatrix buys a carpet to carpet her small bedroom. | |
| Claude, a butcher, buys the meat from 30 cows at a discount price from a farmer. | |
| Denzil, who likes beef, buys the same amount of meat from the farmer and stores it in chest freezers all round his garage. | |
| Elaine buys a joint of beef from Claude for her Sunday dinner. | |

Table 18.2

satisfactory quality (s 14(2)), fitness for the purpose (s 14(3)) in the Sale of Goods Act 1979 (see section 17.2) (s 6(2)). (This is important or otherwise sellers would just exclude liability for Sale of Goods Act terms and the buyer would have no remedy for defective goods.)

- The same applies to the similar terms in ss 2, 3 and 4 of the Supply of Goods and Services Act 1982 (s 7(1)). (The same obviously applies in respect of goods provided in the course of providing a service, eg inferior and unsafe wiring when a house is being rewired.)

## ACTIVITY

### Activity 5

In the following statement fill in the missing words from the list of words below

The ........................................ Contract Terms Act 1977 helps consumers in several ways. Some contracts cannot be ........................................ against the consumer at all. An example of this is where the consumer is a victim of a breach of one of the ........................................ terms in the Sale of Goods Act 1979.

Use words from the following list:
- unreasonable
- unfair
- included
- enforced
- express
- implied.

## 18.4.4 Types of exclusion clause that will only be enforceable against the consumer if they are reasonable

In contracts between businesses the validity of exclusion clauses mostly depends on the use of the clause being reasonable. This is because businesses are in a more equal relationship and in a better position to negotiate terms.

The Act also identifies some situations where an exclusion clause could be enforced against a consumer if it was reasonable.

- a clause excluding liability for loss, other than death or personal injury, caused by the negligence of the party inserting it will only be enforced if it is reasonable (s 2(2)).
- where a person contracts as a consumer, or deals on the other party's standard business forms, a clause excluding liability for breach of contract, or for a substantially different performance, or for no performance at all is not enforceable against the consumer unless inclusion of the clause was reasonable (s 3).

## 18.4.5 Testing whether it is reasonable to use the exclusion clause

In the Act there are some guidelines on what reasonable means and there are also some examples of things that can be considered in deciding whether to use the clause is reasonable.

Whether to include the clause is reasonable depends on what was known by the parties at the time that they contracted (s 11(1)).

 **EXAMPLE**

A person buying a house had to pay for a valuation report on the house for the building society lending him the money to buy the house. In fact the surveyors carried out the survey negligently and a defect in the house was missed which later resulted in a loss to the buyer. The surveyor was not able to avoid liability for the accuracy of the report as a clause in the contract said he could. This was unreasonable.

*From the case of Smith v Eric S Bush (1990)*

In any case it is the person who inserts the clause in the contract and who is trying to use it against the consumer who has to show that it is reasonable. Reasonable means 'reasonable in all the circumstances' (s 11(5)).

 **EXAMPLE**

A husband and wife were very upset when a firm of photographic developers lost the film containing photographs taken at the couple's silver wedding party (this is when they have been married for 25 years). The firm tried to rely on small print in the contract that limited its liability to supplying a replacement film. The firm had to try to prove to the court that this was reasonable. In the light of the significance of what was on the lost film, the court would not accept that it was and the couple were given extra compensation.

*From the case of Warren v Trueprint Ltd (1986)*

## 18.4.6 Some comment on the Act

The Act is certainly a significant area of consumer protection:

- It particularly helped consumers by removing some of the inequalities in bargaining strength between consumers and the businesses that they buy from.
- It ensured that some of the most unfair exclusions, eg for negligently causing death or injury, would be completely invalid and can never be relied on by the seller.
- It introduced a test of reasonableness in respect of some other types of clause.

However, it must be remembered that the Act still has limitations:

- It does not cover all exclusion clauses.
- It is mainly restricted to exclusion clauses.
- It ignores a lot of unfair terms that consumers may find in contracts that they make.

It perhaps in these senses is limited in its scope and application.

## 18.4.7 The Unfair Terms in Consumer Contracts Regulations 1999

These regulations were introduced to comply with an EU directive. They are quite different to the Act in two ways:

- because they cover contractual terms in general and not only exclusion clauses
- because they only cover consumer contracts, not inter-business contracts. Therefore, they purely concern consumer protection.

The definitions of seller and consumer are also different to those in the Act.

- A seller or supplier is defined as '. . . any person who sells or supplies goods or services and who in making a contract is acting for purposes related to his business.' This is wider than in the Act.
- A consumer is defined as '. . . any natural person who is acting for purposes which are outside his trade, business or profession.' So this is much narrower than the scope of the Act.

The regulations also only apply where the consumer has not individually negotiated the term in question with the seller. Therefore, the regulations are particularly appropriate to standard form contracts. The seller or supplier can only really then avoid the effect of the regulations if he can show that the contract has been negotiated with the consumer and is not just his standard form contract.

## 18.4.8 The types of term that are covered by the regulations

The regulations control the use of what are described as 'unfair terms'. An unfair term is defined as

66  . . . any term which contrary to good faith causes a significant imbalance in the parties' rights and obligations under the contract to the detriment of the consumer.  99

Therefore, the regulations are definitely aimed at trying to prevent businesses taking unfair advantage of consumers.

A seller can try to argue that he acted in 'good faith'. There are various factors that must be looked at in order to be able to show that the seller did in fact act in good faith.

- the relative bargaining strength of the parties to the contract (consumers of course rarely bargain but just buy at the price and under the conditions that the seller lays down)
- whether the seller or supplier gave the consumer some sort of inducement so that he would agree to buy with the unfair term included in the contract (this could be something like a significant discount on the usual price)
- whether the goods sold or services supplied under the contract were to the special order of the consumer (in other words this means that the seller had to do something unusual at the seller's request)
- the extent to which the seller or supplier has dealt fairly and equitably with the consumer (in other words there should be no trickery).

There are also general guidelines listing many different types of term that generally can be considered unfair and therefore would be invalid under the regulations. The common feature in all of these examples is that the contract puts the seller in a better position than the consumer.

For instance:

- a term that is absolutely binding on the consumer but which is at the discretion of the seller or supplier
- a term that allows the seller or supplier to back out of the contract at any time where the consumer is not allowed to back out of the contract at all

- a term that allows the seller or supplier to change the terms of the contract without any valid reason and without consulting with the consumer
- a term that allows the seller to decide the price of goods when he delivers them or to change the price at any time without the consumer having the chance to cancel the contract and go elsewhere.

These are just a few examples but it is easy to see that these would be terms that would be very unfair on the consumer and that mean that the regulations are good consumer protection.

The regulations also say that the terms in a contract should be expressed in plain and easily understood language. So if any term is then found to be unfair under the regulations it will not be enforced against the consumer.

## 18.4.8 Some comment on the regulations

The regulations still have certain limitations:

- They do not apply to any term that has been individually negotiated. (This is fair because the buyer does have the chance to negotiate terms but it also presumes that consumers always have this chance of equal bargaining strength and that consumers would feel capable of negotiating prices or conditions, which they often do not.)
- Consumer groups that may have wished to police contracts have no power under the regulations, so a significant degree of help that consumers may have had is not available to them.

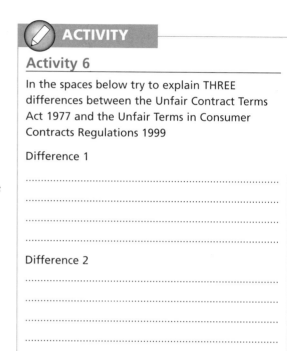

**ACTIVITY**

**Activity 6**

In the spaces below try to explain THREE differences between the Unfair Contract Terms Act 1977 and the Unfair Terms in Consumer Contracts Regulations 1999

Difference 1

......................................................................

......................................................................

......................................................................

......................................................................

Difference 2

......................................................................

......................................................................

......................................................................

......................................................................

Difference 3

......................................................................

......................................................................

......................................................................

......................................................................

**KEY FACTS**

- An exclusion clause is a term in a contract where the seller is trying to avoid liability for any breaches of the contract or for negligence; a limitation clause is one where the seller is trying to reduce the amount of damages he has to pay.

- We are generally bound by contracts that we have signed.

- Judges developed controls on the use of exclusion clauses because of their potential unfairness to consumers.
  - An exclusion clause will not succeed unless it is incorporated into the contract:
    - so the party subject to it must be aware of it at the time of contracting
    - although the consumer may be bound by the term because he actually knows of it through past dealings.
  - The seller must do everything he can to let the consumer know of the clause.
  - If the seller makes false statements about the clause he cannot then use it.
  - If the clause is ambiguous it cannot be relied upon: *Hollier v Rambler Motors*.

- There are some statutory controls on the use of exclusion clauses in the Unfair Contract Terms Act 1977 and the Unfair Terms in Consumer Contracts Regulations 1999 (which both comply with EU law):
  - In the Act some clauses are not enforceable against a consumer, eg exclusion of liability for death or injury caused by negligence – s 2(1); exclusions of liability for breaches of the implied terms in the Sale of Goods Act and Supply of Goods and Services Act – ss 6(1), 6(2) and 7(2).
  - Some other clauses have to pass a test of reasonableness, eg damage caused by negligence – s2(2); standard term contracts.
  - The regulations apply to unfair terms generally, not just exclusion clauses, but they only apply to consumer contracts.
  - In general they do not allow unequal conditions.

# CHAPTER 19

# PRODUCT LIABILITY AND PRODUCT SAFETY

## Aims and objectives

After reading this chapter you should be able to:

- understand the essential requirements for making a claim in negligence for damage caused by a defective product
- understand the essential requirements for making a claim for damage caused by a defective product under the Consumer Protection Act 1987
- apply knowledge of the rules concerning claims for damage caused by defective products to factual situations
- respond to sources or arguments concerning claims for damage caused by defective products.

## 19.1 Product liability and negligence

Although consumer protection is something which really developed in the second half of the twentieth century, there are actually some very old examples of courts being prepared to impose liability for the damage caused by defective goods.

 **EXAMPLE**

A gun was given to a young servant who knew nothing about handling guns. He was injured when the gun went off. It was accepted that the goods were potentially dangerous and 'capable of doing mischief', so there was liability for the injuries caused by the defective product.

*From the case of Dixon v Bell (1816)*

Originally, general claims for defective or dangerous goods were only accepted where there was also a contract. Later on, some claims were possible where there was no contract but only where the seller knew of the defects and gave no warning about it.

The first real acceptance of liability in negligence for defective goods was from Lord Atkin's judgment in *Donoghue v Stevenson* (1932) (see section 16.4).

## 19.1.1 The basis of liability for defective products in negligence

In *Donoghue v Stevenson* Lord Atkin identified that

> 66 . . . a manufacturer of products which he sells in such form as to show that he intends them to reach the ultimate consumer in the form in which they left him with no reasonable possibility of intermediate examination, and with the knowledge that the absence of reasonable care in the preparation or putting up of the products will result in an injury to the consumer's life or property, owes a duty to the consumer to take reasonable care . . . 99

There are three important elements here that must be satisfied in order to claim successfully:

- The goods must reach the consumer and be intended to reach the consumer in the form that they left the manufacturer (this is easy, for instance, where the goods are sealed).

- There is no chance of any examination of the goods between leaving the manufacturer and reaching the consumer (again, in the case, this was straightforward because the ginger beer was in a sealed opaque bottle – nobody would have known that the snail was there).
- The manufacturer knows that taking insufficient care over the goods may put the consumer at risk of some harm.

In diagram form:

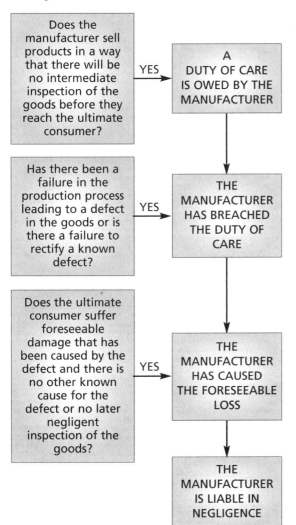

Figure 19.1 What needs to be proved in a successful negligence claim for damage caused by a defective product

## The scope of liability

A negligence claim for defective products has nothing to do with the quality of the goods themselves. All claims over the quality of the goods, in other words for replacement goods, should be made in contract law (probably under the Sale of Goods Act 1979; see section 17.2). It is the damage caused by the defective goods that the consumer is trying to recover compensation for.

At first, product liability in negligence applied only to foodstuffs following the first case. However, it has been extended to cover many other situations:

- anything that is manufactured, eg woolly underpants still containing a chemical which caused the consumer to get dermatitis when he wore them

    *Grant v Australian Knitting Mills* (1936)

- defective motor cars

    *Herschtal v Stewart and Arden Ltd* (1940)

- defects in the house, which can also include fixtures and fittings

    *Batty v Metropolitan Property Realisations Ltd* (1978)

- defective lifts causing injury

    *Haseldine v Daw Ltd* (1941)

- A more modern example includes computer software

    *St Albans City and District Council v International Computers Ltd* (1996)

## 19.1.3 People who can be sued (potential defendants)

The most obvious person who can be sued for a defect in the goods is the manufacturer.

**ACTIVITY**

### Activity 1

In the right-hand column below place a tick against the types of damage in the left-hand column for which compensation could be claimed in negligence.

Alison bought a new electric toaster last week and the first time that she used it, the toaster burst into flames. When Alison bought it, the toaster was in a sealed package and when she used it she followed the manufacturer's instructions precisely. Alison is not in any way to blame for the damage that has resulted:

| 1 | Alison's hand was badly burnt when the toaster caught fire | |
|---|---|---|
| 2 | The work surface was badly burned when the toaster caught fire and will need to be replaced | |
| 3 | The decorating in the kitchen was also damaged by the smoke from the fire and the kitchen will need to be redecorated | |
| 4 | The toaster was destroyed and Alison wants a new toaster or her money back | |

Table 19.1

This has now been expanded to include:
- wholesalers (the people that shopkeepers buy their goods from)

**EXAMPLE**

A wholesaler failed to test hair dye which was defective and caused damage.

*From the case of Watson v Buckley, Osborne Garrett & Co Ltd (1940)*

- retailers (shopkeepers)

**EXAMPLE**

A shopkeeper failed to follow manufacturer's instructions on testing before labelling the product which then caused damage.

*From the case of Kubach v Hollands (1937)*

- Suppliers of goods (other possible suppliers, eg mail order)

**EXAMPLE**

Where the duty owed by the supplier goes beyond distributing the goods and requires that the goods are inspected etc, then the supplier can also be sued by the consumer for damage caused by a defective product.

*From the case of Herschtal v Stewart and Arden Ltd (1940)*

- repairers of the goods

**EXAMPLE**

An expert in lifts and equipment for lifts carried out a repair on a lift. This also involved fitting spare parts as part of the contract. When the lift later failed and dropped down a number of floors, the injured people were able to claim compensation from the contractor that had repaired the lift.

*From the case of Haseldine v Daw Ltd (1941)*

 **ACTIVITY**

## Activity 2

The chart below on the left identifies descriptions of six types of defendant in a claim for negligence numbered 1–6. The chart on the right names six different types of defendant A–F.

| | | | | |
|---|---|---|---|---|
| 1 | This person actually makes the goods in his factory. | | Supplier | A |
| 2 | This person has assembled various component parts in his factory in order to make a finished product. | | Repairer | B |
| 3 | This person sells the goods from his supermarket. | | Wholesaler | C |
| 4 | This person has a large warehouse and sells goods to shopkeepers. | | Manufacturer | D |
| 5 | This person has repaired goods that have become broken. | | Assembler | E |
| 6 | This person does not make the goods or sell them in a shop but you can buy the goods from him by mail order. | | Retailer | F |

Table 19.2

In the chart below insert the correct letter A–F next to the number 1–6 for the name of a potential defendant in a claim for negligence described in the left-hand column.

| | |
|---|---|
| 1 | |
| 2 | |
| 3 | |
| 4 | |
| 5 | |
| 6 | |

Table 19.3

• assemblers of goods

 **EXAMPLE**

A business that assembles parts to make them into a finished product can also be liable to the consumer for damage caused by defects in the goods if it is also under a duty to inspect the goods.

*From the case of Malfroot v Noxal Ltd (1935)*

• This gives the consumer a reasonably wide range of people to sue. However, it is not as wide a range as under the Consumer Protection Act 1987: see section 19.3.1.

## 19.1.4 People who can sue (potential claimants)

Clearly, the people who could sue the manufacturer for the defective goods were described only as 'ultimate consumers'.

This is a reasonably broad description. It obviously for instance was wide enough to cover people who had not bought the goods themselves. This is obviously wide enough to include gifts.

Again, however, a claimant is anybody that the manufacturer 'should have in his contemplation' as being likely to be harmed if the goods are defective. So the definition has been broadened to include some other foreseeable situations.

• suppliers injured by the goods

 **EXAMPLE**

Where some sharp metal protruded from the goods and injured a shopkeeper who was storing them the manufacturer was liable to compensate the shopkeeper for the injury.

*From the case of Barnett v H and J Packer & Co (1940)*

• mere bystanders.

 **EXAMPLE**

A pedestrian was injured by a faulty reassembled component that fell off a lorry and injured him.

*From the case of Stennet v Hancock (1939)*

## 19.1.5 The elements that must be proved when bringing a claim in negligence for damage caused by defective products

Clearly, suing in negligence for damage that has been caused by defective goods is the same as for negligence claims generally (see section 16.4).

The claimant must show:

• the existence of a duty of care owed by the manufacturer to the 'ultimate consumer' of the product
• breach of that duty by the defendant manufacturer
• that the damage suffered was foreseeable and was caused by the defendant's breach of the duty of care he owed.

### Duty of care

Since 1932 it has been established that a manufacturer does owe a duty to consumers of his products not to cause them harm. The duty applies only where the goods reach the consumer in the form that they left the manufacturer and there is no chance of an intermediate examination.

### Breach of duty

A breach of the duty of care by the manufacturer is any failure in the production process or failure to rectify a known defect before it reaches the end consumer. The breach can occur in many ways:

• failing to check products that have been exposed to chemicals during the manufacturing process that then may cause harm

**EXAMPLE**

A man bought woollen underpants which contained traces of chemicals which then caused him to develop a very painful skin disease. Underpants should not cause such a reaction and so there was a breach of the implied term.

*From the case of Grant v Australian Knitting Mills Ltd (1936)*

• failing to do anything about a known fault.

 **EXAMPLE**

A manufacturer failed to recall cars with a dangerous defect once the defect had been detected so the manufacturer was liable for negligence.

*From the case of Walton v British Leyland (1978)*

Negligence is fault-based, so the manufacturer will be able to avoid liability if he can show that the cause of the defect did not arise through want of care on his part. Since detailed knowledge of manufacturing processes is generally unavailable to most consumers, this can make it hard for a consumer to prove the breach of duty. As a result, in some circumstances, the consumer is able to make the manufacturer prove that he was not negligent. This will be where:

• the manufacturer was in control at all material times (eg such as the sealed opaque bottle in the snail in the ginger beer case)
• the thing causing the damage or injury was of a type that could only be caused by negligence (again, foreign bodies cannot get into food unless there is some failure to take care in the production process)
• there is no other explanation (obviously if the consumer has proof of the negligence, then he should present it).

# Foreseeable damage caused by the defendant's breach of duty

The consumer will only be able to recover compensation if he can prove that the damage was actually caused by the defect in the goods.

If there is another possible cause of the damage or even of the defect, then the consumer may struggle to gain compensation.

 **EXAMPLE**

A windscreen on a car shattered without explanation while the owner was driving the car. The manufacturer of the windscreen was not liable because it was impossible to prove why the windscreen shattered. The fault in the glass could have occurred any time after the glass left the factory, for example when it was fitted to the car.

*From the case of Evans v Triplex Safety Glass (1936)*

 **ACTIVITY**

## Activity 3

Read the short description of a claim in negligence for damage caused by a defective product below. The consumer is successful in her claim.

At each point you are given alternative statements to complete the story (a) and (b).

Cross out the statement (a) or (b) in each case so that the remaining description means that Angela will have a successful claim.

Angela buys a new electric food mixer.

The mixer is:

a) in a box that is sealed and stapled

b) not in any kind of packaging.

Angela wants to try the food mixer out so she

a) plugs it in

b) reads the instructions that come with the mixer before she plugs it in.

When Angela switches on the food mixer, it explodes and bursts into flames.

a) This is because of a faulty wiring arrangement in the food mixer

b) This is because the socket that Angela plugs the food mixer into is faulty.

The fire

a) startles Angela momentarily

b) causes severe burns to Angela's hand.

Angela wants

a) compensation for her burnt hand

b) a replacement food mixer.

Angela succeeds in her claim.

## Comment

Negligence is clearly very useful for consumers in a number of ways:

• It allows any end consumer the chance to sue a manufacturer for damage caused by defective products – so even someone who receives the product as a present and has no contract with the supplier can sue.

• It allows the consumer to gain compensation for the consequential loss caused by the defective product, eg any damage caused to property and also personal injury or even death can be compensated.

However, there are two important problems associated with negligence:

• Trying to prove that the defect in the product actually caused the damage can sometimes be hard.

• Sometimes it is hard trying to prove that it is the manufacturer's fault (in other words that he has in fact breached his duty).

 **EXAMPLE**

The Thalidomide cases (which were settled out of court) are evidence of both these points. Thalidomide was a drug to help pregnant

woman during their early pregnancy but it had not been properly tested and it caused many children to be born with deformity such as short or non-existent limbs.

*From the case of S and Another v Distillers Co (Biochemicals) Ltd; J and Another v Distillers Co (Biochemicals) Ltd (1969)*

## 19.2 EU product safety

In the same way as has happened with employment protection, it is our membership of the EU that has led to the introduction of major developments in consumer protection. This is definitely true of product safety where EU legislation has meant that consumers have much broader rights in the case of unsafe products.

One of the major aims of the EU is to harmonise the law in the different member states so that citizens can expect the same rights anywhere in the EU. The EU uses a type of legislation called directives to achieve this.

The most significant measure was the Product Safety Directive 85/374, which required member states to introduce the following:

• strict liability on producers for all loss or damage suffered as a result of defective products

• a broad definition of 'producer' – so this could include anyone in the chain of supply and distribution, including manufacturers, importers and suppliers – meaning that a consumer would always have someone to sue

• all that the consumer needs to prove is the defect in the goods, the damage caused and that the damage was actually caused by the defective goods

• a number of defences to protect innocent producers – for example, due diligence.

## 19.3 Statutory product safety

The UK put the EU Directive into national law by passing the Consumer Protection Act 1987.

The Act includes criminal sanctions as well as civil liability in Part 1. It has also been supplemented with the Product Safety Regulations 1994. The civil liability is found in s 2(1):

66 . . . where any damage is caused wholly or partly by a defect in a product, every person to whom subs 2 applies shall be liable for the damage . . . 99

The important features to know about the Act are:

- who can be sued under it
- the types of product covered by the Act
- the types of defect in the goods that are covered by the Act
- the types of damage that can be compensated under the Act
- the available defences.

### 19.3.1 Those who can be sued under the Act

One thing that the EU Directive was trying to achieve was that the consumer should always have somebody to sue – so the Act covers practically everybody in the chain of manufacture and distribution.

There are four categories listed in s 2(2):

1. producers
   which includes:
   - the manufacturer (this also includes manufacturers and assemblers of component parts, and also producers of raw materials used in making the goods)
   - a person who extracts minerals from the ground
   - a person carrying out any industrial or other process which adds to the essential characteristic of the product, eg freezing vegetables.

2. importers
   - includes anybody who in the course of a business imports a product from outside of the EU

3. suppliers
   - these are retailers and wholesalers (usually these would be sued in contract law under the Sale of Goods Act 1979 (see section 17.2); however, when it is impossible for the consumer to identify either a 'producer' or an importer, the consumer can sue the supplier if he has asked the supplier to identify the producer and the supplier has failed to identify or refuses to identify the producer)

4. own-branders
   - these are bodies that sell goods that they have not produced but under their own name, eg supermarkets like Sainsbury's and their baked beans or Asda and their curry sauce (they can be sued if they have not indicated who is producing the goods for them under their own label).

### 19.3.2 Products covered by the Act

Section 2 (1) defines a product as including:

66 any goods including a product which is comprised in another product' 99

So this could, for example, refer to a car component that is defective.

Goods are defined as:

66 substances, growing crops, and things comprised in land by virtue of being attached to it and any ship, aircraft or vehicle. 99

However, some things are specifically not covered by the Act:

* buildings – although building materials are included
* nuclear power
* agricultural produce which has not undergone an industrial process.

### 19.3.3 Defects covered by the Act

Defect is defined in s 3(1):

> **❝** if the safety of the product is not such as persons generally are entitled to expect, taking into account all the circumstances . . . **❞**

There are many things that a court will take into account in deciding if the goods are unsafe:

* the manner in which and purposes for which the product has been marketed
* the use of any mark in relation to the product and any instructions for, or warnings with respect to, doing or refraining from doing anything in relation to the product
* what might reasonably be expected to be done with or in relation to the product
* the time when the product was supplied by its producer to another
* the market, eg toys and children
* the use of warnings
* the way that the consumer has used the product, eg setting off fireworks indoors, or drying wet pets in microwaves.

 **ACTIVITY**

**Activity 4**

In the right-hand column below, write either TRUE or FALSE against the statements in the left-hand column.

| | | |
|---|---|---|
| 1 | Amos has a defence under the Act because he sold Brendan a defective product but it was a private sale and Amos is not a businessman. | |
| 2 | Calum has a defence under the Act because he sold Dalvinder the defective goods at a very cheap price. | |
| 3 | Euan has a defence under the Act because he has offered to repair the damage caused by the defective goods. | |
| 4 | Faisal has a defence under the Act because terrorists put the poison in the baby food that killed Georgina's baby and Faisal had no idea that the food was poisoned as it was still sealed. | |
| 5 | Haiki has a defence under the Act because although it turned out that the products that he supplied were dangerous, they had been checked and complied with EU safety regulations. | |
| 6 | Ian has a defence under the Act because at the time the product was sold, nobody was aware that the chemicals in the product could explode when coming into contact with water. | |

Table 19.4

**ACTIVITY**

**Activity 5**

In the spaces below identify THREE types of defendant that a consumer could claim against under the Consumer Protection Act 1987.

1. ................................................................
2. ................................................................
3. ................................................................

## 19.3.4 The type of damage to which the Act applies

The Act covers death, personal injury, and loss or damage to property caused by unsafe products.

It does not cover:

- small property damage under £275 (the consumer should use contract law instead – probably under the Sale of Goods Act)
- business property (the Act is for the protection of consumers – so the property must have been intended for private use, occupation or consumption)
- damage to the defective product itself (again this should be taken under contract law).

## 19.3.5 Defence

There are five possible defences in s 4 of the Act:

- The product complies with statutory or EC obligations (for example, a chemical required

**ACTIVITY**

**Activity 6**

In the right-hand column below, place a TICK next to the three statements in the left-hand column which represents types of damage caused by a defective product that a consumer CANNOT recover compensation for under the Consumer Protection Act 1987.

| | | |
|---|---|---|
| 1 | Amy has bought an electric hairdryer which does not work and she wants a replacement. | |
| 2 | Baljit has bought an electric hairdryer which bursts into flames when she switches it on, causing her to suffer extensive burns to her hands and head. | |
| 3 | Claudia has bought an electric hairdryer which fuses a socket when she turns it on which costs £60 to repair. | |
| 4 | Dominique, a hair stylist, buys an electric hairdryer for her business. The hairdryer blows up when it is switched on, causing severe damage to Dominique's business premises. | |
| 5 | Ebukwe has bought an electric hairdryer. It bursts into flames when it switches on and causes a fire in Ebukwe's house. The damage from the fire will cost £2,000 to repair. | |
| 6 | Falia buys an electric hairdryer which electrocutes her when she switches it on, killing Falia instantly. | |

Table 19.5

to be in a product by law which then turns out to be dangerous).

- The defect did not exist at the time it was supplied by the defendant (this could be where animal rights campaigners put poison in food).
- The product was not supplied in the course of a business.
- The defendant can show he did not supply the product.
- Where the state of technical or scientific knowledge was such that when the product was supplied the defendant could not be expected to have discovered the defect.

## 19.3.6 Comment on the Act

The Act has improved the protection of consumers in a number of ways:

- Producers have to take more care and need appropriate quality control systems.
- There is also more likelihood now of product recall when a common defect is discovered.
- It also means that the consumer has more chance of getting a remedy because he has a greater range of potential defendants from which to choose.

However, the Act is also not perfect because of the following limitations:

- Not all products, nor all defects, nor all damage is covered by the Act.
- Consumers only have a small time frame in which to bring an action.
- There are probably too many defences, making it difficult for a claimant to succeed.
- The Act is supposed to provide strict liability

(the consumer does not have to show fault, just the existence of the defect and the damage) but the consumer still has to show that the defect caused the damage and the standard of care is very similar to negligence, so it is possibly no better than suing for negligence.

### ACTIVITY

**Activity 7**

In the spaces below, try to discuss how the limitations in the Consumer Protection Act 1987 might prove harmful to consumers.

...................................................................

...................................................................

...................................................................

...................................................................

...................................................................

...................................................................

...................................................................

...................................................................

...................................................................

...................................................................

...................................................................

...................................................................

...................................................................

...................................................................

...................................................................

...................................................................

**KEY FACTS**

- Consumers can recover compensation for damage caused by defective products in two ways:
  - under basic negligence principles
  - under the Consumer Protection Act 1987.
- In negligence the manufacturer of the product can be sued for compensation if:
  - he owes the consumer a duty of care (which he will if the goods are received in the state that they left the manufacturer and there is no chance of an intermediate inspection of the goods)
  - he has breached the duty of care (by a failure in the production process or a failure to remedy a known defect in the goods)
  - the defect has caused foreseeable damage (so it must be proved that there is no other possible cause of the damage).
- The Consumer Protection Act allows consumers to sue a wider range of defendants:
  - producers
  - suppliers
  - importers
  - own-branders.

- The consumer can sue for a defect in any goods which also includes a product comprised in another product.
- Defect is defined as 'if the safety of the product is not such as persons generally are entitled to expect, taking into account all the circumstances . . .'
- The Act covers death and personal injury and damage to property.
- It does not include:
  - small losses under £275
  - damage to business property
  - damage to the defective product.
- Defences include:
  - product complies with EC or statutory requirements
  - defect did not exist when the product was supplied
  - the product was not supplied in the course of a business
  - the defendant did not supply the product
  - the state of technological knowledge when the product was supplied.

# INDEX

Note: references ending with 'k' refer to Key Facts charts.